MARINA

THE STORY OF A PRINCESS

Sophia Watson

MARINA

THE STORY OF A PRINCESS

Weidenfeld & Nicolson, London

First published in Great Britain in 1994
by Weidenfeld & Nicolson Ltd
The Orion Publishing Group
Orion House
5 Upper St Martin's Lane
London WC2H 9EA

The right of Sophia Watson to be identified
as the author of this work has been asserted
by her in accordance with the Copyright,
Designs and Patents Act 1988.

British Library Cataloguing-in-Publication Data
is available on request.

ISBN 0 297 81467 2

Filmset by Selwood Systems, Midsomer Norton
Printed and bound in Great Britain by
Butler & Tanner Ltd, Frome and London

CONTENTS

ILLUSTRATIONS

ACKNOWLEDGEMENTS

There are many to whom I owe gratitude for their help in this project, which has at times been very difficult. Among them are friends of Princess Marina who would prefer not to be named. Those who discussed some of the more sensitive areas of her life did so because they believe that she is now owed the truth and that only when the Princess's causes for unhappiness are known can she really be understood and respected as she deserves. Lady Carew-Pole, Valentine Dawnay, Fiona Douglas Home, Philip Dunne, Celia and Nicholas Djivanovic, Edward Hay, Daska Maclean, Elizabeth Maxwell, Jimson Parsons, Sir Steven Runciman, Stephanie Tanner and Hugo Vickers are among those who helped me in various ways. Others were less helpful for reasons of, I hope misplaced, loyalty. Alastair Forbes, a regular visitor at Coppins, wrote that although 'I know everything about Princess Marina, her sisters and cousins,' he would not talk to me 'because it would take too long. And besides, why should I?' He did appear at proof stage for some late suggestions, for which he can be thanked.

My husband Julian Watson must also be thanked for supporting me (in every sense) during the writing of the book.

Perhaps most thanks are due to Caroline Dawnay for the enormous act of faith which saw this work through some dark hours.

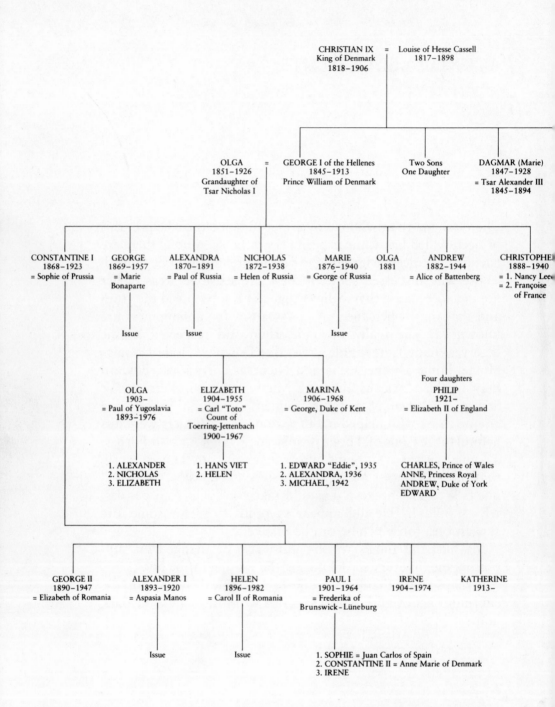

CHRISTIAN IX = Louise of Hesse Cassell
King of Denmark   1817–1898
1818–1906

OLGA = GEORGE I of the Hellenes   Two Sons   DAGMAR (Marie)
1851–1926   1845–1913   One Daughter   1847–1928
Grandaughter of   Prince William of Denmark   = Tsar Alexander III
Tsar Nicholas I   1845–1894

CONSTANTINE I   GEORGE   ALEXANDRA   NICHOLAS   MARIE   OLGA   ANDREW   CHRISTOPHE
1868–1923   1869–1957   1870–1891   1872–1938   1876–1940   1881   1882–1944   1888–1940
= Sophie of Prussia   = Marie   = Paul of Russia   = Helen of Russia   = George of Russia   = Alice of Battenberg   = 1. Nancy Lee
Bonaparte   = 2. Françoise
of France

Issue   Issue   Issue

OLGA   ELIZABETH   MARINA   Four daughters
1903–   1904–1955   1906–1968   PHILIP
= Paul of Yugoslavia   = Carl "Toto"   = George, Duke of Kent   1921–
1893–1976   Count of   = Elizabeth II of England
Toerring-Jettenbach
1900–1967

1. ALEXANDER   1. HANS VIET   1. EDWARD "Eddie", 1935   CHARLES, Prince of Wales
2. NICHOLAS   2. HELEN   2. ALEXANDRA, 1936   ANNE, Princess Royal
3. ELIZABETH   3. MICHAEL, 1942   ANDREW, Duke of York
EDWARD

GEORGE II   ALEXANDER I   HELEN   PAUL I   IRENE   KATHERINE
1890–1947   1893–1920   1896–1982   1901–1964   1904–1974   1913–
= Elizabeth of Romania   = Aspasia Manos   = Carol II of Romania   = Frederika of
Brunswick-Lüneburg

Issue   Issue   1. SOPHIE = Juan Carlos of Spain
2. CONSTANTINE II = Anne Marie of Denmark
3. IRENE

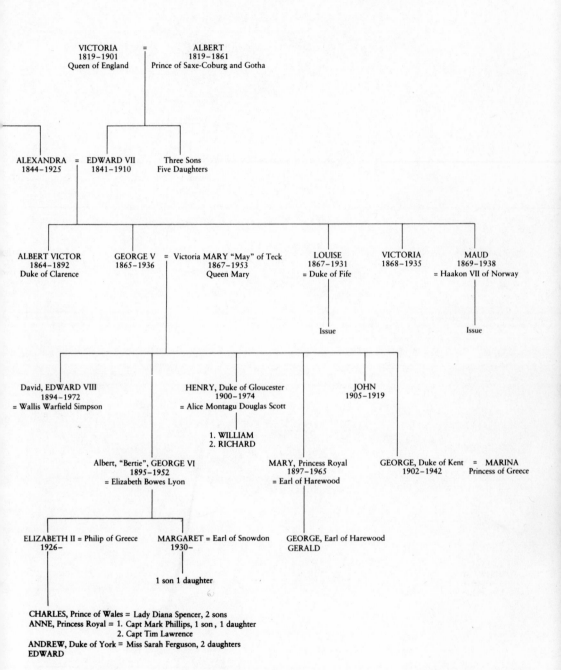

VICTORIA = ALBERT
1819–1901 1819–1861
Queen of England Prince of Saxe-Coburg and Gotha

ALEXANDRA = EDWARD VII   Three Sons
1844–1925   1841–1910   Five Daughters

ALBERT VICTOR   GEORGE V = Victoria MARY "May" of Teck   LOUISE   VICTORIA   MAUD
1864–1892   1865–1936   1867–1953   1867–1931   1868–1935   1869–1938
Duke of Clarence   Queen Mary   = Duke of Fife   = Haakon VII of Norway

                                                          Issue   Issue

David, EDWARD VIII   HENRY, Duke of Gloucester   JOHN
1894–1972   1900–1974   1905–1919
= Wallis Warfield Simpson   = Alice Montagu Douglas Scott

                                  1. WILLIAM
                                  2. RICHARD

Albert, "Bertie", GEORGE VI   MARY, Princess Royal   GEORGE, Duke of Kent = MARINA
1895–1952   1897–1965   1902–1942   Princess of Greece
= Elizabeth Bowes Lyon   = Earl of Harewood

ELIZABETH II = Philip of Greece   MARGARET = Earl of Snowdon   GEORGE, Earl of Harewood
1926–   1930–   GERALD

                                  1 son 1 daughter

CHARLES, Prince of Wales = Lady Diana Spencer, 2 sons
ANNE, Princess Royal = 1. Capt Mark Phillips, 1 son, 1 daughter
                       2. Capt Tim Lawrence
ANDREW, Duke of York = Miss Sarah Ferguson, 2 daughters
EDWARD

For Constance and Beatrice, with my love

PROLOGUE

Princess Marina, Duchess of Kent, was an exceptional woman. She was beautiful, loyal and warm, inspiring a love and loyalty to meet hers. She was not always happy, indeed she often had cause to be deeply unhappy, but her sense of duty, her love for her family, her religion and her own strong character always upheld her. 'Her loyalty, her gentle sweetness and charm, which equals her beauty and her saintly character, make her an outstanding woman,' her friend Chips Channon (Member of Parliament and father of Paul) wrote in his diary on 1 May 1942. Writer and aesthete Harold Acton, a neighbour of Marina's sister Olga in Tuscany, wrote of Marina, 'whose nobility was printed on features of the utmost refinement, endowed with a gallant sense of humour which enabled [her] to rise above misfortune'. And on her death the photographer Cecil Beaton mourned, 'For people of my age the loss is great for she was so much part of an era and she added so much to the early days. She was always so vividly around, even until now, so that with her going she leaves a very great gap.'

The gap Marina's death left has of course closed over the years. She is now remembered mostly as a tragic beauty who gave a certain chic to the dowdy Windsors. Little is said or thought of her work for the royal family: perhaps the most enduring image is of an elegant princess walking with a slight limp on to the Centre Court at Wimbledon to give the winners their prizes. Others with longer memories may give her credit for being the only woman ever to look stylish in a uniform (she was Commandant of the Wrens).

To her friends Marina was essentially a family woman who put her children before everything and was close above all to her daughter (Princess Alexandra) and her sister Olga (Princess Paul of Yugoslavia). Marina was reserved, yet loved company and cards and jokes. She was a nervous smoker, a woman who would never sit in an armchair but would always perch on its arm. She was a loyal and true friend. Nevertheless her friends were always aware of the Princess's serious side: Edward Hay, son of her Private Secretary Philip Hay, stressed how hard she worked for Kent University; the academic Steven Runciman points to her work with the Anglo-Hellenic League, with which he was closely involved. Her friends echo each other when they say that she never 'played at' her job. Anything she undertook was done properly.

On her death, there were many who mourned her personally, but there were many more who mourned her for her public persona. Writer Kenneth Rose (author of the definitive work on George V) was among those more aware of her public importance: on her death he wrote that 'She continued ... to uphold those tenets of duty and dignity and courage that were part of her Royal upbringing and to enhance an ideal of dynastic harmony that seemed to belong to another age.' In this she was truly exceptional. Other women have been beautiful, loyal, good company, happy or sad. But her past, and the way she brought it to bear upon her future and that of her adopted country, make her more than just a footnote in history.

When Marina died in August 1968 she was given credit for her part in the shaping of the modern monarchy, but now her contribution is usually forgotten in the romance of her life story. Her obituary in *The Times* shows how seriously she was taken at the time of her death:

From the day of her marriage thirty-four years ago Princess Marina had been one of the most popular members of the Royal Family. Her good looks, her ease of manner and the tragedy of her early childhood are sufficient explanation of this but she achieved something more than simple popularity. She made a decisive contribution to the evolution of the subtle relationship between the Royal Family and the British public. It is not so easily explained of someone of foreign birth, who was widowed after only eight years of marriage ... Despite, or perhaps even to some extent because of, these handicaps she was able to respond particularly well to the need for some adjustment of attitude by royalty at a time of rapid social change. She could react warmly to public interest and attention without any loss of dignity. Her presentation of prizes at Wimbledon each year was a case in point. She became in a personal sense part of a great popular occasion but remained as gracious as ever. It was this capacity to meet in substance both the old and the new demands upon royalty that won a depth of respect and affection among the British public.

Everywhere in the tributes that followed her death the same sentiments are repeated. The RNLI remembered her for her conscientiousness, her many visits to the lifeboat stations and her attendance of virtually every general meeting, and also for her personal touches: 'She had a great interest in the wives of the crew, talking with them woman to woman.' H.F. David, Chairman of the All England Lawn Tennis and Croquet Club, stressed that 'Princess Marina was indeed President in the full sense of the word. This was no nominal appointment.' Lord Butler, President of the National Association for Mental Health, another body for which Marina had worked hard, wrote to *The Times* with his own tribute to her, in which he pinpointed her working methods:

Princess Marina chose to interpret her duties in the most personal and conscientious manner. The late Lord Feversham, Chairman of the Association, used to pay her regular visits and from these occasions she derived a close knowledge of the organisation. She was not content with memorising her impressions, she collected them on paper ... she was fully briefed ... on all aspects of our work. One had, in fact, to put one's best foot forward to keep level with her supply of information.

Marina, for her individuality, was part of something much larger than herself, something she had been brought up to believe in implicitly: the monarchy. Her strength, and the reason for her success, was not her beauty, it was that belief. It carried her through some dark years and in return she gave of her best to the institution. The monarchy Marina worked for in her last decade was very different to that into which she had been born and which had shaped her early years, but it was still at the heart of her life.

CHAPTER ONE

The World into which Marina Was Born

Marina of Greece was in fact anything and everything but Greek. Her mother, Grand Duchess Helen and paternal grandmother, Queen Olga, were Russian. Her paternal grandfather, George I of Greece, was born Danish and her maternal grandmother was a German duchess of Mecklenburg-Schwerin. Yet her father, Prince Nicholas of Greece, had been brought up to regard himself as Greek and, as the historian C.M. Woodhouse declares, 'the only practicable definition of a Greek is that he is somebody who thinks he is a Greek'. To that extent Marina was Greek until the day she died.

Prince Michael of Greece wrote

The Greek royal family is the fruit of an unlikely union, a union between the descendants of Vikings with those of antiquity and Byzantium. Yet, as frequently occurs in such odd alliances, the result has been, and still remains, a happy one. Although we did not start in Greece we belong to Greece. Unless one speaks with a racial bias, Greekness does not imply membership of an ethnic group. On the contrary, it always used to mean (and, I like to think, still does mean) partaking in a certain spiritual outlook, religion and language; sharing a common body of knowledge and appreciation of a way of life.

Greece has had a troubled recent history, and to understand its ups and downs one must look further back than Marina's immediate family. Throughout the centuries boundaries changed and different nationalities emigrated to Greece, adding their blood and cultures to the ancient Hellenic race. Despite, or because of, their mixed blood the Greeks are a fiercely patriotic breed.

After four hundred years of subjugation to the often cruel overlordship of the Turks, the Greeks finally won independence in 1830. With the Turks gone, there remained the vexed question of who should rule. The Greek leaders immediately fell out and their squabbling continued until they agreed that the answer was to find themselves a king. The three Protecting Powers – Great Britain, Russia and France – exempted themselves and their ruling families from the search for a king, and the last Emperor of Greece, Constantine XI, had been killed so long ago (at the siege of Constantinople, 1453) that nothing of his dynasty was left.

Queen Victoria's uncle, Leopold of Saxe-Coburg, was advanced as a candidate for the Greek throne by the British, and though he pretended not to be interested, he worked hard to secure the position. When it was offered him in 1830 he accepted, but as soon changed his mind. (He later succeeded in finding himself a kingdom, becoming ruler of Belgium in 1831.) Finally, in 1832, King Ludwig of Bavaria's seventeen-year-old son Otto packed his bags and moved to Greece as its first king for centuries. Darkly handsome, he arrived at Nauplia in a British frigate at the end of January 1833; with him came three Bavarian regents and three and a half thousand Bavarian troops. His was an unenviable position, for he arrived as a Bavarian, not a Greek, and therein lay his mistake.

King Otho (he did change the spelling of his name in recognition of his new country) ruled Greece for almost thirty years. And rule it was. His three Bavarian regents (only one of whom had any previous experience of Greece) ran the country autocratically, bickering among themselves, raising ruinous taxes, and behaving in an almost insultingly anti-Greek fashion. They did do some good, but they never became less than Bavarian and Otho himself never embraced the Greek Orthodox faith.

At first Otho retained the affection of the people – after all he was a minor and could not be blamed for his regents' heavy-handedness. As well as building himself a splendid palace in Athens he was also linked with the foundation of a university. He wore national dress and his naiveté was appealing. On the other hand the constitution which had been promised the Greek people by the Powers (and confirmed by the Bavarians in 1832) showed no signs of appearing. Furthermore his Queen, Amalia (a princess of Oldenburg), was unpopular and he, a weak man, was swayed by her influence. To add to her crimes she failed to produce an heir for the Greek throne. They lived in a grandeur to which the majority of their poverty-stricken subjects could not even aspire, and held court balls at which the Greek women refused to dance and Greek men wore day-time boots.

Finally, after an uprising in 1843, Otho agreed to dismiss his Bavarian advisers and call a National Assembly. The move did not really solve the Greek problems. His reign continued to be rent with troubles until his eventual deposition in 1863. Perhaps his greatest handicap was that, although well intentioned, Otho was stupid.

As he grew older and became more involved with the politics of his adopted country Otho made many mistakes, some of which (for example, his stubbornness towards the British) made him more liked by his people. The Greeks are always ready to be swayed by patriotism, and Otho thought he had found the answer to his worries in a continuous stirring up of patriotic fervour. However, such tactics did not pay off; in 1853 a brief and humiliating attempt to capture Thessaly and Epirus from the Turks led to the French and British occupying Piraeus and ordering Otho to renounce his burgeoning alliance with Russia.

Otho's eventual downfall came after a characteristic piece of manoeuvring, this time against the much respected Admiral Kanaris. Otho accepted him as head of government, accepted his proposed reforms, but undermined him by making sure that no good men would work under him. Otho and Amalia were on tour when revolution broke out and although they tried to return home, they were forbidden entry at Piraeus. So, twenty-nine years after he had arrived in a British warship, Otho left his country by the same means, affirming his love for Greece and refusing to give up his claim to the throne.

Without much ado the Greeks chose Queen Victoria's second son, Prince Alfred, as their new king. The Powers still stood by the decision they had made when searching for a king in 1830, that none of their own royalties should accept the job, so the hunt was on once more. The Earl of Derby was offered the throne, but refused, preferring an aristocrat's life in the English countryside to what would certainly prove a troubled crown. Finally Prince William, second son of Prince Christian of Denmark, was chosen by the British government and the decision confirmed in a Greek election on 30 March 1863. His position would be 'to regulate the function of the constitution, and to be the figure to whose supreme authority the political parties would submit their controversies'. His father (who acceded as Christian IX a few months later) was doubtful as to the wisdom of allowing his son to accept such a tricky job, but the will of the Greeks and the enthusiasm of the young prince prevailed.

Prince William was eighteen when he learned he had been chosen as King of Greece. He opened the lunch pack he had taken to the naval academy and, wrapped around a sardine sandwich, found a newspaper report that he had been elected king. His father had told him there was interest from the Greek government, but he learned his fate in the most prosaic of ways.

Prince William, who became George I of the Hellenes (Otho would not abdicate and so remained 'King of Greece'), took up his job with open eyes. Like Leopold of the Belgians, he 'kept a portmanteau ready packed' from the day he arrived in his adopted country. He learned from the fall of Otho and knew that although, unlike Otho, he had been elected by the Greek people rather than imposed upon them, his would be no easy task. As well as his ever-ready suitcase, he was protected by a guarantee from the Powers of an income of £20,000 a year for life should he be forced to give up the throne.

George I arrived in Greece with a guaranteed welcome: with him came the Ionian Islands, ceded to Greece by Britain as an accession present. Otho had retained a degree of popularity by adhering to the Great Idea – that the Greeks should reconstruct the long-gone Byzantine Empire with a capital at Con-stantinople – and while this was clearly unlikely ever to come

to fruition any enlargement of the Greek boundaries was sure
to be greeted with fervour by the people. Nicholas, George's
third son and Greek by birthplace if not ancestry, learned to
understand the strength of this feeling:

For every Greek there lingers deep in his soul the haunting yearning for
'the city' of his ancestors, where stands the undying glory of St Sophia,
the 'Basilica' of his dreams, which 'time and years will once again make
his'. In moments of great popular enthusiasm, ever since we were little
children, we can remember that the cry of the people was *'ke stin poli'*,
which means 'to the city' – to the city, the city of Constantine, to take it
from the Turks and once more hear Mass at St Sophia.

George also brought with him a Danish advisor, Count
Sponeck, who showed no more tact than any of the three
Bavarian regents. But yet there was a difference. Although
also very young – George was only eighteen when he became
King – he was made of different mettle from the young Otho.
George was no weak-minded boy happy to play manipulative
games with older and wiser men. From the moment he arrived
George showed a gravity and commitment to his task that
marked him apart from the earlier King, combined with an
informality and approachability that soon won him friends.
George was not Greek either, but he realised that his becoming
Greek would take more than the wearing of national dress.
Remembering the unpopularity of Otho's Bavarian advisors,
he soon asked his father to recall Sponeck to Denmark and
chose to be guarded by Greeks, not soldiers, from the
Protecting Powers.

Like Otho, George found a country torn apart by rival factions. Fewer than two hundred houses were left in Athens after
Otho's war, and the population of the whole country was only
a million. Corruption and protection rackets made the King's
early years hard and his government was run more by clan
loyalty than a party system. But unlike Otho, George's priority
was to see a new constitution written and working. He hurried
along the National Assembly and on 28 November 1864 he
took his oath to the new constitution. The diplomat Horace
Rumbold found the sight of the 'slight delicate stripling' swear-

ing his life away 'painful and saddening', but Greece became in truth a democracy under a King, a King who had more powers than many constitutional monarchs, but who could not act without the approval of his ministers. There was new hope among the Greeks. Maybe all would be well.

George spent the first four years of his reign learning to be Greek and growing ever more beloved of his people. Sir Horace Rumbold described the King during his first year in Greece:

Although still boyish in many ways, and with a flow of animal spirits that made it sometimes difficult for us, his daily companions, to maintain the respectful reserve and gravity due to his regal station, [he] already showed much of the simple dignity and charm of manner which have made his sister the Princess of Wales the beloved of all England.... His truthfulness and straightforwardness united to form considerable firmness of character and personal courage, and assured him an exceptional position with his subjects.

And so the new King travelled the length and breadth of the land, learning the language thoroughly and acquainting himself with every region of Greece. Although homesick for Denmark, he did not leave Greece once for four years.

George then decided it was time he found himself a wife. Otho had left no heir. George would not make the same mistake. The obvious place to look for a bride was Russia: the two countries were bound together historically and by religion, and it was to Russia that many Greeks had fled to escape the hardship of Turkish rule. George's sister Dagmar had married the Tsarevich Alexander in 1866, and his own search was soon rewarded: he found the Grand Duchess Olga Constantinovna, a sixteen year old whom he had first met on his journey to Greece through Russia in 1863. The Grand Duchess's pedigree was impeccable: niece of Tsar Alexander II, daughter to Grand Duke Constantine and Princess Alexandra of Saxe-Altenburg, Duchess of Saxony, Olga was fair, blue-eyed and much admired at the Russian Imperial court. The marriage was popular in Greece, where high hopes of Russian support for Greek expansion remained, but George showed much wisdom in choosing someone who was in fact little more than a child. Olga had lived in Poland for a year while her father was viceroy, and had even suffered with the family when an assassin made an attempt on his life, but otherwise her experience was that of the cosseted daughter of a very rich man. There were few signs that this immature girl would become a strong and much-loved queen, 'Olga the Good', and bear with fortitude the violent deaths of so many of her close relations.

The marriage was solemnised with magnificent Russian pomp in the Winter Palace in St Petersburg on 15 October 1867. Olga came to Greece with a trunk full of dolls from which she could not bear to be parted, but despite this sign of childishness she was immediately welcomed by the Greeks. 'Her shy youth and beauty conquered their impressionable hearts that day and, through all the vicissitudes of our House, she at least never lost their love,' wrote her son Christopher in his memoirs. Doubtless, the Greeks would have welcomed any Russian bride, especially one who had made the effort to please by dressing in the Greek colours of blue and white for her arrival. At first Olga's homesickness confined her to the palace – a hovel compared to the magnificence from which she came – and she admitted in later years that she spent hours playing with her dolls and avoiding public functions. Nevertheless she mastered Greek within a year, gave birth to a son, Constantine, in 1868, and began her lifelong work of visiting hospitals, orphanages and schools.

The Queen missed Russia for the rest of her life and never allowed herself, or anyone else, to forget that she was first a Russian. Although she was genuinely loved by the Greeks this remained a bone of contention. Her apartments were hung with icons, a room was converted into a Russian Orthodox chapel and while George did all he could to bring his children up as Greeks, Olga was insistent they should also be Russian. One of her sons, Prince Andrew, took this so far as to refuse to speak anything but Russian. George never converted to Orthodoxy and, indeed, had built a Danish dairy in the grounds of Tatoi, the summer residence, but although he never forgot he was a foreigner he did his best to help his people forget. Olga did not do the same. Much as she was loved and her work for the country respected, she remained Russian. This was summed up in a commentary written in 1905, while the Greek monarchy was still on the throne:

Queen Olga is a kind-hearted, benevolent woman, deeply religious, and interested in all good works, particularly in hospitals and the relief of the suffering. But like many other good people she is deficient in tact; and although she has lived so many years in Greece, she is just as Russian as when she first set foot on Greek soil. While respecting her deep love of her own country, her subjects think that it goes too far.

George, though, was keen for his children to be wholly Greek and in theory at least his Queen shared this aim. 'Our parents had determined from the first that all their sons and daughters should be truly Greek children. Though Greece was but his adopted country, my father impressed upon our minds, in and out of season, that we were Greeks, and that we were born and educated to serve Greece alone.' So well was this lesson learned that when George's daughter Marie was told on a foreign trip that she was not Greek, but Danish, she burst into tears.

Olga bore George eight children: Constantine (born 1868), George (1869), Alexandra (1870), Nicholas (1872, Marina's father), Marie (1876), Olga (born and died in 1880), Andrew (1882, the Duke of Edinburgh's father) and Christopher (1888). Of these eight, three, Nicholas, Alexandra and Marie, married Romanovs: Alexandra and Marie's husbands both died in St Petersburg on 30 January 1919. Alexandra had already died in childbirth in 1891. Marie, in England at the outbreak of the Great War, survived the Revolution and later married the Greek Admiral Joannides.

Her passion for Russia notwithstanding, Olga helped the poor, working hard to raise the standard of living for Greek women in particular. In 1888 she founded the Annunciation Hospital in Athens, helped by funds from the Tsar and her father, and she also set up a nurses' training school. Among her other charities were a boys' reformatory and the Association of Christian Brotherhood, designed to help prisoners both morally and materially. Olga's unshakeable Christian faith sustained her through both the best of times and the worst of times. One of her projects was to have the New Testament adapted into modern Greek for the people: she paid for the work, printing and distribution, with the backing of the Church in Greece. (Plotting Greek politicians managed to use this as a way of forcing the current Prime Minister's resignation, and the books were later suppressed.) Olga was an old-fashioned queen, charitable, conscientious and religious. It is unlikely that King George could have chosen a wife more wisely.

Both Prince Nicholas and Prince Christopher were to write their memoirs, telling of their upbringing in the Greek court. Their blood was thoroughly royal on every side, but their early years were relaxed and informal. It made for a family whose loyalty was unquestionable, whose respect for their father went beyond that owed to a king and whose love for their monarch was deep and abiding.

'Both my parents' aim was to make us forget we were princes; we were to become true gentlemen, capable and disciplined, well-informed, with a high sense of duty and humble about our attainments' wrote Nicholas. And Christopher said, 'we were not allowed to be conscious of our rank except through the responsibilities it entailed and, consequently, it was not regarded by any of us as a matter for congratulation.'

Theirs was a multi-lingual family. King George and Queen Olga spoke German to each other and English to their children. The children spoke Greek in the schoolroom and English in the nursery. Helen (Princess Nicholas) spoke Russian to Queen Olga and English to everyone else. Although George I never converted to Greek Orthodoxy, all the children were brought up in the faith of their country. 'You must never forget', George told them, 'that you are foreigners in this country, but you must make them forget it.' Their daily regime was strictly organised but in between lessons they were allowed to run wild. They tell tales of bicycling along the enormous corridors of the palace, of roller-skating in the stables, of practical jokes played on visiting dignitaries – jokes that seem to have gone unpunished – and of long summers at Tatoi, a house set in a 40,000-acre estate 30 miles from Athens. George bought this summer home in 1871, and in 1886 began work on a new, larger house on the estate. Tatoi was much loved by the Oldenburgs and was in many ways their real home.

Of course they were royal, and although George and Olga were anxious for their children to have no false pride in their position, their lives were such that it could not really be forgotten. Their 'grannies' were after all members of the royal families of Europe. Their Aunt Alexandra, Princess of Wales, welcomed them at Sandringham, they visited their Danish and Russian grandparents. Greece was indeed democratic and relaxed, but Russia's was the most sumptuous court in Europe. As Nicholas grew older his pleasures included shooting boar in Germany, bison in Russia and pheasant in England. He was young, royal and popular. Not all the visits were just holidays, either: Nicholas attended Nicholas II of Russia's coronation and Alfonso of Spain's coming of age celebrations. It seemed as though the party would never end. As he wrote in classic understatement of the Spanish jaunt: 'Little did we think then that in so few years so many of the countries represented at this pageant of princes would have notified their Royal families that their services were no longer required.'

There were also royal occasions at home: George introduced a Greek court dress, a glorified version of the Greek peasant costume, which was worn once a year at the New Year's Day Ball. 'My parents were so used to these functions that they thought little about them and never found themselves at a loss to find an amiable word for everybody. We of the younger generation, however, were self-concious and shy, and often used to torment ourselves beforehand as to what to say to this or that person.' Prince Nicholas managed, though, and earned himself a reputation as a wit and an expert mimic, characteristics which would be inherited by his daughter Marina.

The upbringing of the Greek royal children inculcated in them a love of their country and a lasting religious feeling. It also gave them a strong sense of family – the extended family of Europe, but more importantly their immediate family. This last perhaps strengthened them most of all in the years ahead. For Marina, too, her sense of family was to uphold her during both the years of the Second World War and the early years of her widowhood.

While the Greek Princes and Princesses grew up and were trained to take responsible places in the family, Greece continued to work towards peace and stability. Problems came from various quarters, among the most troublesome being the Cretans, who rose regularly in revolt against the Turks who still ruled over them. The troubles started before George came to Greece, and broke out again in 1866 when Crete declared itself free of Turkey and part of Greece. The Greeks were overjoyed, and many took themselves to the island as military volunteers. The King and government, however, were more cautious, waiting for the decision of the Protecting Powers. Russia and France were in favour of a referendum in Crete; England, which had heard tales of misgovernment in the Ionian Islands since their cession to the Greeks, opposed it. For two years violence prevailed and the Greeks and British grew further apart. Meanwhile the Russians, keen to extend their own influence, were growing increasingly hostile to both the Greeks on the one hand and the Turks on the other. All came to a head with the declaration of war by Russia on the Turks in 1877.

Greece was once again in a difficult position: a country with a king and government of her own, she nevertheless had to please not only her people but also the Powers. While the Russians advanced on Constantinople, the Greeks could make noises about 'occupying the Greek provinces of Turkey,' but could do little other than wait and see. When the Turks accepted an armistice the Russians found themselves more or less redrawing the map of Eastern Europe: Rumania, Serbia, and Montenegro were given independence, but the enlarging of Bulgaria's borders worried Britain enough to make her insist on a full conference of the Powers before any changes were ratified.

As usual the Greeks' concern to increase their empire only landed them in trouble. In 1880 the Powers decided the border question to Greece's advantage, granting lands which included Mount Olympus. However, when the Turks cut up rough on the subject the Greeks ordered mobilisation of the troops, the

Powers crossly thought again and finally in 1881 a settlement including Thessaly but not much else was agreed.

And so it continued. Greek ministers swept into office on waves of nationalistic fervour, were forced to settle for less than they had hoped or promised under threat of war (or even under blockade from the British) and were then replaced by other ministers promising the earth (or the dream of Constantinople). 'Political feuds in Greece may well be considered as a national heritage,' wrote Prince Nicholas. 'They opened the door to the Roman conquest; they sowed the seeds of the fall of the Byzantine Empire; they facilitated the advent of the Latins in the Levant; and they brought about the ultimate subjection of the Greek people to the Turkish yoke.'

Crete remained a problem, with riots between the Christians and Muslims becoming more intense and violent. Finally, in 1897 the Greek leaders left Khania (Crete) for Akrotiri and there declared an independent government. One of their number was Eleftherios Venizelos, destined to play a major role in Greek affairs.

This time Greek government, King and people were in accord. Enough was enough: it was time for the slaughter of Christians to stop. The Greeks felt that the Powers were not doing enough to halt the troubles:

European Diplomacy, unable to cope with the insurgents whom they had no means of bringing to reason, nor with the Turks themselves, whom they did not want to offend, blockaded the island, and prevented the Turks from sending reinforcements to Crete; whilst, at the same time, their united fleets, at Suda Bay, bombarded the Christians fighting for their liberty. In this way they maintained the role of impartial arbiters.

This is fighting talk from Prince Nicholas, and indeed the Greeks decided they had to go to the rescue. But even Prince Nicholas admits that this heroic gesture was short-sighted: the Greek army was in no shape to contend with any major opposition. The troops set off in good spirits (with Prince Nicholas in charge of a battery and Crown Prince Constantine Commander-in-Chief), but the wait for action only depressed them.

When war finally began in March the Greeks did not have a

hope. There were fewer of them, their positions were not good, and despite Constantine's best efforts they remained dispirited and disorganised. For a week they defended the mouth of the passes on to the Thessalian plain from the Turks, but Nicholas wrote in sorrow,

it was on the evening of Good Friday that for no apparent reason our troops suddenly lost courage, and a most disorderly retreat was the consequence. This degenerated very soon into a panic. Unless one has been an eye-witness, it is impossible to picture to oneself the appalling impression produced by human beings running for their lives.

That was really the end. The war dragged on until an armistice in mid-April but the Greeks were defeated and retreated, defeated and retreated, until they were little more than a physically and morally bruised mass of humanity. George sent telegrams to his sister Alexandra, begging her to ask Queen Victoria's help, but with the approaching Jubilee British thoughts were elsewhere. 'The Princess of Wales came down last night in an awful stew about Greece, imploring the Queen to do something to stop the war and stay the hand of the triumphant Turks,' Victoria's lady-in-waiting Marie Mallet wrote to her husband. 'We live for nothing but the Jubilee and seem to ignore the doings of the world in general, and we snort at the Greek question.' Peace was at last signed in October and some good did come to the Cretans as a result of the war: the Powers granted the island self-government (but still under the Sultan's supremacy) and in 1898 gave King George the right to name the high commissioner. He appointed his second son, George.

The whole conflict affected the Greek monarchy badly: the people forgot how loudly they had bayed for war and held the King to blame for entering battle and Constantine to blame for incompetence. The royal family retired to spend the autumn at Tatoi to lick their wounds and wait for the emotions of the moment to pass.

They returned to Athens for Christmas 1897, believing that matters were on the mend. They could not have been more wrong. In February 1898 while King George was driving in an open carriage outside Athens with his daughter Marie, an attempt was made on his life. Six rifle shots were fired at close range, the first three finding targets in the horses' harness, the lantern and the coachman's epaulette. 'I had a red velvet bow on my hat which my father thought would make a good target for them so he quickly stood up, put his hand on my neck and forced me down. With his other hand he menaced them with his walking stick,' remembered Marie in her memoirs. The coachman whipped up the horses and they galloped out of danger. When the attempted assassin was caught, he said he had acted alone to revenge Greece for her defeat, for which he held the King responsible. The man was executed and his action helped the return of the King to popular favour. In the spring Marie and Nicholas accompanied the King and Queen on a tour of the provinces, during which they were, according to Nicholas, greeted with 'unbounded enthusiasm' everywhere they went. Money was raised by public subscription to build a church on the spot on which the assassination attempt had failed, and the King was reinstated in the people's hearts. Meanwhile Queen Olga kept the part of the harness through which the bullet had passed as a memento.

As the third of five sons Nicholas had on the whole a fairly easy life. He undertook royal duties, such as the tour of the provinces, and enjoyed the privileges and pleasures of his position and his royal connections to the full. His memoirs of his youth are packed with tales of visits abroad, of summers at Tatoi, spring cruises on the King's yacht, of visits to and from Grand Dukes, princes and kings. However, in times of trouble the royal family certainly did its duty. Nicholas was the only officer in his regiment to take no leave during the 1897 war. This discipline was an important part of the training of the Princes, and one which Nicholas in turn instilled in his own family.

While the political manoeuvring continued and wars were waged, the royal family of course carried on with its personal life. Despite the troubles, it seemed on the whole as though the monarchy was fairly stable and so there were parties to go to, weddings to arrange.

In 1889 the Oldenburgs celebrated two marriages. The first was between Princess Alexandra and Grand Duke Paul Alexandrovitch of Russia, Tsar Alexander III's younger brother. Nicholas's description of his sister's wedding spells out the impressive grandeur of the Romanovs.

We all travelled over Vienna and Warsaw to St Petersburg. Grand Duke Paul came to meet his bride at the frontier . . . . There were flags everywhere and at night illuminations, all along the route we passed, and, wherever we made a few hours' halt, a guard of honour was at the station, to salute the bridal party.

No one can imagine the brilliance of the functions at the Russian Imperial Court. This marriage was a glittering pageant from end to end.

The bridal dress worn by all the Grand Duchesses was made according to a fashion instituted by Empress Catherine II. It was of silver cloth, décolleté, in a point, with twelve large diamond buttons reaching to the end of the dress, and open sleeves, hanging from the shoulders to the waist.

Besides the diamond ear-rings, the three strings of pearls, which were the Tsar's personal present, Imperial brides always wore a set of diamonds belonging to the Crown jewels. The bride used to wear the Russian head-dress . . . of diamond rays, on a foundation of silver cloth . . . behind the head-dress a miniature Imperial crown in diamonds.

This diamond head-dress had been bequeathed by Catherine the Great to all imperial brides. Twenty-five years after Marina's parents' wedding Prince Christopher of Greece was shown the crown by the jeweller Cartier in his New York showroom. He had bought it in a Paris antique shop, and knew it had been sold by the Bolsheviks but not how it had come to Paris. He would not break it up, saying to Prince Christopher, 'I am keeping the Crown intact until the restoration of the Imperial House and then I shall present it myself to the Emperor.'

Attended by young pages and court functionaries, the bride was attired in red velvet and ermine before meeting her family and observing a one-minute silence. Then the royal families, headed by the Emperor and Queen Olga, walked in procession through state rooms full of bowing nobility until they reached the chapel of the Winter Palace. The wedding was followed by a state banquet, at which wine was drunk from glass placed on gold plates. 'The ordinary food and wines of the Russian Court were probably the richest in the world; and I had never seen, nor imagined, so gorgeous a pageant of gold and flowers, glittering jewels, decorations and exquisite gowns.'

Three years later the Russians treated their adopted daughter with similar pomp when she died after the birth of her son Dimitri. (Grand Duke Dimitri was later involved in the murder of Rasputin.) This time Alexandra lay under gold cloth covered with ermine, the coffin was placed in a special railway carriage draped in white silk and gold hangings, and as the train passed from Moscow to St Petersburg, 'peasants assembled from all sides, and kneeling with their caps in their hands, prayed fervently'. It was the first tragedy for the Oldenburg family.

Four months after Alexandra's wedding, George's heir, Constantine, married the Kaiser's sister Sophie. The Greeks may not have had the money of the Russians, but they went out of their way to welcome the bride. It was a great moment for the royalist Greeks. The first Greek-born Prince for centuries was to take a wife and with the birth of his son a true dynasty would be founded. If there was a shadow on the event, the sunshine of the wedding dispelled any vaguely anti-German feeling that may have been lurking. After all, this bride was a kaiser's daughter, a granddaughter of the Empress-Queen of England. Greece could only be honoured by such a match.

The Kaiser did not take quite the same view. When (on the birth of her first son) his sister declared her willingness to convert to the Orthodox faith he ranted and roared, then forbade his sister to set foot in Germany for three years. Later, he relented and the sentence was somewhat reduced, but the young Princess's stand against her brother was something which should have been better remembered in the First World War, when Constantine and Sophie were accused of pro-German feeling.

The wedding was carried out with as much grandeur as the Greeks could muster. Never mind that there was not enough room for all the foreign royalty to fit into the palace, and Athens society was asked to entertain royal visitors; never mind the overloading of horses and carriages on the palace stables, and that extra coachmen had to be drafted in and squeezed into borrowed blue livery: a good time was had by all. 'There were, of course, at our small Palace none of the gorgeous ceremonies prevailing at other Courts – where functions and etiquette are based upon historical traditions,' Nicholas apologises, 'but, despite the fact that everything in this respect had to be created, we managed "to cut quite a good figure".' And the bells rang out and the artillery fired a salute and the Crown Prince was married.

Princess Marie, who had been with her father during the attempted assassination, was the next of George's children to be married. Like her sister Alexandra, she was sent off to Russia, where she was united with Grand Duke Mikhail Nicolaievitch (despite the fantastically ugly King Alexander of Serbia's late attempt to win her away from her Russian suitor).

And then it was Nicholas's turn. He too turned to Russia to find a mate, and the girl he chose was Grand Duchess Helen, only daughter of Grand Duke Vladimir and Princess Marie of Mecklenburg-Schwerin. Helen was in the very heart of the imperial family: Tsar Alexander III was her 'uncle Sasha' and although her father had his own palaces – the Vladimir in St Petersburg and a summer house at Tsarskoe Selo – much of her childhood was spent in the imperial palaces. The youngest child, born after three boys, she grew up a young lady who knew her own mind.

She had been engaged when she was sixteen to Prince Max of Baden, but the engagement lasted only a few months. It was he who broke off the match. Helen had already met Nicholas, but it was another four years before they were engaged.

Like her sister-in-law Alexandra and so many Grand Duchesses before that, Helen was decked out in the traditional diamonds, silver dress and false ringlets for her marriage to Nicholas. The wedding took place at Tsarskoe Selo on 29 August 1902, attended by an army of kings and queens, princes and princesses, Grand Dukes and Grand Duchesses. The *New York Herald*'s correspondent described the procession of carriages leaving the bride's house as 'like a line of living gold', but this glory was the last Helen was to see for some time. The three-month honeymoon began at Ropcha, the palace 40 miles from

St Petersburg where Peter III had been assassinated. Prince Nicholas shot wild duck on the lake in the park and acquainted himself with his wife. Then he took her to Denmark to meet her new relations where she had the first hint of the more provincial life she was to expect from now on.

The young couple returned briefly to Russia for the bride's final farewells to her family. 'At the station of St Petersburg a crowd of friends came to see us off. I remember even to-day how conscience-stricken I felt taking my wife away from her old home. Life was so simple with us at Athens, where luxury was unknown and comforts often missing,' wrote Nicholas. Helen was more mature than her mother-in-law had been when she left Russia for Greece. She left the dolls behind, but, like Olga, arrived in her new country dressed in its national colours of blue and white. For her there was no hiding in the background: she was immediately interested in Greece and threw herself into charitable works and social life. She was not her father's daughter for nothing. Grand Duke Vladimir, the senior of the Grand Dukes and most powerful man in Russia after the Tsar, was a patron of the arts and a playboy. From him Helen inherited a strong social sense which made hers the most lively of the royal homes in Greece and stood as a barrier between her and her shyer, deaf sister-in-law Alice (Prince Andrew's wife).

The Tsar's wedding present to the young couple was a palace, but until it was built (and it took almost three years to finish) they joined the other members of the royal family in the Royal Palace in Athens.

The Royal Palace had been built by King Otho in 1850 and was splendidly uncomfortable. On his arrival in Greece George had honourably packed up most objects and returned them to the ex-King before beginning the refurbishment needed for a modern king with a growing family. He did keep some rich bronze and crystal candelabra and curtains woven with the Bavarian coat of arms which hung in the ballrooms. There were only two marble baths in the whole palace, which were more for ornament than sanitation, and the whole royal family relied on tubs for cleanliness. What Otho had neglected in the way of warmth and modernity he had compensated for in grandeur. It was a glorious combination of the Germanic and the neo-Grecian. Otho had been chosen as King of Greece partly as a compliment to his father, Ludwig I, who had supported Greek independence and brought Greek-style architecture back into fashion, and Athens's palace was designed by Ludwig's chief architect. It boasted three ballrooms, of which the largest was about a hundred and forty square metres. There was a marble staircase, a huge hall hung with Turkish flags and banners captured in war; there was the balcony from which King George exhorted his people in times of crisis; state apartments (including the Room of the Heroes which was decorated with medallions of the leaders of the War of Independence) and a throne room. King George converted the room over the central hall into a private theatre in which the royal family, Diplomatic Corps and high society entertained each other with performances of French and Greek plays.

The family rooms were no smaller, with the schoolroom alone measuring over thirty-six square metres. Nicholas described how the family, led by the King their father, would bicycle or roller-skate down the corridors – probably as much to keep warm as for amusement. So if Helen was impatient as she waited for the building of the Nicholas Palace, if she fretted as she remembered her home where grandeur could go hand in hand with comfort, can she be blamed? Nicholas himself was aware of the difference in his wife's life and probably just as keen for the new palace to be ready. But while she waited there was Greek to be learned – a job she undertook alongside her new sister-in-law Alice (daughter of Prince Louis of Battenburg, later Marquis of Milford Haven) who had married Prince Andrew in 1903.

Children were immediately born to the royal couple. First, in June 1903, Olga was born at Tatoi. The Norland nanny had already found her place in upper-class life and so Miss Kate Fox was imported from England to bring up this new branch of the Greek royal family. Eleven months after Olga's birth a second daughter, Elizabeth, followed; she too was born at the family's summer retreat. In 1905 the family moved to their new palace in Athens, and there, on a rainy night in December 1906, Marina was born. For some reason the bells and cannon of Athens greeted a baby prince, rather than a princess, but the real news was soon made known and greeted enthusiastically. Helen was very seriously ill after her third daughter's birth. For months she could take little or no part in public life, and for the following two years she left Greece for 'treatment' at the health spa in Franzensbad. There were no more children born to the Nicholases after Marina.

So when Marina was born the Greek monarchy looked to be stable. The King had survived forty-three years and many crises with his throne steady beneath him. He had provided Greece with more than one son, and by 1906 the eldest of these had three sons and a daughter of his own (another daughter was later born to the Crown Prince). Through marriage the Greeks had strengthened their ties with Russia and Germany, while the King's own sister was queen of the other great power abroad, England. Considering the history of the country, the Oldenburgs had much with which to congratulate themselves.

Marina's godparents were chosen from among the various branches of her enormous family: they included George I of Greece, Edward VII of England and his daughter-in-law Princess May (Queen Mary), Prince Andrew of Greece and Grand Duke Boris, another uncle. Once again the family came first.

Not long after Marina was born an old gypsy woman appeared at the Nicholas Palace and made a prophecy about her future: 'She is a child of destiny, and there is both sunshine and shadow for her. She will be beautiful and make a great marriage with a King's son. Love will be her guiding star. It will bring her sorrow, for she will lose her husband while she is still young and at the height of her happiness. But she will find consolation in her children.' So ran the prophecy, or so the story goes, and it was fulfilled in uncanny detail.

Marina and her sisters were, like the generation earlier, brought up with a very un-royal freedom and lack of pomp. 'We endeavoured to bring them up on the simple principles of our own home life, to be unpretentious and full of consideration for others,' said their father. And if they needed anything grander, they saw it on their frequent visits to their Russian relations, or at the Danish and English courts. Life in Greece was passed in commendable happiness under the sun.

Each summer the family would leave the heat of Athens for cooler parts of the world. As well as the royal summer residence at Tatoi, there were numerous relations to visit elsewhere in Europe. Marina's first recorded visit to England took place in 1910, when she was four years old, and from then on it became a regular summer holiday. The stay would begin at Buckingham Palace, where the girls were fussed over by Princess Victoria, Edward and Alexandra's eldest daughter, and given lessons in English history by Queen Mary, Marina's godmother. Then they would separate from their parents and be taken by Miss Fox to a south-coast resort, staying at Westgate-on-Sea near Margate or in one of the flats owned by the Norland Institute at Bognor. From the seaside they would occasionally venture back up to London, or their parents would come to visit them where they were, but these English holidays were totally free and uninhibited.

The girls would also be taken to Russia at least once a year, travelling by boat to the Crimea and then boarding the imperial train to St Petersburg. The very train was of a luxury unknown in Greece. In winter they would stay in St Petersburg with their grandparents, the autocratic Grand Duchess Vladimir and the loud Grand Duke. The Vladimir Palace was built on the banks of the Neva. 'Everything is exquisite,' wrote Miss Fox in a letter home.

My nurseries consist of eight beautifully furnished rooms; dining-room, two saloon ante-rooms, night nursery, dressing-room, bathroom and so on.... There must be a regular army of servants here.... The King's Palace in Athens is supposed to be big, but it is nothing like this. We are such a distance from the Grand Duchess's rooms that when I take the children along to their mother I have to wait for them. It is too far to go again to fetch them.

In the summer the family would visit the Vladimirs' palace at Tsarskoe Selo, another retreat for royalty. In either place there were young cousins for the three girls to play with, and indulgent adults to cosset them. These were carefree days, and the only shadow over the future was the health of the sickly little Tsar-evitch.

Far from the strict nanny of the story books, Miss Fox was much loved by the whole family from the moment of her arrival in Greece and, in the tradition of much-loved nannies, stayed with them (with a few interruptions) until Olga's marriage. 'The nurse used to let them crawl in the sun, attached by a long cord to the trunk of a tree. My poor father was in despair when he saw these children become as brown as berries, and predicted that their complexions would be ruined for ever. English hygiene, however, proved quite satisfactory,' wrote Prince Nicholas of his daughters' childhood.

Miss Fox did more than allow the girls to run wild in the sun. She dosed them with camomile tea once they were weaned from their peasant foster mothers, sponged them down with cold sea water, taught them physical jerks. She complained at the foreign food, longing for the regular hours and simple cooking of an English nursery.

She was also determined to be ruler in her own nursery, never mind which member of which country's royal family contradicted her on her methods. Queen Alexandra was horrified at Marina being left to sleep in a room on her own without a nursemaid, but Miss Fox was not to be swayed. The Grand Duchess Vladimir was a tougher proposition, but even she could not overcome the 'I know what I'm doing' approach of the Norland nanny. First there was the battle of the opened windows, with the ferocious Grand Duchess and self-righteous Fox determinedly closing and opening all the windows in the nursery suite. Then there was the disagreement over spanking – according to their Russian grandmother, the little girls were 'knocked about' by their English governess. Later friction between the Grand Duchess and Miss Fox grew to the point where Princess Nicholas was threatened with the withdrawal of her vast income from the Apanages (the fund set up by Tsar Paul I to provide for the Russian royal family) unless Miss Fox was sacked.

Princess Marina was born with one leg marginally shorter and thinner than the other, and with the left foot very slightly twisted. It was not a major deformity, but might have become more troublesome without 'Foxy', who massaged the injured foot twice a day for the first five years of her youngest charge's life. In 1911 the foot was successfully operated upon, although the left leg remained weaker then the right and to the end of her life Princess Marina had to have her shoes especially made to compensate for the slight difference in the length of her legs.

The Nicholases were now installed in their own palace, and their life ran with a smoothness that they must later have regretted. The Nicholas Palace (Le Petit Palais) was more comfortable than the Royal Palace by far – it boasted central heating, real bathrooms, even heated towel rails. Whitewashed and elegant, it stood in its own garden (complete with fountain and rockery) off a wide boulevard. At last Princess Nicholas had the comfort of home. Prince Nicholas left most of the running of the palace to his wife, except for his decision that male servants should cut off their long moustaches and appear clean-shaven. The servants nearly mutinied over the pointless order.

Greece was the most democratic of European countries, its King the most approachable: the young Princesses were not even addressed as 'Your Royal Highness' until they were old enough to understand the responsibilities as well as the privileges that went with the title. The girls had a liberal upbringing, but within a strict religious background. When Princess Elizabeth decided she needed a boy doll to join her family of girl dolls, rather than ask a grown-up, she knelt down to pray. When, after a week, no boy doll appeared, she complained to Marina. Her younger sister told her, 'God probably has not had any time yet to make even half a little boy. Just wait and keep on praying.' A week later a boy doll appeared. At that stage of their lives prayers were simple and easily answered.

The girls were taught their prayers in English, and every Sunday before tea were told Bible stories by Miss Fox. When Queen Olga asked her granddaughter why she did not say her bed-time prayers in Greek, Marina answered, 'I've arranged it with God. I told Him I liked to talk to him in English best, and he said: "Please yourself, Marina. All languages are the same to me."' God became, and remained a real figure in her life, one whom she used on more than one occasion to outface her parents with irrefutable logic. Once, on being told it was bedtime, she argued 'lots of other little girls are going to bed now. God must be terribly busy listening to all their prayers. If I go to bed later on, the rush will be over and God will have more time to listen to me.' Another time, on being ticked off for some mis-demeanour and told she should tell God she was sorry, she looked her father in the eye and said, 'What would be the use? If God knows everything He must know I'm sorry without being told. I don't want to waste His time.'

Princess Marina was intelligent and well informed, but not an intellectual as an adult. She was, however, a precocious child, often the leader of the three girls, and her straightforwardness and logic remained with her throughout her life. 'All the family met at lunch ... Princess Olga and Princess Elizabeth used to ask all sorts of questions. Princess Marina did not ask questions. She *answered* them, sometimes very cleverly,' remembered a French governess in later years. She was 'on the whole a good baby, but likes her own way and does not hesitate to scream hoping to get it,' commented Miss Fox. Even as a child, Marina was noted for being reserved, but with a powerful personality.

There were the approved numbers of nurses and governesses, but the Nicholases took a modern approach to their children: the parents were as at home in the nursery as were their off-spring, and certainly did not limit themselves to the tea-time glimpses of children in party frocks to which many other aris-tocracies were accustomed.

Aged seven Marina joined her sisters in the classroom where three governesses taught them languages (at which Marina excelled, speaking Russian, French, German, Italian and English fluently), literature (the study of which was backed up prac-tically by the plays Nicholas produced in his theatre, combining to create a genuine and lasting love of Greek and French drama) and geography. Marina could or would not succeed at her music lessons – Prince Nicholas attempted to persuade her into trying to play the piano by sitting beside her and playing nursery rhymes. 'Come along, you see Papa trying, don't you?' he coaxed. 'Yes, that's why I don't,' she answered.

Her history lessons were a similar struggle, but from an early age Princess Marina took an interest in art. She would follow her father to his studio and attempt to copy him at work, and as she grew older he would take her out and the two of them would sit side by side, painting together. Prince Nicholas always believed that his second daughter, Elizabeth, had the most artistic talent, but she preferred riding to sketching. So it was Marina and her father who visited sites of archaeological excavation together, learning about their country's past in the most practical of ways. It was a love that drew the father and his youngest daughter closer together.

As the girls outgrew the need to be tied to a tree, the emphasis on outdoor activity increased. They began most mornings with a ride, accompanied by Prince Andrew's two eldest daughters Theodora and Margarita, Princess Helen (Constantine's daughter) and an English groom, Taylor. They learned to swim – Marina when she was only three threw herself into the water to keep up with her sisters. They were taken out in an open carriage, and were taught to acknowledge the cheers of passers-by with regal waves (often finding themselves in trouble for making their dolls bow and wave rather than bothering to do so themselves).

The girls also took part in the theatricals so much loved by the Greek royal family. For a while Marina's ambition was to grow up to be an actress – but then there was also the allure of travel, and becoming an explorer ... or babies and working as a children's nurse. All flights of fancy for a princess. With Nicholas as the most cultured and Helen as the most social and stylish of the younger members of the family, Olga, Elizabeth and Marina were given a good foundation for a royal life. 'Foxy' was there to care for them, but there were also French and German governesses. And there was *The Times* newspaper. Years later, Marina was asked which newspaper she had as a child. '*The Times*,' she answered. 'I was spanked with it! So I am familiar with it since my earliest days.' The Nicholases were old-fashioned enough to hold with discipline, even if they had given up swaddling clothes for the babies.

Athens was the Nicholases' home, but it was Tatoi that was really the centre of family life for the Greek royal family. Oh, they mingled regularly in the capital – on Sundays everyone gathered at the Royal Palace, on Tuesdays at the Nicholases and on Thursdays at Constantine and Sophie's house, but it was at Tatoi that the family was truly on holiday and together. 'Tatoi represented our real home – the place that belonged to us, where everyone was free to do as he liked. For my parents [George and Olga] it meant a rest in their life devoted to its many duties .... For us it represented liberty, independence .... Tatoi was a refuge, a haunt of freedom ... it was my father's own beautiful creation,' writes Nicholas. He describes an idyll, a house loosely based on an English-style cottage belonging to Tsar Alexander II close to Peterhof on the Gulf of Finland.

Tatoi was the one place where the basically foreign royal family could feel at home. The agent of the estate was always a Dane, 'firstly because he [King George] believed them to be experienced and competent men, and, secondly, because the fact of speaking to them in his own language kept him in touch with his old country.' Here too was the Danish-style dairy, whose produce could bring the tastes of home back to him.

There was also a home farm, where the individually named pigs and cows fed from white marble troughs and where the royal family would play at being farmers. There was a deer paddock, and vineyards which provided the grapes for the royal household's wine. Surrounded by forest, Tatoi was alive with the sights and sounds of wild animals – not just the deer (which King George would allow no one to shoot), but wolves, boar, peacocks and of course foxes were all to be seen on the estate. From Tatoi they would go on excursions: picnics on the beach at Phaleron, visits to local villages where they were always warmly welcomed with cheers and flowers, trips to the island of Spetsai. Even Queen Olga was not homesick for Russia when she was there.

Despite the influx of blood from more modern European courts, the Oldenburgs knew how to celebrate in good old-fashioned feudal style. And according to Nicholas at least, the local peasantry knew how to enjoy such feasting. On Queen Olga's name-day, all the estate workers, soldiers from the garrison and nearby villagers, were invited to the festivities. Courtiers drove out from Athens for a service of thanksgiving in the church and refreshment and entertainment afterwards. After an outdoor lunch at three the peasants began to arrive. Twenty sheep were roasted on spits, wine was poured 'and all those people, sitting cross legged, eating their mutton and drinking their wine, were as happy as kings, or, rather, as kings ought to be,' remembered Prince Nicholas years later.

The luncheon over the dance began. They all danced in a chain, to the weird tune of a kind of horn pipe, whistle and drum. What horrible music! But they played until the poor musicians were blue in the face with heat, and until deep into the night .... When the band was at its hottest and the perspiration was streaming from the musicians' faces, my father, following an old custom, used to place a sovereign on every man's forehead, and, the perspiration acting as glue, the coins generally remained safely in position.

This was the old-fashioned, paternal style of monarchy to which Marina was born. As a child she would have understood little of the implications of her position, but she would have experienced the roar of a crowd, seen the awe in an old lady's face when confronted with the small royal child or her father. Try as Nicholas and Helen might to bring their daughters up to be unaffected and modest, they could not deny them the essential fact of their royalty – it was around them every day of their lives. And although Marina was not arrogant, she carried a pride in her heritage which she never lost, neither when she was an exiled princess, nor when she was a loved princess in a new country. Even as a princess of England, Duchess of Kent, she never forgot her inheritance as Princess Marina of Greece.

CHAPTER TWO

That World Crumbles

Of course the idyll, if idyll it was, of the king was not destined to last. While Marina was growing up in the comfortable security of a happy family, she was too young to understand the problems which consistently beset her grandfather.

Marina's uncle Prince Christopher described the mess in which Greece found itself almost lightheartedly:

In the years immediately preceding the World War the whole Balkans was a sort of witches' cauldron in which wars and rumours of wars simmered perpetually over a fire assiduously fed by the great protecting powers. The inevitable end was a conflagration that spread throughout Europe, but no one had the wit to realise it at the time. So Greece, Turkey, Bulgaria and the rest of the little Balkan States hammered away at one another with good heart until the issue became so confused that the former allies turned upon one another and the rest of the world lost count of who was fighting whom and why.

However small the countries battling out questions of borders and independence, the Balkan Wars overshadowed most of George I's last years as King.

Although the First Balkan War did not break out until 1912, the trouble started brewing as early as 1908 when Marina was little more than a baby. And as usual, as far as the Greeks were concerned, the Turks were the chief troublemakers. With every one else raising their heads and demanding independence, a group of Turks, made up mostly of officers and intellectuals, began talking about nationalism. The Young Turks (officially if not colloquially known as the Committee of Union and Progress) began their revolution with an army mutiny. The rebels' base was in Salonika, an important port, and soon their success was such that Constantinople was threatened. In July 1908 the Sultan promised a constitution and the election, when it came, was easily won by the Young Turks. However, the next spring saw a counter-revolution in Constantinople, whereupon the army moved on the capital, deposed the Sultan and the Young Turks regained control.

Neighbouring Balkan states could not resist taking advantage of Turkey's internal confusion. The Bulgarians announced their own independence, the Austrians annexed Bosnia and Herzegovina, and in October 1908 the Greek population in Crete proclaimed the island's union with Greece. This was the kind of talk the Greeks, ever with an eye to expansion, liked. So Venizelos, one of the committee of five set up to carry on government in Crete in the name of the King, was first heard of by the general Greek population as something of a hero. Prince George, who had already had some dealings with Venizelos, was more wary of the ambitious Cretan lawyer, and warned his father against the man's machinations, but Venizelos was destined to play a large part in Greece's history.

His first appearance in politics had been in 1899 when Prince George, as High Commissioner of Crete, had chosen him to become part of the Cretan administration. The son of a carpenter, and of mixed Turkish, Jewish and Armenian origin (it was said that at his birth his father had representatives of all three religions concerned – the Greek Orthodox priest, the rabbi, and the imam from the mosque – waiting in different rooms), Venizelos was as crafty as he was gifted. Prince Christopher describes him as

a shabby young man with a fox-like smile and an amazing gift of oratory and a still greater gift of putting other people in his pocket. He could talk so convincingly that even my father [George], though diametrically opposed to many of his theories, had to admit that, after listening to him for an hour, he generally found himself being reluctantly convinced. He was never forceful or compelling; he was smooth as silk, gentle, obsequious, with a mind as agile as a rapier and a never-failing flow of words. On brains less alert he had a hypnotic effect; he could sway crowds in whatever direction he wished and twist cabinets this way and that until they did not know their own minds.

Such was the man who was to play so large a part in Greece's future.

For a while George and the administration worked together for peace and calm on Crete and all was briefly well, until in 1901 Venizelos thought of making Crete independent. Prince George and Greeks of all parties were against this plan but Venizelos (who was, according to all commentators, nothing if not a wild enthusiast) continued working towards his goal, gathering supporters. In March of the same year Prince George sacked Venizelos, an act which may have been prompted by a wish to keep unity but which made him an enemy for life. Venizelos continued to work behind the scenes, undeterred by an election defeat in 1903 (only four of sixty-four deputies returned to the Chamber were Venizelos's men), until in 1904 he changed his opinions and declared himself the leader of those who wished for immediate union with Greece. His political manoeuvrings succeeded in at least one aim – that of more or less forcing Prince George to resign as High Commissioner in 1906.

Venizelos failed to gain a majority in the Cretan elections of 1907, but before long he turned his thoughts to a wider field of political activity. In 1909 Greece was in a hopeless muddle. The army and the government came into direct confrontation, which ended only after months of coming and going by ministers. A military league was formed to force reform on the government; it succeeded in bringing about the Theotakis ministry but Mr Ralli, who formed the new government, refused to enter into conversation with the officers. In August military sedition forced the resignation of the government; the Crown Prince, who had reorganised and reformed the army, was accused of favouritism and all the Princes resigned their commissions before a bill expelling them from the services could be passed. Had the bill gone through, their father would have been forced to sign it, and all the brothers agreed that this must be avoided.

Their forced resignation from the army was a humiliation for the Princes that it is perhaps difficult for us to understand, and the memory was one that remained with Prince Nicholas for the rest of his life.

I remember ... attending a Requiem Mass at the Catholic Church for the repose of the soul of our aunt Marie (Princess Valdemar of Denmark). It was particularly painful for my brothers and me to make our first public appearance in plain clothes. We had a feeling of real humiliation. Before the Mass, waiting for the King's arrival, the Prime Minister came up and said to me: 'Are you not cold without your uniform?' 'I am morally cold,' I answered.

Worse was to follow.

Venizelos (born a Greek citizen) arrived in Athens in 1909 and stepped into the fray. Never mind that a few – headed by Prince George – spoke out against him; the Greeks were in the mood for a saviour. King George was told that Venizelos could form a cabinet without causing a civil war, and so he sent for this remarkable man. Prince Christopher wrote,

He was so poor in those days that he wore cracked boots and frayed trousers. His smart frock-coat ... had been borrowed for the occasion. But there was about him a certain unconscious dignity, the marks of a dominant personality. Underneath his silken urbanity one glimpsed an iron will and an absolute ruthlessness. He was the born political adventurer, piratical and opportunist.

In the 1910 elections Venizelos entered Parliament with about eighty deputies behind him and was asked by the King to form the cabinet. At the next elections, in December of the same year, Venizelos won with a majority of three hundred. He was there to stay.

King George, despite warnings from many men he trusted, including his son, took to the man. And he trusted him, despite many proofs of Venizelos's double dealing. On one occasion a loyal statesman brought the King a letter from Venizelos which had been intercepted. It read: 'I have kicked out one George already, and I've come to Athens to kick out another.' At the next audience, George casually showed Venizelos the letter. 'For once his extraordinary aplomb deserted him. Every vestige of colour went out of his face. "What are you going to do?" he stammered.

My father shook his head: "Nothing. Take that letter. I give it to you as proof of my faith, for in spite of it I trust you." '

As even Prince Nicholas later agreed, the state of the country did at first improve under Venizelos. Once again the royal family had survived what had appeared to be an earthquake but now seemed to have been little more than a tremor. The little Princesses could go on playing in their shady garden, tended by their governesses and maids, and if their father no longer wore his country's uniform they were too young to know the difference.

Until war broke out. Then once again the Princes were needed. In May 1912 Prince Nicholas managed to kick himself during a game of tennis and cause an injury severe enough that he was sent, without his family, to Bagnoles de l'Orne in France to recover from a case of phlebitis. On his way home he stopped in Paris and learned from the Greek minister the apparent seriousness of the Balkan troubles. By the time he reached Venice, where he was joined by his father, the royal yacht was on the way to pick them up. On arrival in Greece they were met first by Venizelos, then by Prince Constantine, then by an excited crowd baying for war. The Turks were facing revolt in the Yemen, insurrection in Albania, and were continuing their oppression of the Christians in Thrace and Macedonia. All the Balkan states were officially neutral, but preparing for war. Bulgaria and Serbia declared war on Turkey, and Greece followed. The King had no choice. Public opinion and the state of his world forced his hand.

Crown Prince Constantine was reinstated as Commander-in-Chief of the army, and all the other Princes were given back their commissions. Once again Greece was at war.

Every soldier was proud to follow the lead of the Crown Prince and his well-trained staff. The continual Turkish persecutions, which had driven the population to a state of exasperation, made everyone feel that this war was being fought for the deliverance of their Christian brothers. An army with that moral, skilfully led, was certainly sure of victory.

So wrote Nicholas. In many instances history does not bear out his theory, but in this case he was right.

This time the Greek army was disciplined and ready. Military operations began on 18 October, and by 9 November the Greeks were at the gates of Salonika. On the 10th Crown Prince Constantine entered the city at the head of his army and was greeted by an exuberant crowd of dancing and singing Greeks, 'but the large majority wept, which is always the highest expression of emotion,' Nicholas, who had taken part in the campaign, recorded.

This victory marked the first real change in Marina and her sisters' lives. Bulgaria had had its eye on Salonika and was not wholly pleased that what she regarded as her inferior ally had won the city. It was decided that to keep the claim open, King George should go to live in Salonika for some time. He arrived in the city the day after his eldest son and decided to stay there for eighteen months.

When Prince Constantine left Salonika for the north of Macedonia, he made his brother, Prince Nicholas, Military Governor. It was not an easy job. With the Bulgarians ever on the doorstep trying wily new ways to ensure at least a shared occupation of the valuable seaport, Nicholas and his King had to use all their tact to preserve the status quo. Meanwhile the three girls waited until it was safe for them to be sent for, and grew accustomed to life without their father and grandfather.

It was not until March 1913 that it was deemed safe enough for the three small Princesses to join their parents in their new home. They had spent the war with their maternal grandmother, Grand Duchess Vladimir, in Russia and Paris. For some of that period Marina had for the first time been separated from her sisters, having gone with Miss Fox to stay with Nicholas's sister Marie, the wife of Grand Duke George, in the Crimea. But now they were all to be reunited.

On 12 March Princess Nicholas left Salonika for Vienna, where she was to meet her mother and take the three girls back to their father. King George accompanied her to the station. A week earlier his wife, Queen Olga, had also left Salonika, to resume her duties at her military hospital in Athens. All George's sons but Nicholas were with Constantine in Epirus – two weeks earlier the Greek army under the Crown Prince had taken its capital, Janina, in another glorious victory. For George the future looked as happy and as stable as it ever had.

In October of that year George was to celebrate his silver jubilee, and he had decided that it was time to abdicate in favour of his eldest son. 'I think I'm entitled to a little rest in my old age,' he told his sons when they tried to dissuade him. 'Besides, Jino will be able to do far more with the country than ever I could. He has been born and bred here, while I am always a foreigner.'

Although George had always been aware of his 'foreignness' to the Greeks, it was a foreignness which by now he felt perhaps more than did the majority of his subjects. It is certain that in Salonika, a city only recently Greek, he felt safe enough to walk the streets unguarded.

On 13 March he lunched with his son Nicholas, and they discussed the design of a new decoration for military valour during the recent campaigns. Two special medals of a higher order were to be awarded to Constantine and Admiral Coundouriotis, his ADC and Commander of the Fleet. Nicholas, the artist of the family, was to put some ideas on to paper. After lunch George, accompanied only by an ADC, with no armed guard, took his customary stroll through the streets. A man, sitting alone on a low stone wall, aroused no suspicion. Just before reaching him the King and his ADC turned and made back towards the city centre. The man stood up and shot King George through the back. The bullet went clean through the heart and although a passing horse-drawn cab immediately stopped and took him to the military hospital, the King was dead on arrival.

Nicholas was in his garden when a soldier burst in on him saying, 'They have struck the King.' Nicholas acted with great speed, knowing that no time was to be lost if a riot was to be prevented. The town was full of Bulgarian troops, loathed by the Greeks and sure to be suspected of the murder. Before knowing the truth, Nicholas announced that the assassin had been a Greek. The Bulgarians kept to their quarters and major bloodshed was avoided. In fact the assassin turned out to be a Macedonian, a madman with no particular motive. It was all the more bitter that King George, having survived so many blows during the fifty years of his reign, should have fallen, not to a politician, but to a stray lunatic. (The murderer later committed suicide while in custody.)

The family gathered in Salonika. Princess Nicholas heard the news in Belgrade, from where she turned back without her daughters. Constantine and Christopher learned the news in Janina and travelled via Athens, where Constantine as new King took the oath. The Queen travelled from Athens on the royal yacht with two of her sons.

On a foggy day after prayers, the King's body left Salonika on the royal yacht, accompanied by foreign battleships. He lay in state in Athens and from there was taken to be buried at Tatoi, on a hill covered with cypresses and pine trees. Princess Marina, considered too young to attend her grandfather's funeral, had returned to Russia with her grandmother, but, at Grand Duchess Vladimir's insistence, without Miss Fox.

George I was deeply and genuinely mourned by the Greeks. But then Constantine was Greek born. His name was one which augured well for the Greeks (many wished him to be known as King Constantine XII, underlining his succession from the last Emperor of Byzantium whose name he bore and whose wife had been another Sophie). He was a respected soldier who had won great victories for the Greek nation – Salonika and Janina had wiped out all earlier resentments. A new reign had begun.

There was even harmony between King and Prime Minister. Venizelos had achieved much in the political field – friendship with the Serbs, a peace with Bulgaria and Turkey which both the former enemy and the most nationalist Greeks could accept – and Constantine had carried out his part in the battlefield. The Second Balkan War, which broke out after Constantine had come to the throne, came in the form of an attack by the Bulgarians on the Serbs and was a disaster which was soon over. By the beginning of 1914 the future looked good for Greece. Venizelos was securely in power, with the backing of the King who had awarded him the Grand Cross of the Redeemer for his services.

With peace signed, Prince Nicholas's post as Military Governor of Salonika was now redundant and he travelled back to Athens to prepare for the triumphal entry of his brother to the capital. No longer in active service, he was able to devote himself to princely pursuits of a more aesthetic nature, collaborating with academics in the founding of a Byzantine museum, attending meetings of the Archaeological Society. The family was still in mourning, but life was better for them than it had been for some years. Constantine's picture hung in every peasant's house, and he stood godfather to the sixth child born to every family.

Princess Marina rejoined her family in Athens and the royal family was able to resume its pattern of family entertainment – lunch after Mass on Sundays with Queen Olga, dinner on Thursdays with the King and Queen and on Tuesdays at the Nicholases. The new King lived no more luxuriously than had his father, although he had built himself a smaller, more comfortable palace while Crown Prince and remained there after succeeding to the throne. He took an interest in gardening and botany while his Queen fulfilled the time-honoured charitable functions of the monarchy, which included forming a society (of which Prince Nicholas was vice-president) with the aim of replanting Greece's forests. Greece was rebuilding itself socially and morally. 'I think at last we can look forward to peace,' said King Constantine to his brother Christopher. And the little Princesses played on.

Their lessons continued, too. German and French were added to their curriculum, Prince Nicholas resumed the art lessons which had been interrupted by his time in Salonika, a Swedish lady gymnast taught them keep-fit exercises, and they bicycled and rode. Every night (until they were all grown up) Princess Nicholas read to them in either English or French.

In the summer of 1914 Prince Nicholas took his family to Russia for their summer holiday with Grand Duchess Vladimir. They travelled by boat to Sebastopol. At Constantinople the Greek minister and Russian ambassador boarded the boat, told Nicholas of worrying developments between Austria and Serbia, but insisted that the news was not serious enough for him to return to Athens. At Sebastopol the family was as usual met by the imperial train. Travelling at 20 miles an hour in luxury beyond imagining, met at every station by officials bearing gifts, coming from a country which, if not so rich, was every bit as loving towards them, neither the little girls nor their parents had any idea how soon this story would end.

The family arrived at Tsarskoe Selo on 30 July. The holiday had barely begun when news arrived of war. On 1 August Prince Nicholas heard that Germany had declared war on Russia. The Tsar moved from his summer palace at Peterhof to the Alexander Palace at Tsarskoe Selo which was deemed to be safer for him. In an interview with Prince Nicholas, he stressed the gravity of the situation he had tried so hard to avoid. Nicholas realised that he must take his family home, and the Tsar gave his permission for the journey.

Marina had few memories of the war, but as an adult she recalled hearing the soldiers singing as they turned out for exercise in the streets of Tsarskoe Selo. Not understanding what it meant, she loved the music.

It was 28 August before a route was organised which was thought safe enough for the Nicholas family to take. As they set out from Tsarskoe Selo they saw for the first time the signs of military activity. 'The military movement was intense; we met soldiers everywhere; at the stations, in the trains, or marching in never-ending columns on dusty high roads in the sweltering September heat.'

They were forced to break their journey in Rumania, staying as guests of the Crown Prince Ferdinand and his wife Marie, while the next stage of the journey was organised. On their last evening the Queen arranged a special cinema performance for Olga, Elizabeth and Marina. The journey had been more uncomfortable than the children were used to, but treats were still laid on for them.

The King lent the family his train, and the Crown Prince and Princess travelled with them as far as the Rumanian border. There they stayed with 'a kindly Rumanian bourgeois', who lent them clothes and fed them. The children delighted in the adventure of being without their baggage, dancing in outsize nightgowns around the room. The next morning the family waited irritably for a boat to take them across to the Serbian coast, and the Crown Princess of Rumania sat with the children around her telling story after story to while away the time.

The next stage of the journey was by train, and once again the heat and the discomfort were overpowering. Prince Nicholas and his daughter Marina both long remembered 'the heat and the flies and the long dreary day, and eventually the water melon which was so good'.

The journey was again halted at Salonika, where the family visited the monument Queen Olga had had raised to King George. The visit made the three girls unhappy for a while, but by then their journey was nearly over. Back in Greece, the children often spent hours in a cellar, frightened by the sounds of explosions and shouts from the streets. Then they were sent to the villa Prince Nicholas had rented at Kiphissia, in the foothills of Mount Pentelikon, half way between Athens and Tatoi. And the holiday continued. So, alas, did the war.

Other members of the Greek royal family had been recalled from holiday to face the newest crisis together. Prince Christopher and his nephew, Crown Prince George, were staying in England with Queen Alexandra at Marlborough House when war was declared.

We stood at the window to look down at the immense crowd in front of Buckingham Palace, waiting in a silence that could almost be felt while the last moments of the ultimatum to Germany expired; and when at length the clock boomed out the hour, one deep breath was drawn by all those thousands, like a mighty sigh. Then the tension relaxed and a second later everyone was laughing, singing patriotic songs and shouting for the King and Queen. King George went out on to the balcony. His face was white and drawn; he had grown years older in the last week. Tears stood in his eyes as he listened to the frantic cheers.

Recalled to Greece, Christopher and George found themselves, like many others, stuck somewhere they did not want to be. Finally they procured themselves a cabin on a P. & O. steamer and after an eventful journey arrived home.

Greece immediately declared itself neutral, but was urged to join the war by all sides. Venizelos, 'his smile as fox-like as ever, but ... no longer obsequious, could even be called arrogant' by now (wrote Prince Christopher) and he had his own plans for the war. While the Kaiser plied King Constantine with unwelcome telegrams, urging him 'as a brother-in-law and Field Marshal of the German Army' as well as arguing expediency as reasons for Greece to join the Germans, Venizelos made promises to the Allies. Constantine, determined not to put Greece's new-found peace and prosperity at risk, returned his German decorations and Field-Marshal's baton to the Kaiser and stubbornly clung to neutrality. With Queen Sophie the sister of the Kaiser, it was easy for Venizelos to spread the rumour that the King was in fact pro-German. In England factions were also claiming that King George and Queen Mary were secretly siding with the Germans, but although Mary spoke with a slight guttural accent she was the first consort for over four hundred years to speak English as her first language. Both she and George were in everything except blood totally English.

In fact the Kaiser had never been personally popular with the Greek royal family. Every April he was accustomed to holiday in Corfu where he gave presents of toothbrushes and combs to the Greek peasants and soap to their children. Each year King George had arranged to arrive at the Greek palace, Mon Repos, a few days before the Kaiser and to leave a few days after his holiday ended. 'Why on earth do you always go to Corfu to meet the Kaiser? You know you can't stand him,' Queen Olga once asked. 'If I don't, he'll think he's the King of Greece,' came the reply. The distrust of the Oldenburgs for the Hohenzollerns went back in history to Prussia's taking of Holstein from Denmark in 1864. While Constantine's marriage to Sophie had healed the rift somewhat, the royal Greek's inclination was certainly not to make life easier for the Kaiser and Sophie herself described her position as being one of 'a horrible no-man's land of distraction'.

Constantine did all he could to help the Allies without actually joining battle: he gave practical advice, loaned the Serbians artillery munitions to help drive back Austria, and allowed them to form a base at Salonika. When the Bulgarians began military manoeuvres close to the Serbian frontier, Constantine telegrammed a warning to the Kaiser that he too would mobilise his armies unless the Bulgarian troops were demobilised. The next day manoeuvres were halted. Although refusing to join in the battle of the Dardanelles, he gave the Allies the plans the Greeks had drawn up for attacking Constantinople by land instead of sea.

Nevertheless Venizelos's insinuations did their work. While

Venizelos took advantage of a Prime Minister's prerogative to change his mind occasionally, sometimes even taking the same view as his King, he did his best to undermine the King's popularity both at home and abroad. Although Constantine sent his German decorations back, he had after all received them along with a wife from Germany. His Chief of the General Staff, Colonel John Metaxas, who supported Constantine in the decision to remain neutral, was trained in Germany, but so had been many other Greeks, including George Papandreou, Liberal Prime Minister and a staunch ally of the Western powers. Later history shows that Metaxas was not pro-German (in 1940 he joined Greece in the war against the Axis powers), but in the early days of the First World War many did not look beyond the obvious German links.

The question of whether Greece should provide practical help for the battle for the Dardanelles was a vexed one: Venizelos was all for it, although Prince Nicholas noted his brother Constantine's views down in his diary:

Mr Venizelos' scheme is certainly alluring, and it appeals to me as much as it, probably, will appeal to every true Greek. I should not object to our participation in the enterprise – how could I? I am reluctantly convinced it is impossible. The object of the Allies' attack against the Dardanelles is to reach Constantinople. The Straits can never be forced by a fleet alone. There must be a simultaneous attack by land and by sea, and a very big army would be needed to carry it through.

At first, despite his doubts, Constantine reluctantly agreed to Venizelos's plan, but when Metaxas resigned over the issue, the King withdrew his consent. He stuck to his refusal through the resignation of Venizelos, and appointed Dimitrios Gounaris Prime Minister despite his reputation for being pro-German. Even after new elections were held in June 1915 Venizelos retained a large majority in Parliament and finally in August Constantine had no choice but to recall his enemy. Going against the democratic will by keeping Venizelos out, and undermining his power while he was in, was perhaps Constantine's biggest – and most unforgivable – mistake.

While the King still could, he did his best to keep the Allies aware of his good intentions. Himself weakened by a near-fatal illness, he sent Nicholas to Russia and Andrew to France to persuade the Allies of his good faith. Christopher stayed at Kiphissia with Helen and the children.

By 1916 the King's position was very shaky. He and Venizelos were open enemies. Tatoi and the surrounding forests were burned to the ground by arsonists – eighteen of the household died in the fire. Princess Nicholas and her daughters watched the red glow from the house at Kiphissia while estate workers headed by King Constantine fought the blaze. Only the King's intimate knowledge of the goat tracks around the palace saved his life as he finally gave up the battle and escaped the fire with his wife and two of his children. Constantine's ADC was warned that all the wines at Kiphissia had been poisoned in a plot to kill the King. In September Venizelos went to Salonika where he set up a triumvirate of himself, Admiral Coundouriotis (King George's former ADC) and General Danglis.

Constantine still refused to join the war, until on 2 December Allied troops marched into Athens. They were forced to retreat but later the same day the French bombarded Athens into submission 'without warning and without evacuating the popu-lation'. Olga, Elizabeth and Marina were back in Athens and watched the violence from their windows until they were sent into the basements of the palace.

And so the King was left defenceless in his capital. The Allies had control of his fleet, his army, his railways and his lines of communication. Finally, they asked for his abdication. Con-stantine, threatened with the renewed bombardment of Athens if he did not comply, realised that he effectively had no choice. He agreed that he and the Crown Prince (also regarded as pro-German by the Powers as his early military training had been in Germany), would leave the country and that his second son Alexander would rule in his place. It is important to note that this agreement did not in fact amount to an abdication, but the Powers were so delighted at his departure that they did not, at the time, notice that he left the country without signing a formal act of abdication.

The High Commissioner sent by the Protecting Powers, M.

Jonnart, promised that Venizelos would not be recalled and that the Greeks could re-elect the King if they so chose once the war was over. It was hoped that his promise would help to avoid unpleasant scenes on the King's leaving.

Such a hope was in vain. Prince Nicholas recorded the scene in his diary:

As soon as the Powers' ultimatum and its acceptance by the King became known, confirming their worst suspicions, the people came hurrying to the Palace from every direction. Alarm and dismay were written on every face, and they firmly decided to prevent the King from going away. All the church-bells began to toll mournfully, and the whole town was plunged in despair. The Palace was surrounded on all sides, and the soldiers of the King's body-guard ... received orders to close the gates and to allow no one to enter. The crowds were thickly massed outside and peremptorily, almost angrily, forbade the exit of anyone who wished to leave the Palace.

Throughout that night of 11 June the King received delegations begging him not to leave: again and again he explained that he had little choice, that his action was for Greece. Twice Constantine and Sophie tried to leave the palace, but each time the crowds prevented them. The whole royal family spent the night in the palace, roaming its corridors sleeplessly.

At six the next morning Princes Nicholas and Andrew tried to leave with their wives to return to their own homes, but they too were turned back by the crowds. At ten an official declaration from Constantine was distributed among the people:

Obeying necessity and accomplishing a duty towards Greece, I am departing from my beloved country with the Crown Prince, leaving my son Alexander on the Throne. Even far from Greece, the Queen and I will always retain the same affection towards the Greek people. I beg you all to accept my decision with serenity, trusting to God, Whose blessing I invoke on the nation. And that this sacrifice for the country may not be in vain, I adjure all of you, if you love God, if you love your country, if, lastly, you love me, not to cause any disturbance, but to remain submissive. The least disorder, even if prompted by a lofty sentiment, may today lead to the most terrible disaster. At this moment the greatest solace for the Queen and myself lies in the affection and devotion which you have always shown to us, in the happy days as well as in the unhappy ones. May God protect Greece. Constantine R.

Not surprisingly, this did little to calm the inflamed folk of Athens, who came in even greater numbers to besiege the palace and rang their bells ever more dolefully. M. Jonnart decided that the Greeks needed a little reminder that insubordination would not be welcome and began landing foreign troops on Greece, sending a polite message saying how much the soldiers were looking forward to Greek hospitality. Meanwhile young Prince Alexander, blinded by tears, took the oath of allegiance. This was announced to the public, and then Jonnart issued another statement, also designed to calm the crowds. In it he promised that the provisional government in Salonika was dissolved, that the Powers were not intending to put Venizelos in office as Prime Minister, and that Greece was free to remain neutral.

With the troops marching towards Athens, it became imperative that the King and Queen should leave at once. Finally the crowds were tricked into gathering by the wrong entrance and the royal family made its escape through a private garden into waiting cars which took them to Tatoi. As they left the palace it began to rain. At Tatoi the sad preparations for the King's departure continued: he received a stream of people wishing him goodbye, and then he and his family visited George I's grave on the hill for private prayer. On the night of 13 June the royal yacht *Sphacteria* arrived at the small fishing village of Oropos. The next morning the King and his family, accompanied by his brothers, made the journey by road to Oropos, where once again they were met by crowds of well-wishers strewing flowers before them.

In later life Princess Marina would always claim to have forgotten the details of those hard times, but she was old enough for that to be a question of selective memory. It is certain that her own family's departure from Greece, very soon after the King's, remained in her mind. Constantine's expulsion was followed by that of the rest of his family except for the new young King, and the Nicholases were the next to leave.

On 4 July the new King came to see Nicholas and his family off on their journey away from Greece. Nicholas and Helen explained what was happening to their daughters, and the family stood together on the deck of the *Amphrite*, watching Greece

47

slip away from them and repeating 'God bless and help Greece' together. Alexander was left behind without his family, and with his household replaced by new faces. Despite promises to the contrary, Venizelos was recalled to Greece within a week of the royal family's leaving the country.

Royal families in exile are lucky if they can keep their friends, and the Greeks were lucky. With no income, they had to live on borrowed money. It was, as Christopher said, 'an unpleasant test to apply to one's friends, but people were amazingly kind. Just when we were wondering where in the world the next quarter's rent was coming from, someone always stepped into the breach. Our household servants had all followed us from Greece and served us out of pure devotion.' The Nicholases were to learn a new kind of life from that which had sheltered them for so long. Had Greece's troubles come upon her sooner, Russia would have been the obvious home for Nicholas's family, but Russia was now facing her own disasters. Revolution was raging, and many of their Russian relations were facing much worse than exile in the Swiss mountains. So the Nicholases first home was in St Moritz, where they spent the next three winters.

Prince and Princess Nicholas did all in their power to keep their daughters' lives on an even keel: lessons were resumed and in place of riding the girls took up skiing and skating. Marina's interest in art continued and she found inspiration in the mountains about her. At first Marina was taught to draw by her father, but as it became clear that her interest was more than passing and that she had genuine talent, a professional art teacher was engaged. It was a pastime that the Princess was to keep up for the rest of her life.

Although the family was on a black list, mail censored, forbidden to leave Switzerland, and surrounded by spies, the Nicholases tried hard to continue with some kind of normality. However, they could not keep everything from the girls, and it was a real blow when in the summer of 1918 Miss Fox, who had been with the family since the Princesses were born, was sent for by the British consulate in Lausanne where the Nicholases were spending the summer. She was cross-questioned about the family and told that if she continued to work for the 'traitors to England' her passport would be removed. She returned in tears, and left for England the next day, promising to rejoin them as soon as she could.

The Swiss exile lasted for three and a half years, years which passed on the whole calmly and in which the family, while still hoping for a return to Greece, learned to live away from their country. Lloyd George claimed that Constantine was 'surly and suspicious' and too sympathetic to the Germans. The King had good cause to be the former and no reason to be the latter. For the older generation 'time hung heavily on our hands' as they watched the development of affairs in Greece, but the girls were young and adaptable. Family life continued to be as important as it had in Greece – with Nicholas, Constantine, Andrew and Christopher all in the country the network of family feeling and support helped to keep up their spirits. King Constantine's health was a constant worry and when he fell victim to the Spanish flu epidemic his life was in danger. However, during the Easter midnight Mass he took a turn for the better and survived.

Both Marina's grandmothers had been caught in Russia when the Revolution broke out. Queen Olga, a Grand Duchess by birth, had been running a military hospital and found herself marooned in her homeland. At first her children did not worry: 'We imagined that she would be perfectly safe among the people who had known her since her childhood,' wrote Christopher, and indeed apart from a few near misses Olga was able to pass between Pavlovsk (in the summer) and the Marble Palace in the newly renamed Petrograd without too much danger. On one occasion Olga was saved by the habit she had had of visiting Russian ships calling on Greece. Her maid recognised in an angry Bolshevik one of the sailors to whom Queen Olga had shown kindness, and read him a riot act which ended in him and his companions slinking away in shame. Olga's clinging to Russia, which had so irritated the Greeks, did in the end save her.

Finally, when she heard of Constantine's illness, she determined that she must join her family and after strenuous efforts by the Danish Embassy she was at last, in July 1918, free to leave. Her jewellery was smuggled out of her home by a Greek student and taken to the Danish Legation, from where it was forwarded to Copenhagen.

Olga did not leave a moment too soon. In July the Tsar and his family were killed by the Bolsheviks, and in the slaughter that swept Russia many aristocrats were murdered. Princess Nicholas lost seventeen of her closest relations (the Tsar himself was of course both her and Nicholas's first cousin) and her children (now fifteen, fourteen and twelve), were old enough to mourn the Grand Duchesses and Tsarevich, who had been their playmates in easier times.

The Grand Duchess Vladimir, Helen's mother, had a harder time of it. She too had been running a military hospital in the Caucasus, but she was rarely left in peace by the Bolsheviks. After over twenty searches of her home, more than one flight into the mountains, including one when she had time to do no more than pull a dressing gown on before leaving, it finally became clear that the Grand Duchess must leave the country if she was to have any chance of survival. Being a woman of stern and noble character, she did not leave by night. She left Kislovodsk in an open carriage with a maid of honour and a box of jewels. The Cossacks drove her 50 miles to the nearest railway station where a special train had been commissioned to take her away. Her staff and other refugees followed in other carriages.

Novorǒssisk, from where a boat was to carry them to Venice, was full of Russian refugees, including the Tsar's sister Olga, an old enemy, who later told of Grand Duchess Vladimir's arrival:

I was amazed to learn that she had reached the town in her own train, manned by her own staff, and still had her ladies with her. For all the dangers and privations she still appeared every inch a Grand Duchess. There had never been much love between Aunt Miechen and my own family but I felt proud of her. Disregarding peril and hardship she stubbornly kept to all the trimmings of bygone splendour and glory. And somehow she carried it off. When generals found themselves lucky to find a horse and cart to bring them to safety, Aunt Miechen made a long journey in her own train. It was battered all right but it was hers. For the first time in my life it was a pleasure to kiss her.

Grand Duchess Vladimir's character was difficult, and made her many enemies, but under such circumstances she could not but be admired.

She arrived in Switzerland in the summer of 1920, and was reunited with the family she had not seen for six years. Despite her privations, her courage and humour were undimmed, but her health had suffered. After some weeks spent in Switzerland, the Grand Duchess went to Contrexeville, a French spa which had long been a favourite with her. On 6 September she died, with her three sons and daughter beside her. Although the war was long since over, Nicholas and his daughters were still not allowed to leave Switzerland to be at her bedside.

Grand Duchess Vladimir's death did give some financial relief to the Nicholases. As well as the jewels she had managed to bring out of Russia with her, others, the main part of her collection, had been rescued from Russia by an intrepid Englishman, Bertie Stopford, a figure half way between Bertie Wooster and the Scarlet Pimpernel. He had gone to Russia with the sole aim of saving the Grand Duchess's jewels, disguised himself as a workman, removed them from her palace in Petrograd in two old Gladstone bags, and smuggled them back to England. Most of the jewels were left to her daughter Helen. However, there were so many magnificent jewels in the hands of suddenly impoverished aristocrats that their value had fallen. To realise any real money, they could only be sold slowly and cautiously. Queen Mary bought some fine pieces, including a diamond tiara with opals and drop pearls (often worn by the present Queen Elizabeth II) and a diamond bow clasp which she later gave to Marina.

Prince Nicholas had already begun to earn money for the first time in his life as his interest in art was turned to more practical use than mere princely dabblings. Living off borrowed money, with three daughters and many other relations in similar straightened circumstances, Nicholas decided to hold a small exhibition at Montreux under the pseudonym 'Nicholas le Prince'. The pictures sold well and from then on Nicholas's work contributed to the family finances.

Meanwhile, in Greece King Alexander continued as a puppet monarch. Probably the only act he perpetrated of his own volition was his marriage in November 1919 with Aspasia

Manos, the daughter of his father's ADC. He married her secretly without either parental or religious approval, and when the marriage was discovered both politicians and the populace were furious. Greece may have been proud of her democracy, but she was not democratic enough to take a commoner to the throne. The young girl was immediately separated from her husband. Never recognised as queen, 'Madame Manos' as she became known, gave birth to a daughter, who was given the title of Her Royal Highness Princess Alexandra.

Alexander's reign was not to prove long, but even as it was nearing its end the Powers realised that Greek feeling was veering back towards the return of the monarchy. Greece had finally joined the war in May 1918 and played a late but honourable part in the defeat of the Turks. But by 1920 Mustapha Kemal (Atatürk) was leading a nationalistic upsurge and the Turks were ready to recover their lost name. Venizelos ordered Greek troops at Smyrna to advance against Mustapha Kemal's still disorganised army, thus opening yet another episode in what to many Greeks seemed an endless war.

In June the British minister in Athens, Earl Granville, reported the growing swell of monarchism:

I have always felt confident that provided the decisions of the Peace Conference were favourable to Greece, Venizelos was safe to secure a majority – and probably a big majority – at the elections, but I confess that during the last few days my confidence has been a good deal shaken; any number of people have told me stories of strong feeling existing in the country against him.

With the elections due in November, it was time for the pro-Venizelists to worry about the future.

In fact matters came to a head even sooner. In October 1920 King Alexander was bitten in the arm by a pet monkey. On 25 October he died of blood poisoning. None of his family was near him. Only his mother, Queen Olga, was given permission to return to Greece when it became clear that his illness was fatal, and she arrived twelve hours too late.

Greece was now without a monarch and with an increasingly unpopular Prime Minister. Venizelos offered the throne to Constantine's third son Paul, who refused it on the grounds that both his father and his elder brother were alive. Less than a fortnight later Venizelos was roundly defeated in the elections, gaining only 120 out of the 370 seats in Parliament. He handed in his resignation and 'discreetly left Athens by night', leaving the Allied Powers in total confusion.

It was announced that Princes Nicholas and Andrew were to return to Greece with their families, which gave Lord Granville more cause for concern. Should he or should he not call on them formally and sign their book? 'Nobody outside Greece can realise the complete change of popular opinion that has taken place and the almost insane enthusiasm at this moment for Constantine,' he wrote to England, but was told in answer than he should do nothing which might implicate the British government in an ultimate recognition of the King.

The British could not stop the popular movement, and the first step in the restitution of the monarch came with Queen Olga (in the country since Alexander's death) being made regent. It was in this role that she welcomed back Andrew, Christopher and Marie, the first of the family to return to Greece.

Nicholas, Helen and the girls were not far behind, although they almost did not survive the journey home. The family travelled to Brindisi, where a luxurious liner was waiting to carry them to Greece. However, at the last moment Nicholas decided that they should re-enter Greece in a Greek ship. All that was to be had was an uncomfortable little 'cockleshell' of a ship in which they nearly drowned near the Greek islands. Luckily a nearby Greek warship came to the rescue – and the family did re-enter Greece in a Greek vessel.

Each return was met with almost crazy enthusiasm by the Greeks, and it was a time that none of them ever forgot. Such a welcome almost wiped out the waiting years, and led them all to believe that the time had come when Greece could live happily ever after with its monarchy.

On 5 December a referendum was held throughout Greece (at Constantine's instigation) to decide Constantine's fate: only 10,883 out of 1,010,788 voters were against him. Two weeks later he arrived back in a snowstorm.

It is no use to pretend that the English behaved well under the circumstances: although the Greeks had been soothed on Constantine's departure with the promise that he could be reinstated by a general vote after the war, there can have been no intention on the Allies' part to allow the monarch back on his throne. The speed with which Venizelos had been invited back, despite another promise, seems to prove this. However, there was nothing they could do. The Allies even went so far as to inform the Greek government that

though they had no wish to interfere in the internal affairs of Greece, they felt bound to declare publicly that the restoration of the throne to a King whose disloyal attitude and conduct to the Allies during the War had caused them great embarrassment and loss could only be regarded by them as a ratification by Greece of his hostile acts.

The Greeks paid no attention. The cry, '*Erchetai ... erchetai*' ('he is coming ... he is coming') was heard again and again as each of the members of the royal family returned. The return of the King and Queen themselves was greeted with almost frenzied fervour. Flags flew from almost every house and the anthem 'Son of the Eagle' was heard once again. No one really seemed to mind that the flag was missing from the British Legation or that Lord Granville, instructed from England to have nothing to do with either Constantine or the government, could only lie low and wait and see.

Marina never forgot the return to Greece (she was just fourteen when her family went home), but perhaps for her one of the most important effects of the restitution of the monarchy was the return of Miss Fox, who true to her promise rejoined the family almost immediately.

Unfortunately for Constantine, Venizelos's last legacy to Greece was the mobilisation of her troops in Asia Minor. Constantine was against this war, as he had been against the other, and for the same reason. He could see that Greece was not ready for more confrontation. But the Greeks themselves were in such a state of overexcitement that they could not be dissuaded from continuing what Venizelos had begun, even though France and Great Britain had both withdrawn their backing (as much as an anti-Constantine move as anything else). The Greeks were back on their favourite track of empire-building and nothing could stop them.

The family had returned in triumph in November and December of 1920. By January 1921 the country was back in the full-blown throes of a war. The children were sent to Tatoi, which although still badly scarred by the fire, meant so much to them all, while the Princes returned to soldiering and their wives to hospital work.

There were moments when royal life resumed its old patterns. In 1921 there were two royal weddings: On 27 February in Bucharest Crown Prince George married Princess Elizabeth of Rumania. George had first proposed to the fat Rumanian Princess in 1914, when she was sixteen and he twenty-one. She, advised by her namesake the Queen of Rumania that she could do better, refused. 'God started him but forgot to finish him off,' she said of her suitor. In 1920, when the offer was renewed, she accepted a loveless match. Between the engagement and wedding George had returned from exile and taken his place as Crown Prince of Greece. George took his sister Helen on his engagement visit to Rumania. There she met and soon became engaged to the wicked Crown Prince Carol.

Greek Orthodox Church law specifies that when brother and sister marry brother and sister the two weddings should take place within the hour. Queen Marie of Rumania was given dispensation to break this law so that she could attend both her children's weddings: the superstitious Greek peasants prophesied trouble, and on this occasion they were proved right. Within a year of her marriage Helen was back in Greece for four months, alone with her baby. On her return to Rumania Carol was back at his womanising and the marriage which had begun on both sides with genuine hope had started its slide into vicious cruelty and recrimination. They were divorced in 1928.

George and Elizabeth's wedding was also to end in divorce, after Elizabeth's lack of wifely support was manifested by telegrams she sent to her mother's adviser and Prince Paul of Yugoslavia, begging to be rescued from Greece.

Marina, dressed in Irish lace, was bridesmaid to the ill-fated Helen.

Aside from the pomp of royal weddings, normal life continued. There were cousins to play with, island picnics, games of bows and arrows, figs to eat, trees to climb. Life was grand.

At first the war went satisfactorily enough for the Greeks, but that was not to last. While all was well they were encouraged in the campaign by the British, who did not, however, see fit to give any actual help. The French remained firmly set against the whole struggle. By the end of June 1921 the Greeks had nearly reached their objective of Ankara, the new capital, but from then on they were struggling. In August Mustapha Kemal counterattacked and the Greeks began what was to be a long and slow, though orderly, retreat. They held on throughout the winter, but by March 1922 were ready to accept an armistice proposed by the Powers. Mustapha Kemal was also prepared to accept it on condition that Asia Minor was evacuated, a condition the Powers (not Greece itself) rejected. Mustapha Kemal chose to enforce his condition and at the end of August 1922 launched a vicious and successful attack against Smyrna. Smyrna was sacked, its Christian inhabitants murdered in their thousands and the Greek army fled.

Someone had to be blamed. And that someone was King Constantine. Anti-royalists began to agitate until both the British and French governments feared for the King's life. Nicholas requested a British man-of-war to come and evacuate the whole of the Greek royal family, but the British were at first more worried for themselves than for the Greek royalty. 'It is certainly to be hoped that we shall not become involved in the misfortunes of the Greek Royal Family ... on the other hand we would, of course, intervene to avoid actual bloodshed,' went a dispatch from the Foreign Office.

On 30 October King Constantine abdicated in favour of his eldest son George. His leaving was the more bitter as it was demanded this time not by outside powers, but by his own people. Prince Nicholas, who had been at Tatoi with the King, Queen and Crown Prince, left the country with his brother.

The farewell greetings in 1917 had been heart-breaking, but there *was* always the hope of it being only a temporary exile. This time it seemed to be good-bye for ever .... It was dark when the steamer started – the wind was howling; one by one the lights of the little village, as we sailed away, faded into the distance; this was the last time King Constantine gazed on his beloved Greece.

This time Marina was spared the sad humiliation of departure. She was already in England, on holiday with Miss Fox. Her sisters and mother were also out of the country, staying in Paris and with Prince Christopher and his American wife Nancy in Cannes. And Queen Olga had also already left Greece, much against her will, for urgent eye treatment. Prince Andrew, whose first son and fifth child Philip had been born in the summer of 1921 when there was still some hope of stability, was less lucky. He was arrested as a traitor, kept in custody (he was allowed a valet but no dentist when he broke a tooth) and only saved from the death sentence by the intervention of the Kings of England and Spain and the President of France.

Constantine, Sophie and Nicholas went to Palermo, from where Nicholas sent for his family to rejoin him. Princess Marina looked at her parents and said, with the mischievous glint in her eye that her friends knew so well, 'We really needn't have unpacked our trunks.'

Constantine died in Palermo in January 1923, only three months after leaving Greece. His health had been poor for some years, but it is not fanciful to suppose that his end was hastened by an old-fashioned complaint: a broken heart.

After his family had gathered in Palermo, Prince Nicholas had to decide on where to live next. They stayed in San Remo until spring 1923, then moved to Merano. At first their life was quiet, as they were in deepest mourning for the King, but as usual their studies continued and there was no reason for the girls not to enjoy outings to local beauty spots and historical buildings.

They all knew that this time there was little hope of the monarchy being restored, and they all believed that they were now looking for a permanent home. England was mooted as a possibility and was Prince Nicholas's preference, but the combination of their rickety finances and precarious political position made this unfeasible. So it was decided that after 'doing' the London season they should settle in Paris. Prince George and his rich wife Marie Bonaparte lent a house in their grounds to Prince Andrew and his family, and the Nicholases also settled in St Cloud.

This was a different Paris from the city in which they had all stayed in great luxury as royal visitors. The three sisters had often visited the French capital with their maternal grandmother, and those days had been full of treats and excitement. Now the carriages were traded for taxis, the grand hotels for a small hotel near the Bois de Boulogne. Not all their friends were as assiduous as they had been in the palmy days. After all, Paris was a city of exiles, overrun with the Russians who had succeeded in escaping the Revolution. And as Prince Andrew's daughter Sophie later said, 'We never had any money. The Greek royals never used their position to hoard money.'

It was as a Russian that Princess Nicholas found a new purpose in her life. She sold many of her jewels and founded a home for the children of Russian refugees – a place which would enable their parents to find employment. She worked wholeheartedly for her charity, and encouraged her daughters to do the same. As Princess Nicholas had been a leading figure in the *haut monde* of Greece (even among her royal sisters-in-law), so she became a success in Paris. Her presence at a charity gala was sure to draw others to the ball. Her daughters, too, soon earned a name for their sweetness and naturalness. They were drawn in to programme selling at the galas, to performing in tableaux designed by their artistic father. But Marina most enjoyed actively helping in the home: putting the children to bed, playing with them and being part of the household.

The family was not together for long. The summer season of 1923 was spent in London. They stayed in a Kensington hotel from which the older girls were taken to cocktail parties and dances, polo matches and shopping outings while Marina visited museums and art galleries. In October Olga married Prince Paul of Yugoslavia. It was not her first engagement: in the year before, while staying with her uncle at Cannes, she had met and become engaged to Crown Prince Frederick of Denmark. The engagement was almost as short as the courtship. It is not entirely known why the engagement did not last; rumours included hints that Prince Frederick's drinking was more than recreational and there is a story that 'Rico' was once so drunk that he raised Princess Elizabeth's hand to acknowledge a cheering crowd rather than Olga's. Whatever the reason, by September the wedding plans had been officially shelved.

Marina had been in England during the happy days of the courtship and engagement, but she was reunited with her family by the time the wedding had been called off. Sitting in a window as the adults heatedly discussed the rights and wrongs of the whole sorry affair, she suddenly proffered her own view: 'Why the hell should Olga marry him if she doesn't love him? I wouldn't.' And that was the view that was allowed to hold sway.

It was just as well. Prince Paul of Serbia was the nephew of King Peter I and was later to become regent of Yugoslavia during the minority of his nephew (also Peter). At this time he was a glamorous and carefree bachelor, with an Oxford degree and living in Mount Street, London. Paul saw Olga across a crowded ballroom (at a dance given by Lady Zia Wernher) and pursued the Greek beauty with intent. This too was a speedy courtship – he proposed on 29 July and the marriage took place in Belgrade three months later. The family approved of the match, Prince Christopher writing, 'Paul, brilliantly clever, sensitive, artistic, an idealist, is precisely the right husband for Olga, who is merry, philosophical and practical to the last degree.'

The wedding was the day after the christening of Prince Peter, and royalty from all over Europe and the Balkans was assembled including the Duke of York (the future George VI, who stood godfather or 'Koom' to the baby and also exchanged rings at the wedding) and his Duchess. The marriage ceremony, solemnised by the Patriarch of Serbia, was rich in pageantry and symbolism. Afterwards Olga carried out the Serbian customs of stepping across a strip of cloth (which symbolised the moat of her husband's house), scattering corn and kissing a baby boy (Prince Peter).

After the excitement of the wedding was over Elizabeth and

Marina were left together to help their mother in her charitable enterprises. All who knew Marina confirm how wholeheartedly in later years she entered into her work as a British Princess, that she would never take on any charity without intending to give of her best. This was an attribute she must in part have learned from her mother's example during those Paris days. Princess Nicholas was not rich by the standards to which she had been brought up, yet she sold her jewels not for herself but to help her fellow Russians. Her daughters were dressed by Paris couturiers, and they were not by any means on the bread line, but Paris was full of people in similar situations to themselves, and Princess Nicholas gave much of what she had to them.

As well as the Paris home, she also patronised homes for poor Russians on the Riviera and would take Elizabeth and Marina with her to charity galas. Their bank balance might have shrunk but the grandeur of their social circle had not. 'I remember King Emmanuel of Portugal winning a motor-car in the tombola over which the two young Greek princesses presided,' wrote Helena von der Hoven, adding that the King and Crown Prince of Sweden and King and Queen of Denmark were also wont to attend these events. Charity galas they may have been rather than private balls, but the guest list was still extremely grand.

And, of course, the British royal family remained on friendly terms with the Greeks. Queen Alexandra was after all Prince Nicholas's aunt, and whenever Nicholas and his family were in England they visited their English relations at court, albeit unofficially. Even when alone in England with Miss Fox Marina would visit Queen Alexandra regularly, saying later, 'she was so lovely and sweet and such a good friend'.

When in 1924 Olga was expecting her first child she was lent White Lodge in Richmond Park by the Duchess of York for the birth, and Marina stayed there with her sister. Once again the Nicholases had brought their daughters to England for the season. Olga's son, Alexander, was born on 7 August and was baptised a month later, numbering King Alexander of Serbia, the Infanta Beatrice of Spain and the Duke of York (an old friend of Prince Paul's) among his godparents.

Marina already had great affection for the English, and her

charity work in Paris deepened her faith in her English friends. 'It's the poor who help the most,' she said once, 'especially the English people. They are so kind. Once you have gained their friendship they never let you down.'

In December 1923 King George, the last member of the family to remain in Greece, was forced to leave the country with his wife, Queen Elizabeth. They went into exile in Rumania, along with Queen Sophie and her younger daughter. Elizabeth ate rich cakes and played mahjong before falling in love with another Greek and divorcing George (by now living in England), whose only ally was his mother-in-law, the Rumanian Queen. George learned of his divorce in the British Press. Greece was declared a republic and the Greek royal family was denied Greek nationality – they were forced to travel on Danish passports. Any remaining hope of return seemed finally doomed. Nicholas had already arranged the leasing of his Athens palace to the owners of the capital's leading hotel, and this shrewd move ensured not only an income but also the return of many of the family's possessions. On the proceeds they were able to leave their hotel and rent themselves a flat in the Boulevard Jules Sandeau, not far from the Bois de Boulogne.

Nicholas was not without some bitterness, writing in 1926:

Few people can realise that Royal Families are just human beings, that their 'blue' blood is just as red as anyone else's, and their tears every bit as bitter; few of them are able to indulge in the luxury of Palace Hotels and Transatlantic liners. To be born a prince is an accident, but not always a privilege and by no means a career. Although he may be conspicuous, although his position may be envied by those who know nothing about it, he is less protected by the law of the land than the humblest boot-black and chimney sweep. Without notice or compensation no one would dream of expelling a servant. Nor would it be possible, as with us, to confiscate a private fortune. But revolution led by discontents, and not inspired by the apt claims of the oppressed, finds excuses for all its crimes and turns them into laws.

His future at the time looked pretty black, but once again the family clung together and gave and took strength from the contact.

It was decided to send Marina to finishing school. With Olga gone and Elizabeth officially 'out' she was left alone in the school-room. Her parents decided on a school at Auteuil run by another Russian refugee and former lady-in-waiting to Helen, Princess Mestchersky. Marina was not entirely pleased with the decision, but bore it philosophically. She was to board, but to have her own bedroom and Sundays would be spent with her family.

The girls at the school were taught architecture, French language, literature and history. Trips were organised to Fontainebleu and Versailles during the day and concerts and theatres in the evenings. Marina took extra art lessons and soon learned to mix with the other girls, although many remained in awe of her for her mixture of outspokenness and shyness which could be taken for standoffishness. Her own family was aware that this trait sometimes made others wary of her. 'By those who do not know her well she is sometimes misjudged, for her very shyness and ultra-sensitive air of reserve create a false impression of hauteur. Underneath it she had a kindness and sympathy that one rarely encounters, an unfailing sense of humour for her own troubles and an unlimited compassion for those of other people.'

Her reputation as a mimic won her friends and admirers and had she not been a Princess she would have considered taking up acting as a career. Cinema outings were certainly among her favourite forms of relaxation, and Marina still painted for pleasure. Travelling around Paris on her own, or with a few other girls, gave Marina a freedom and independence to which she had not been used but which she soon learned to enjoy.

After the year in school, Marina officially came out. She was allowed to go with her sister Elizabeth on holiday to North Africa. They went without their parents, but accompanied by a few trustworthy friends. The two girls took their sketchbooks and visited Morocco, Tunis and Algiers. Marina rode a camel, which made off with her into the desert to the considerable alarm of her party. It was a tourists' holiday, but once again was something entirely new to both girls, and a happy time they always remembered with affection.

Another visit was to her uncle Christopher in Rome, where he had settled with his mother after his wife Nancy's death. He had decided that, with no home of his own, he should provide

one for the ageing Queen Olga so that in the last days of her
life she might have some of the stability which had been missing
for so many years: 'Her rooms were arranged to resemble, as
far as possible, those she had had in Athens. The decorations
and furniture were the same; all her books and little odds and
ends were brought out; her pictures were hung on the walls.'
The pair of them lived a 'placid, rather lotus-eating existence'
for two years before Olga died in 1926. Her funeral service was
held in Rome, and she was buried in Florence in the crypt of
the Russian church. Her death left a scar in the family of which
she had been the matriarch for so long. There is no doubt but
that this fierce Russian Grand Duchess had been a source of
strength and inspiration to her family during the most troubled
times, and that while she upheld them she was in her turn upheld
by her firm religious faith. 'When I used to ask my mother why
it was that some terrible injustice was allowed to happen in this
world, she would answer, "It is impossible to find a reason for
this, but don't forget that human justice differs from Divine
justice, as a man differs from God." '

And so the years passed. The Greek Princesses were admired
for their beauty, but remained poor relations of Europe. (Poor
indeed – Marina had one white evening dress which became a
running joke in the family, so often did she have to wear it and
in so many ways did she ring its changes.) They could not forget
who they were or from where they had come, but became happy
in their new life. They worked at the various charities sponsored
by their mother, visited their luckier royal relations in England
and every summer visited Olga and Paul at Bohinj, the summer
chalet in Yugoslavia. There were later rumours that Marina
earned money as a model for couture houses, but although any
designer was glad to dress her (and to come to an arrangement
over discounts), this was never the case. The closest she came
was being photographed for a Ponds Cold Cream adver-
tisement – and in doing this she was one of many upper-class
young ladies in need of a little extra money. Both she and
Elizabeth posed for Ponds more than once over the space of a
few years, being paid somewhere between £50 and £100 a time.

If Marina's upbringing was unconventional by royal standards, that was not to harm her. As Prince Christopher was to note, 'There was very little money in those days so she learnt things not usually included in the education of a princess ... to make herself useful in the running of a house, to arrange flowers as well as any florist, and to wear a dress from a small dressmaker so charmingly that it looked like a model from one of the grand couturiers.' Marina often did her own hair, inventing different styles for herself. Queen Marie of Rumania would ask her to do hers, too, saying that she was 'better than any hairdresser'. Queen Marie also testified to the Greek Princess's style: 'In those days Marina and her sister had very little to spend, but they had such taste and natural elegance that everything they wore suited them. Marina was so lovely that I used to call her "La Belle Helene".' More important than these somewhat esoteric talents, though, was the fact that 'in the process she developed independence, much knowledge of life and a great understanding of human nature'.

There was one big advantage for Prince Nicholas's daughters in the family's state of exile. Had they stayed in Greece the likelihood is that, at the very least, they would have been guided into suitable marriages at an early age. Their freedom went beyond the power to travel the Paris metro unrecognised and at whim. Olga did marry young, but it was not until 1934 when she was thirty that Elizabeth found her husband. Maybe their statelessness yet high position made them difficult to place, but nevertheless Nicholas and Helen were becoming worried that their younger daughters would remain on the shelf.

However, in 1933 there was a new guest at Bohinj while the Nicholases were there. Count Carl zu Toerring-Jettenbach was one of the many young men Elizabeth's parents had considered a suitable match for their daughter, and during a visit to Munich earlier in the year, Elizabeth had seemed to like the quiet young German. Not long after his arrival at Bohinj Paul, Olga and Marina returned to London leaving the Nicholases and Prince Christopher as chaperones. They did their job well. On 22 September 'Toto' proposed and was accepted; on 10 January 1934 he and Elizabeth were married at Seefeld Castle, near Munich.

Marina was now left alone at home.

CHAPTER THREE

Meanwhile in England . . .

Meanwhile a Prince was growing up in England, under very different circumstances from those of his future bride. George was the fifth child and fourth son of the future George V and his wife, Queen Mary of Teck.

Prince George was born in 1902, the year after the death of his formidable great-grandmother Queen Victoria. The English monarchy was never more firmly on the throne than during this epoch: Queen Victoria's extended mourning had provoked anti-monarchist rumbles but George's grandfather, King Edward VII, was as popular for his blatant consumption as for any reasons to do with tact or statesmanship.

The young Prince's father was not born in the direct line of succession to the throne: there had been an older brother, Prince Eddy, who stood to inherit. From an early age Eddy caused his grandmother and even his more easy-going father worry, and within the family there was much concern as to whether he would ever reform enough to make a good King. George, already a model son, was given the task of looking after his older brother and keeping him to paths which if not straight, would not be too openly crooked. Aged respectively seven and six Eddy and George were given a tutor, Canon Dalton, who remained with them for the next fourteen years, even accompanying them when in 1877 they were sent as naval cadets to the training ship *Britannia*.

George, the second son, was destined for the sea almost from birth. Eddy, as future King, would not have followed such a course but for the strong family feeling – reinforced by Dalton's own views – that the boys should not be separated. 'Prince Albert Victor [Eddy]', he wrote to Queen Victoria who was pressing for Eddy to be sent to public school, 'requires the stimulus of Prince George's company to induce him to work at all . . . . Prince George's lively presence is his mainstay and chief incentive to exertion . . . .'

In 1879, after two years' naval training, the problem of Eddy reasserted itself. And once again it was the elder son who was put under the care of the younger. Prince George's career must continue on its course, and Prince Eddy could not be trusted far from his brother. So in September 1879 the two Princes, accompanied still by Canon Dalton, left Spithead in the warship *Bacchante*. They returned to England in 1882, seasoned sailors but despite Dalton's efforts (sightseeing when in port, lectures while at sea) woefully undereducated. A brief attempt to rectify this shortcoming sent them both to Lausanne for six months, after which George returned to sea and was for the first time separated from his brother Eddy. Eddy was to go to Cambridge with Dalton, George to pursue his career unhampered by an effete elder brother. And he worked to good effect: there is no doubt that had he been allowed to continue in the navy, Prince George would have proved himself independently of his background.

But it was not to be. Prince Eddy showed no signs of improvement. It was not just that he was lazy, he was also stupid. And there was something more serious amiss, a listlessness more worrying than mere idleness. The only subject that could arouse any enthusiasm in him was matters sartorial. (His father, something of a dandy himself, nicknamed him 'Collars and Cuffs'.) Queen Victoria, who took her prerogatives as grandmother seriously, made him Duke of Clarence and decided that the answer was a wife. Various suitable Princesses were suggested: Princess Alexandra of Hesse preferred the prospect of being Nicholas II's Tsarina to Eddy's Queen; William II of Prussia's sister Margaret was another possibility. Eddy, difficult even in simple matters such as bride-finding, preferred the Roman Catholic (and therefore obviously unsuitable) French Helene d'Orléans. The bride finally chosen was Princess May of Teck.

May had good royal blood: a first cousin once removed of Queen Victoria and a direct descendant of George III. She was not beautiful, but was intelligent and well educated. Her parents – the stout, jolly, extravagant Princess Mary Adelaide of Cambridge and the handsome but impoverished Prince (later Duke) Francis of Teck – had provided her with little other than three brothers and a good linguistic and cultural grounding. To them, perpetually in debt, their children tainted in European royalty's eyes by Francis's morganatic blood, the match was more than they could have dreamed. Indeed, the only worry was that May herself might refuse such a brilliant catch: 'Do you suppose Princess May will make any resistance?' the Prince of Wales's Private Secretary wrote to Sir Henry Ponsonby. 'I do not anticipate any real opposition on Prince Eddy's part if he is properly managed and told he *must* do it – that it is for the good of the country, etc. etc.' Eddy's customary listlessness meant he did not oppose the will of his parents and grandmother. In November 1891 May spent ten days with the Queen at Balmoral, presumably being given a thorough looking-over. In December Eddy proposed to May at Luton Hoo. 'Of course I said yes – we are both very happy' wrote the dutiful Princess in her diary that night. Delighted with the young couple's tractability, their elders arranged the wedding for the following February and May was invited with her parents to Sandringham for shooting and Prince Eddy's birthday on 8 January.

He spent most of the day ill in bed with influenza. The next day the illness spread to his lungs and five days later he was dead. His younger brother George, the sailor Prince, was now at twenty-six in direct line to the throne.

George was to gain more than his brother's position as heir presumptive. Although his career in the navy could only now end, he was given his own quarters – a house at Sandringham known as the 'Bachelor's Cottage' and up until then used by his father for the overflow from house parties – and rooms in St James's Palace. His income increased dramatically as did his staff. He was also given the Dukedom of York.

There was little left that he needed – except a wife. Before his brother's death George had wanted to marry his first cousin,

Princess Marie of Edinburgh. Queen Victoria, the Prince of Wales and Prince Alfred (Marie's father) were all keen on the match, the Waleses even making an offer for Marie after Eddy's death, but Marie's mother successfully spiked it. George's own letter of proposal was answered by a refusal dictated by the Duchess of Edinburgh. (Marie later married Ferdinand I of Rumania.) Despite this the couple remained affectionate and lifelong friends. The royal family, shocked at the Duchess of Edinburgh's refusal, did not, however, have to look far before the perfect answer presented itself. There was, after all, a sweet and willing young Princess whose suitability had already been considered and approved. Would it not be a good idea for George to step into his brother's shoes, not only as heir to the throne, but as bridegroom?

It was certainly lucky for George, and also for England, that Eddy had died before marrying his cousin. For although George and May's union began with the pressures of two families looking on – hers frankly ambitious not to be doubly cheated out of such an alliance, his stern and practical to the last degree – the marriage was one of enduring affection and strength. If both appeared stiff and constrained to the outside world, so did they to each other, although they could at least write to express their feelings: 'It is so stupid to be so stiff together and really there is nothing I would not tell you, except that I *love* you more than anybody else in the world, and this I cannot tell you myself so I write it to relieve my feelings,' wrote May to George before their wedding, and he answered: 'I think it really unnecessary for me to tell you how deep my love for you, my darling, is and I feel it growing stronger and stronger every time I see you; although I may appear shy and cold.' George's cousin Marie remarked on these characteristics:

May ... is fundamentally tidy, orderly, disciplined. She likes possessing, collecting, putting things in order ... She looks into things in detail and is an excellent and vigilant housewife. She has excellent appetite, excellent health, and sleeps beautifully .... Both she and he are scrupulously polite, but their demonstrations of pleasure or affection are always restrained and decorous.

Nevertheless Lady Airlie, who knew them well, recorded that

King George's rough manner and his rather oriental views on wifehood and womanhood sometimes combined to hide the very real love and admiration he had for his wife. But how often when I was sitting reading to her before dinner, while she rested on her sofa, wrapped in a kimono of a lovely pale shade, embroidered cushions behind her beautifully coiffed head, would he come in with some letter about which he wanted to consult her. There was no mistaking the pleasure with which his eyes would light on her.

The couple was married in July 1893 and immediately set about the business of providing an heir to the throne: when their first child was born the following year, he was third in the direct line of succession. Such a birth could not but please the old Queen-Empress.

George and May were to produce six children: Edward (VIII, known to the family as David, born 1894), Albert (Bertie, later George VI, born 1895), Mary (1897), Henry (1900), George (1902) and John (1905). May was not what would nowadays be described as a 'natural mother' and had had no intention of having so many children. As it was, the six tended to divide into two camps: the older three ran together and, for much of their childhood at least, the younger three were also bracketed together.

The family's expectations were of course centred on David as heir. But even when they were small the differences in the children's characters were soon apparent. Mary, the youngest of the elder trio, kept up with the boys and became something of a tomboy while keeping a place in her father's heart as his only daughter. Both David and Bertie could be cowed by their father's disciplinarianism while George was always merry and sturdy.

Of course the royal children had more than one house in which to live, but for them all it was York Cottage, the old 'Bachelor's Cottage' at Sandringham which had been given to George on his wedding, which was home. All of the children but David were born there, and it was Sandringham where they spent most of the year. From mid October to the end of January they were there with their parents. George and May would go to London for February and March, leaving their children in

Norfolk, and returning to spend Easter with them either there
or meeting them at Frogmore, Windsor. In May and June they
lived with their parents in London while the height of the
summer – July and August – were months spent with their
mother at Frogmore while their father shot or yachted. In
September and for most of October the royal family was to be
found at Balmoral, from where they would return to York
Cottage.

The Cottage was perhaps an odd home for such a large family,
with so many other places to choose from. It was neither large
nor pretty – a 'glum little villa' Harold Nicolson called it in his
biography of the King, although to those brought up there it
was dear. His description continues,

[it is] encompassed by thickets of laurel and rhododendron, shadowed
by huge Wellingtonias and separated by an abrupt rim of lawn from a
pond, at the edge of which a leaden pelican gazes in dejection upon the
water lilies and bamboos. The local brown stone in which the house was
constructed is concealed by rough-cast which in its turn is enlivened by
very imitation Tudor beams. The rooms inside, with the fumed oak
surrounds, their white overmantels framing oval mirrors, their Doulton
tiles and stained glass fanlights, are indistinguishable from those of any
Surbiton or Upper Norwood home.

It was a house in which reproductions from the Royal Academy
hung on the walls, although the family had a vast collection of
real art.

This was the home to which George had taken his bride,
moving her straight into the house which he had had decorated
by 'the Maples' man' from Tottenham Court Road in London.
It was a house typical of its period: a study, two drawing rooms,
a dining room and a billiards room on the ground floor, dressing
and bedrooms for George and May and members of the household on the next floor, and, separated by a swing door from the
adults' rooms, the nursery. Despite the six children and nursing
staff, only two small rooms were assigned to the children. The
day nursery was almost too small for toys, but was the room in
which the children ate, played and (while still small) were given
lessons. The night nursery was shared by up to three children

at a time and here they slept and bathed in tin tubs. Lady Airlie wrote,

[May's] boudoir, which had the exquisite daintiness and freshness which I grew to associate with her, was charming, but many of the other rooms were very badly planned. The Lady-in-Waiting slept in a bedroom little bigger than a cupboard, and the nursery and schoolroom quarters were dark and depressing.

But the Duke of Windsor remembered it with more affection: 'Although Sandringham may not have been the place in which to prepare a boy for the world's harsh realities,' he later recalled, 'it nevertheless possessed most of the ingredients for a boyhood idyll.'

When Queen Victoria died and George became Prince of Wales he kept York Cottage as his family's main home, although his residences increased with his promotion. Nor, when George's father died and he became King, did he move his family from the Cottage to the 'Big House'. Queen Alexandra remained in solitary possession of Sandringham itself while her son and his large family continued to crowd into the Cottage. When asked where the servants lived, the King confessed he did not know, 'I suppose they live in the trees' he remarked.

The children's other homes did change as their father was promoted through the ranks of Prince to King. In 1910, when Edward VII died, their London home became Buckingham Palace, rather than Marlborough House; at Windsor they moved from 'the simple comforts at Frogmore' to the 'grand and spacious accommodation' of the royal apartments in the castle, and in Scotland they moved from Abergeldie to Balmoral.

King George and Queen Mary cannot be blamed for their apparent indifference to their young children: much of the fault must be laid on the customs and manners of the time. Upper-class parents did not, on the whole, see their children more than once or twice a day in any household. For those not naturally inclined towards an overwhelming passion for small children, even their own, this did not give much time for what would now be called 'bonding'. May's early years of marriage were spent in childbearing and adapting to the mainstream of royal life. She found pregnancy and childbirth itself uncomfortable and distasteful to the point of offensiveness, and made little attempt to hide the fact. Mabell Airlie, later a lady-in-waiting and lifelong friend, recalled visiting May before the Princess's wedding and when she herself was expecting her first child: 'I think my approaching maternity rather embarrassed her. In all the years I spent with her I never remember her having any enthusiasm for babies. When she was expecting her own she did not like anyone to allude to her condition, and was impatient of the limitations it imposed on her.'

Just after Harry, her fourth child and third son, was born May wrote to her Aunt Augusta, 'I think I have done my duty & may now *stop*, as having babies is highly distasteful to me tho' when once they are there they are very nice.' Despite this plan she went on to have two more children. 'Of course it is a great bore for me & requires a great deal of patience to bear it, but this is alas the penalty of being a woman!' she wrote to George while expecting John, her sixth child.

Lady Airlie tries to explain her friend's attitude favourably:

Although she disliked the routine of child-bearing, and had no interest in her children as babies, she grew to love them dearly when they were older. But the difference between us was that while I, being a commoner, could keep in step with my children as they passed from babyhood into childhood and adolescence, she was prevented by her position and her public life from having this close contact with hers. When they reached an interesting age, and began to develop personalities, her sons were taken from her and delivered over to tutors. Her only opportunity of getting to know them as individuals was during the hour they spent with her in the evening, and that is not enough to create a happy relationship between child and parent.

Indeed, apart from that hour with their mother, or when they were summoned 'for a less pleasurable interview' with their father, the children were expected to keep to their own quarters. Mabell Airlie 'never saw them run along the corridors; they walked sedately, generally shepherded by nurses or tutors'. May's attitude to her children was almost detached: maybe part of the reason was a wish to avoid the clinging relationship Queen Alexandra had with her children. From her first days as a bride May had had to contend with her mother-in-law's jealousy, and there was no danger of her sons' wives having the same problem. She remarked to her brother that David as a baby was 'plain. This is a pity and rather disturbs me.' On another occasion she wrote that the then two-year old Prince was 'jumpy ... what a curious child he is.' Queen Victoria's daughter, Empress Frederick, noticed that May 'does not seem to have the passionate tenderness for her little ones which seems so natural to me. She has something very cold and stiff – & distant in her manner – each time one sees her again one has to break the ice afresh.'

It is probably a sign of George and May's ignorance, rather than their lack of concern, that their two elder sons were abused by a crazy nurse for three years without their noticing. Mary Peters was obsessive in her attentions to David, to the point of pinching him viciously whenever he was handed to his mother so that he should yell and be returned speedily to her. When Bertie was born she neglected him, underfeeding and ignoring him. Both his later stomach troubles and his stammer have been attributed to this treatment at the beginning of his life. Not until Charlotte 'Lala' Bill joined the nursery and dared to report the nurse was she sacked, whereupon she went completely mad and was put into a home.

As the children grew older May did become more of a figure in their lives, but never was she really a true mother in the modern sense. To her – the poor relation with royal but tainted blood – the monarchy was the most important thing in the world. It came above all natural ties of affection (although there is no doubt that she did love her husband). 'I always have to remember that their father is also their King' she said of her children, and the same held true of her own relationship with George. He was her husband but he was also her King. May, a strong-minded young woman who had no compunction in taking on her mother-in-law, never even argued with George. He was the monarch and that was enough for her. Marie of Rumania, visiting her old flame in 1924, remarked on May's submissiveness at a reception: 'King George lets Her Majesty know that if she wishes to speak to anyone, he or she can be brought up to where she is sitting . . . . May does not dare budge, George is a real tyrant and stickler at form like his father, but without his father's renowned ease of manner.'*

The boys were in awe, even afraid of their father. 'The brothers were all jealous of each other,' a member of the household said. 'The only time they were happy was when one of them got into trouble with their father. He considered them dolts, the whole lot of them.'

Away from George, May was more relaxed with her children. 'We used to have a lovely time with her alone – always laughing and joking . . . she was a different human being away from him,' David later wrote. However, the children were never alone with either of their parents – there was always a lady-in-waiting or equerry in attendance.

Although much has been written about the coldness of the royal children's upbringing – pop psychologists making the point that both David and Bertie sought mother figures in their lives while George, the mother's favourite, was the one who married a woman to whom he could relate as an equal – it is only fair to say that the children themselves did have warm feelings towards their mother. David wrote in his memoirs of the hour at the end of the day when the children would be summoned to see their mother as she rested in her boudoir before dinner.

When we gathered around her on little chairs, she would read and talk to us. Looking back upon this scene, I am sure that my cultural interests began at my mother's knee . . . . Her soft voice, her cultivated mind, the cosy room overflowing with personal treasures were all inseparable ingredients of the happiness associated with this last hour of a child's day.

If this scene – with the children knitting scarves for one of May's innumerable charities – sounds impossibly idyllic, it does not matter. In what David claimed was a miserable childhood, it is only important that he remembered such moments with affection.

* On the same visit, Marie wrote prophetically about David: 'Quite irresistible with that delicious face, that short child's nose, that lovely honey-coloured hair and blue eyes. Later if he goes it too hard, his eyes will get tired, the bloom will fade, but for the moment he is "le Prince Charmant" '.

Other witnesses record the homely domestic atmosphere of George and May's home. Mabell Airlie insisted that they were devoted to their children: 'Remembering them in my early days in Sandringham, before their family was even complete, I believe that they were more conscientious and more truly devoted to their children than the majority of parents in that era. The tragedy was that neither had any understanding of a child's mind.' If Queen Mary was short on understanding, King George was even more so.* However, there is nothing to suggest that he was not fond of his 'regiment' of children. When they were small he was positively doting – in his letters at least. 'I have got those two photographs of you and darling Baby on my table before me now ... I like looking at my Tootsums little wife and my sweet child,' and even to outsiders he wrote boasting of his children's prowess. It was, in the early days, he rather than May who would be most likely to be found with the babies at bath-time.

There are other witnesses to the domestic atmosphere of King George's homes. Lord Esher, staying at Balmoral, wrote,

It is altogether different here from former years. There is no longer the old atmosphere about the house – that curious electric element which pervaded the surroundings of King Edward. Yet everything is very charming and wholesome and sweet. The house is a home for children – six of them at luncheon – the youngest running round the table all the while. The Queen knits of an evening .... We go to bed early, which I like, and breakfast is at nine .... Last night the French governess sat on the King's right hand at dinner. Imagine the courtiers of Berlin or Vienna if they could have seen.

Albert Mensdorff, the Austrian Ambassador and friend of Edward VII who remained a friend of George V, also spoke of their 'peaceful life' and said 'the children are very nice and well brought up'.

A letter from Queen Mary to her daughter-in-law Alice, Duchess of Gloucester (Henry's wife), written when her first child was born while her husband was away with the army,

---

* George VI was later to remark to Walter Monckton, Edward VIII's adviser during the Abdication Crisis, that their father had treated them all as though they were the same although their characters were entirely different.

backs up the assertion that King George and Queen Mary were warmer towards their children than some have suggested:

It is a pity Harry is so far away from you at present as I know what a lot of things you want to settle, things which one cannot do alone without one's husband's valuable advice, besides which it is so nice to talk things over together, don't you think so? That is what I miss so dreadfully for Papa and I always talked and discussed things .... What a pity Harry will miss three months of the baby's adorable baby days which one simply loves, especially the first one! You cannot think how Papa enjoyed our first baby (that naughty boy!!!) he was always in and out of the nursery.

It was as the children, particularly his boys, grew older that the trouble began. George was a Victorian and he was royal. He was also, by training and inclination, a sailor. The combination made for a father who was strict even by the standards of the day. David wrote,

My boyhood was a strict one because my father was strict in his own life and habits .... He had the Victorian's sense of probity, moral responsibility and love of domesticity. He believed in God, in the invincibility of the Royal Navy, and the essential rightness of whatever was British .... Through everything cut the sharp concept of duty .... If through my family's position my childhood was spared the mundane struggle that is the common lot, I nevertheless had my full share of discipline. For the concept of duty was drilled into me, and I never had the sense that the days belonged to me alone.

Duty, punctuality and care in dress: these were the three gods of the young children's life.

So for the little Princes their father represented authority, a rigid and repressive authority with very little room for imagination or fun. 'As my mother's room came to represent a kind of sanctuary at the end of the day, so the Library became for us the seat of parental authority, the place of admonition and reproof.'

His manner of chaffing them or interrogating them added to the shyness and tied the tongues of those by nature the most diffident, and the same qualities which gained him the devotion of his staff and servants and the admiration of his wider family as their ideal head, sometimes created a barrier which separated him from his own sons.

So wrote John Gore in his *Personal Memoir* of the King. Add to the King's rigid sense of duty his explosive temper, and it is easy to understand that his children had a difficult life.

Prince George and Marina had one element of their upbringing in common: both sets of parents tried to ensure that their children did not suppose themselves to be different from, or any better than other people, although, as David pointed out, 'by *other people* he meant the children of the well born'. Both the Greek Princesses and the English Princes and Princess had good manners drummed into them and were brought up not to be snobbish.

However, it was one thing to tell the children not to be snobbish, yet another to allow them to play with their peers. Their childhood was remarkable in its loneliness. Occasional parties with children of their parents' friends, rigidly organised dancing lessons in London and even rarer football games put together in a supposedly egalitarian way with sons of Sandringham estate workers did not amount to companionship. They were fortunate in being a large family.

They were fortunate too in their paternal grandparents. King Edward and Queen Alexandra offered George's children all the warmth and affection that he and May could not. Their indulgent behaviour and constant undermining of their authority as parents may have driven George and May wild with despair, but it offered the children something that would otherwise have been lacking.

York Cottage was their home because they spent most of their year there, but perhaps part of the reason why all the children were so fond of Norfolk was to do with the nearness of their grandparents. The arrival of Edward and Alexandra at the Big House, heralded by an army of servants and the delivery of endless supplies of food, meant that their life was to change for the better. An element of licence could creep into their strictly ordered lives. The grandparents made jokes and hugged them. 'It's always jolly up at the Big House' Prince George once said. And indeed it was. The children did not see their warm-hearted grandfather's darker side, although their father had inherited his violent temper. Once Edward VII spilt some spinach on his white shirt front just before a ball. With a complete loss of temper he dipped both hands into the dish and smeared spinach all over himself. 'I had to change anyway,' he said, temper restored.

As with any children, it was important to make decisions about their education. Edward and Alexandra were remarkably relaxed on the subject: 'Queen Alexandra always believed that having fun was more important than having education, and King Edward having had so much trouble with his own education did not believe in it, especially for children he knew and loved,' wrote one of Alexandra's ladies-in-waiting.

Queen Mary had a straightforward view of what her children needed, as she explained to her Aunt Augusta: 'I do so hope our children will turn out common-sense people, which is so important in this world. We have taken no end of trouble with their education and they have very nice people round them so one feels all is being done to help them.'

It was their father who of course would have the final word, and their father believed in a naval education. Therefore David and Bertie were both sent off as naval cadets. Although George knew that his own education had left serious gaps which had to be filled before he could carry out his job properly, he chose the same education for his eldest two boys.

The children all followed the same path at first. After they left the care of Lala (the nurse who had routed the sadistic Peters) they progressed to the schoolroom. May's tutor, Helene Bricka, taught them languages and otherwise they were submitted to Henry Hansell, a tutor whose deficiencies were enormous, a fact hardly made better by his consciousness of them. Hansell came from Norfolk and loved yachting, both factors which commended him to the Prince of Wales. Educated at Malvern College and Oxford he had been a teacher at Rossall and Ludgrove (later attended by William and Harry of Wales) and had tutored Prince Arthur of Connaught. Hansell arrived with the family in the spring of 1902, the year Prince George was born, and stayed for twelve years. When the elder two boys were sent to the Royal Naval College at Osborne (and then on to Dartmouth) the younger children took their place in the schoolroom.

Harry, the fourth child, was never very strong and it was this that finally persuaded George that there must an alternative to a naval education. To Hansell, who had tried to persuade the Duke of York to send David and Bertie to a normal school, this came as a relief. He wrote to his sister:

You know how earnestly I have endeavoured to persuade HRH of the benefit a preparatory school life could offer the Princes, and though I failed in the cases of Princes David and Albert, it is possible that my earlier efforts may have helped to persuade HRH that this would be the best arrangement for his less sturdy third son .... So Prince Harry is to attend St Peter's Court School in Broadstairs ... is that not splendid? Now I can give all my time to Prince George and Prince John – though there is little I can do with the latter alas!

Poor Prince John had more serious problems than Harry's delicacy. The last of May and George's children, born in July 1905, it was not long before it became apparent that something was wrong with him. George and May returned from an eight-month tour to India and Burma to find their eleven-month old baby still unable to sit. When John was four he developed epilepsy, from which he suffered increasingly as he grew older. Other symptoms followed until it was clear that John would never catch up with his brothers. For a while George and John shared the schoolroom, but even Hansell knew that it was doing neither John nor George any good.

It says much for Prince George's character that of all the family – except perhaps for Queen Alexandra – it was he who gave the most time and affection to his disabled brother. John was more and more segregated from the rest of the family until in 1917 he was moved with Lala Bill to a farm on the Sandringham estate, where he was to spend the rest of his short life. His brother George, his grandmother Alexandra, and his erstwhile tutor Mr Hansell visited him every day while they were at Sandringham. George also sent him postcards regularly from Osborne.

John was to die in January 1919, of an epileptic fit. Queen Mary, who was to outlive three of her sons, wrote,

For him it is a great release ... I cannot say how grateful we feel to God for having taken him in such a peaceful way, he just slept quietly into his heavenly home, no pain, no struggle, just peace for the poor little troubled soul which had been a great anxiety to us for many years, ever since he was four years old – the first break in the family circle is hard to bear but people have been so kind & sympathetic & this has helped us much.

For both parents the death was 'the greatest mercy possible', yet May was hurt by her oldest son's cold attitude towards his brother and his death. When he heard how he had hurt her, David did write to apologise, explaining, 'no one can realise more than you how little poor Johnnie meant to me who hardly knew him.' At least the poor child had had one brother who cared about him.

While the eldest two boys continued their naval education, in 1912 Prince George followed his brother Harry to St Peter's Court. George was by far the brightest of George and May's children, indeed when he arrived at St Peter's he was as advanced as Harry, his senior by three years. 'Prince George . . . is as bright as the proverbial button,' wrote Hansell to his sister. 'Thank goodness, H. M. has agreed that he should join Prince Harry at St Peter's Court next term. I shall miss him but it will be best for him. I can even imagine his getting a scholarship into Eton college, if such were needed.'

George fitted into school life, both social and academic, with surprising ease for a boy who had been brought up with few children other than his retarded younger brother and educated by a fairly incompetent tutor. One teacher at St Peter's went so far as to write praising George to his ex-tutor:

Judged by the performance in the classroom of Prince Henry, we were not expecting too much of his younger brother, but he turns out to be a clever little boy who is already showing himself more advanced than his contemporaries – and his brother. I congratulate you on turning out such a nice and bright lad.

All accounts point to George being not only nice, but sturdy, cheerful, and alone of all the King's sons, unbullyable. There is a story told of his plan to while away dull shooting lunches. He decided to fine anyone who used the word 'shoot' (not a sport he favoured) during the lunch. The King, who knew what his son was up to, continued with his own conversations, putting those closest to him at table in grave danger of being fined by the disrespectful younger son.

Harry was of a relaxed enough nature to feel no jealousy for the successes of his younger brother, and indeed the two only overlapped at the school by a year. In September 1913 Harry went to Eton which suited him admirably.

His father's progress up the monarchical ladder made little difference to George – he was the fourth son and still only a child while all the major changes took place. The future George V was the Prince of Wales for most of his fourth son's childhood, and when King Edward died it was Bertie and David who were sent for by the new King, not his younger sons. To little Prince George it was the loss of a grandfather that mattered, not the family's movement up the ranks. Their grandmother Queen Alexandra returned from her holiday in Corfu with her brother the King of Greece the day before her husband's death.

Royal families all over Europe gathered together for the funeral of the King, and among them were the Greeks. This was Marina's first recorded visit to England and the Nicholases stayed at Buckingham Palace for three days. The children – George was seven, Olga one year younger – behaved with normal high spirits despite the looming absence of the dead King and brooding presence of Queen Alexandra. Indeed, Mensdorff later remarked on the 'noisy merriment' of the Greek family in general at the funeral. David later remembered the high jinks.

It all began with a game of croquet. Then George pulled the hoops up, put them in a row and tried to jump them. He failed, and Marina, only four and slightly lame, tried next and also failed. David wrote,

I remember George gallantly helping her up and then both of them falling on the grass, consumed with giggles. After that . . . we started playing bowls with the balls and that, too, soon became somewhat out of hand. One of the balls went into the lake, floating because it was made of wood and Princess Marina took off her shoes and began to wade in, while at the same time Bertie and I, as qualified sailors, launched the rowing boat. All this nonsense was halted by the arrival of the Greek Princesses' nanny. She only had to call out the names of her charges once and they all came to her, Princess Marina with her white dress soaked. Bertie and I apologised, and so did Mary. The nanny admonished Princess Marina but was soon smiling as she took the girls inside.

Young as Prince George was, he attended his parents' coronation with all his siblings but John. This was probably the first time that the boy had any inkling of what his family's position actually meant, but if so he did not appear to be awed by the occasion.

The children rode together to Westminster Abbey in a state coach. Harry and George thought the ride very enjoyable and, as children will, got the giggles. George, dressed in a kilt, tried to tickle his sister, who lost her coronet in the mêlée, and fell to the floor of the coach.

In the Abbey itself all five behaved impeccably. David was dressed in his Order of the Garter robes, Bertie in cadet uniform, Mary in coronet and ermine. David was conducted to his seat in front of the peers' benches first, then his brothers and sister were led to their places. As they passed in front of him, the boys bowed and Mary curtsied. David wrote in his diary,

All the relatives and people were most civil & bowed to me as they passed. Then Mama & Papa came in & the ceremony commenced. There was the recognition, the anointing & then the Crowning of Papa & then I put on my coronet with the peers. Then I had to go & do hommage [sic] to Papa at his throne & I was very nervous. Then Mama was crowned. We got into our cariage [sic], & had a long drive back. My coronet felt very heavy as we had to bow to the people as we went along.

The children's behaviour on the way back from the Abbey was even worse, after the long service, than it had been on the way there. Eventually David's threats succeeded in calming them. Queen Alexandra, who had predicted trouble if all the children were allowed to ride together unaccompanied by any adult, roared with laughter when she heard the tale.

After the coronation, with all its excitements of the parades, the visitors, the comings and goings, life went back to normal for George.

The turning point came when he was fourteen. Along with his siblings, George had spent the evenings in his mother's

Marina aged sixteen with little sign of the sophistication to come

The redoubtable English nanny, Miss Fox, with her three royal charges

Carefree Grecian days: the three little princesses riding with their father

Marina on her mother's knee in a formal family portrait

The children of Prince Nicholas of Greece: Marina, Elizabeth and Olga

Les patineuses: three princesses on the ice

The Royal Palace in Athens where Marina was taught the importance of family loyalty and the meaning of being royal

The youthful Princess Marina as a horsewoman: jumping practice

No taint of common blood: the three royal sisters, Olga (Princess Paul of Yugoslavia), Elizabeth (Countess Toerring) and Marina (the Duchess of Kent) in 1938

A rare photograph of Marina in London, before her marriage. It was while staying with Olga and Prince Paul that Prince George's courtship began

One of the many engagement photographs, 1934

A royal bride steps ashore to be greeted by her fiancé Prince George. Dover, 21 November 1934

After the Greek and English marriage ceremonies, the new Duchess of Kent greets the crowds from Buckingham Palace balcony.

The formal wedding portrait: George's supporters were his brothers, both future King-Emperors, and his youngest bridesmaid was the future Elizabeth II

Sunglasses at San Marco: the Kents cut a dash on holiday in Venice

George and Marina attend a gala performance of Me and My Girl

At Coppins. Continuing a royal obsession – like Queen Mary and Edward VIII before him, George enjoyed clearing brushwood. Here Marina feeds the fire

Marina was at her happiest
with her family about her.
The informal warmth of
these pictures contrast with
the formality of her own
family groups

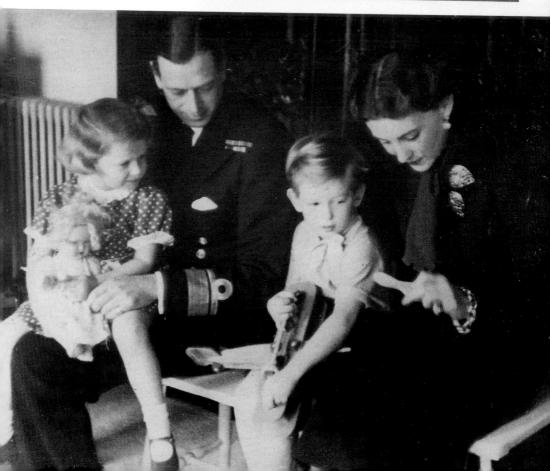

Maternal pride: Marina poses Eddie and Alexandra ready for a photograph at Coppins

Laughing in the garden: despite George's death Marina gave the young Duke of Kent, Princess Alexandra and Prince Michael a secure and happy childhood

boudoir being educated in some of the finer things in life. For all the children, but in particular George, their father's fanatical interests – shooting and stamp collecting – were not enough. Mary's interest in furniture and arts was transmitted to her younger son. Her father, 'Grandpa Teck' to her children, had been interested in music and the arts and these genes did, in George at least, overpower the more prosaic blood of the English royal family. He was also the least willing to follow his father into the navy.

However, his own wishes, and even the rare intercession of his mother, made no difference. Although more intelligent, more hardworking, and more artistic than any of his brothers the King saw no reason for George to be given any other training than the navy. Maybe King George genuinely did not notice his sons' varying needs: in any event Harry alone succeeded in escaping the navy, and George was sent off, as David and Bertie had been before him, to naval college at Osborne and then to Dartmouth.

While his older brothers were both involved in the First World War (David training as an infantry officer in the Grenadier Guards, Bertie as a midshipman on HMS *Collingwood*), George was at St Peter's Broadstairs, then at naval college (Harry was at Eton) where his class placements were consistently better than had been either of his brothers'. In 1920 he left Dartmouth, to join the *Temeraire* for a training cruise. He clearly had not applied himself enough towards the end as 'He has kept up the best traditions of my family by passing out of Dartmouth 1 from bottom the same place as I did!!!!' wrote his father to a friend. Then he was sent to Greenwich for a further course which included languages at which he was a very quick student. He then joined HMS *Iron Duke* as a midshipman (during which time he received the same pay – 5 shillings a day – as the others with nothing extra from his father). It seemed as though, despite his often expressed wish to change his career, a life in the navy lay ahead of him.

Mabell Airlie recalled a conversation she had had with George on the subject of the navy in 1928, seven years after his first commission:

He told me how much he was dreading his next voyage ... he wanted to go into the Civil Service or the Foreign Office, but the King would not hear of it. 'His only reason for refusing is that it has never been done before ... I've tried to make him see that I'm not cut out for the Navy, but it's no use. What can I do?' I advised him not to waste time arguing with the King – which would only make him angry – but to work hard while he was at sea, get the Civil Service papers and do them, and then let his father see the results. He told me some time later that he had acted on my advice, and that it had been successful.

George's rebellion against his father took perhaps the obvious course. At first his dislike of the navy was enough to displease the King, but as he grew older his links with his older brother David, who did not always seem to toe the line as Prince of Wales, drew him into a set of which his family could not but disapprove. As children, David and Bertie had spent most of their time together, but before very long David began to realise how much more he had in common with his younger brother George. David had spent the winter of 1911 at home between leaving the navy and Oxford and with Bertie and Harry at school and John still in the schoolroom he had been thrown much together with George. 'Although George was eight and a half years my junior, I found in his character qualities that were akin to my own: we laughed at the same things. That winter we became more than brothers – we became close friends,' wrote David. George remembered that winter as the turning point of their relationship too:

We got on famously. He used to tell me everything .... Our parents had gone away to India for the Coronation Durbar at Delhi .... I am ashamed to recall how relaxed we all were with our parents away .... Not only did we have the run of the cottage but there was never any fear of bumping into Papa or Mama unexpectedly.

George was to remain David's closest friend for many years, until the arrival of Wallis Simpson, and David was quick to give George praise. 'Possessed of an unusual charm of manner and a quick sense of humour and talented in many directions, he had an undoubted flair for the arts. He played the piano, knew a good deal about music and had a knowledgeable eye for antiques,' wrote the Prince of his brother.

George (Knight of the Garter since 1923) served in the Mediterranean and in China, and although there were moments when life in the navy did not seem all bad, he continued to beg his father to allow him to leave the service. 'Being somewhat Bohemian by inclination,' David later wrote of his brother, 'he had understandably found life in the Navy a bit confining.' His body as well as his mind rebelled against naval life as he was consistently seasick and, like his brother Bertie, he suffered increasingly from digestive problems. Finally, in 1929, his following of Lady Airlie's advice, his persistence, and his illness, combined to persuade the King that he should be allowed to begin another career.

Returning to England, he moved into his brother David's apartments at York House, St James's Palace. Together they raised Cain, enjoying life as young men about town to the full. Their friendship became more equal and now they were allies outside as well as within the royal family. 'He was in some ways more like a son to me,' David wrote to Queen Mary after George's death, 'and his charm and gaiety brought great happiness to York House those years he lived with me.' By day George was in the Civil Service – first in the Foreign Office, then in the Home Office. By night he was a blade. As Chips Channon was later to write, 'they [King George and Queen Mary] made no social background whatever for any of their children. Naturally, their children had to find outlet and their fun elsewhere, and the two most high-spirited ones, the late King and the fascinating Duke of Kent, drank deeply from life.'

George was much the most cultured and artistic of the royal children. He collected art and antiques and loved music, theatre and the ballet. He was friends with Adele and Fred Astaire and Tilly Losch, and actress Gertrude Lawrence once found him trying on one of her wigs in front of her dressing-room mirror. It was George who persuaded his unadventurous parents to see their first 'talking picture' – *The Good Companions*.

George had a good sense of humour. After an operation to remove his two little toes he received a fan letter from an old lady which read, 'I'm so sorry about your poor little toes. Why don't you have them made into a pair of earrings for your dear sister as a wedding present?' No one could have enjoyed the joke more. He also had all his older brother's charm, as well as the advantage of better looks. Wallis Simpson met David and George for the first time together:

I remember thinking, as I studied the Prince of Wales, how much like his pictures he really was – the slightly wind-rumpled golden hair, the turned-up nose, and a strange, wistful, almost sad look about the eyes .... Prince George was considerably taller [than his brother], with neatly-brushed brown hair, aquiline features, and dark-blue eyes. He gave an impression of gaiety and *joie de vivre* .... On closer acquaintance I found [Prince George] to be altogether as attractive as his brother. He played the piano very well, knew all the latest jazz, and loved to bang away at the keys while the rest of us danced after dinner in the octagonal hall. Saturday evenings at the Fort were usually a little livelier when Prince George was on the scene; he was a natural mimic and loved to do caricatures of people he knew well, and often the Prince of Wales joined in. I had a distinct feeling, as I watched them together, that the older brother was at times a little worried, even anxious, about the younger, perhaps because he was too lighthearted.

Ironic, then, that it should be the younger brother who settled down so properly and happily and the older who was to cause disturbance.

George's charm was legendary. 'You've only to be with 'P. G.' for five minutes to feel that you're the only man in the room,' an acquaintance remarked, and once he made a friend he remained tremendously loyal – a characteristic he was to share with his future wife. He was also a younger son which in these circumstances, if no other, could be seen as an advantage. It did not take long for George to be as popular a member of the nightclub set (where he delighted audiences with his performances on the banjolele, a combination of the banjo and ukelele) as was David. As Queen Mary once remarked 'There are no big houses nowadays . . . in which they can be entertained, and therefore where should they and their contemporaries meet and enjoy themselves?' He was full of daring – a pilot (he was given his licence in 1930 and rivalled his brother David in the air), a motorist (one of the first men to put a radio in his car), he even climbed Big Ben in bravado. But if he was keen on cocktails and dancing he was also keen on more romantic dalliance. 'I was told no one – of either sex – was safe with him in a taxi,' said Marina's friend Steven Runciman.

George was lucky enough to live in a time before the tabloid press felt it owned the royal family. Even senior members could pass unrecognised on the streets. George loved to tell a story about going to the cinema with David. When they left they found a big crowd had collected outside and asked the manager to let them out the back way. He obliged, apologising for the inconvenience, 'Sorry, sir, they're waiting for Greta Garbo to come out.'

The King and Queen had stern ideas about duty, but nevertheless if he did occasionally shirk the duty he owed to the public it could be done in a more or less discreet way. That George spent the years before his marriage having a great deal of fun is undeniable. It is generally accepted that George's many affairs were with men as well as women: in his later years Noël Coward used to boast of his own dalliance with the Prince. And the Kaiser's grandson Prince Louis Ferdinand said he liked George because he was 'artistic and effeminate and used a strong perfume.' As long as the affairs were moderately discreet they barely mattered in that they could have no serious repercussions on the monarchy. According to the diplomat Sir Robert Bruce-Lockhart there was one close shave in April 1932 with 'a scandal about Prince George – letters to a young man in Paris. A large sum had to be paid for their recovery.' On another occasion George and a homosexual friend were arrested in a shady nightclub. He was released after police discovered his identity. Otherwise, with the press more at bay than now, George was safe.

David, as Duke of Windsor, wrote about how the intrusion of the press began to change the family's life:

The thought occurs to me that one of the most inconvenient developments since the days of my boyhood has been the disappearance of privacy. I grew up before the age of the flash camera, when newspapers still employed large staffs of artists to depict the daily events with pen sketches . . . . Because our likenesses seldom appeared in the Press, we were not often recognised in the street; when we were, the salutation would be a friendly wave of the hand, or, in the case of a courtier or family friend, a polite lifting of the hat.

This privacy meant that gossip was on the whole restricted

to the circle participating in the same sort of life. So that behaviour which would have horrified the Old Guard at the palace, the sturdy middle classes or the working man was on the whole kept from them. It is worth remembering that the British public did not know about the threat Mrs Simpson posed to the monarchy until after her divorce from Ernest.

Like David, George was not very good at choosing suitable young women. His name was linked with actresses (including the black American Florence Mills) as well as socialites. Helen (known as Poppy) Baring, a twenties fun-lover if ever there was one, caught the eye of both Bertie and George, and both proposed to her. Bertie was accepted by Poppy in 1921 while the Prince was staying with her parents during Cowes week, but the Queen made it clear that the marriage would not be permitted. Six years later, in 1927 George met and fell for Poppy, whose 'fastness' may have contributed to her single state, and who had not forgiven the King and Queen for coming between her and Bertie. But, as Duff Cooper, husband of society beauty and sometime actress Lady Diana, told her, if she were to marry George, 'you don't have to be on slap-bottom terms with Queen Mary and King George'. Duff also reported an evening spent at his London house during which Poppy made jokes about the royal family at which George 'rocked with laughter'. When George proposed and was accepted, society was surprised at the ease with which his parents took the affair. Perhaps they were at first fearful of what else might tempt him if they refused and, as Freda Dudley Ward (David's mistress) said, 'If Prince George sticks to it firmly, the King and Queen can't stop it.' However, after further investigations they decided the match really would not do and it did not take great pressure before the romance was broken off.

The most serious result of George's fast living was an addiction to drugs which began after one of his mistresses, the American Kiki Whitney Preston, introduced him to the pleasures of cocaine. That the rich upper classes should experiment with drugs was nothing new, that the son of the King should was of course a fact that had to be covered up. And David, dilettante himself, sided with the King and Queen in worrying about

George's new affair and did all he could to persuade George to break it off. In the summer of 1929, with the affair still raging, David confronted Kiki and made her agree to leave England. He then took George to the country and sat over him while he recuperated. For a man so often portrayed as living only for himself, David's unselfishness was remarkable. He cancelled a holiday with Freda Dudley Ward, admitting to her how tiring was the job of 'doctor, gaoler and detective combined'. However, by the end of the year it seemed as though the worst was over. Kiki was safely abroad and the Prince was weaned off the drugs that had threatened to destroy him. George V wrote to David thanking him for helping his younger brother through the crisis. This was not quite the last of the matter, though: three years later Prince George met Kiki again by accident in Cannes (one of his favourite watering-holes, where incidentally he once won a dancing contest under an assumed name) and yet again David had to come to rescue, and remove George from the danger.

If George and David behaved like Bertie Woosters – climbing up lampposts to leave top hats as trophies, dancing, playing tennis and squash, drinking too much too often ('the Prince of Wales turned up in the Casino at Le Touquet the other night quite drunk and quite incapable of standing,' reported Bruce-Lockhart in September 1929), getting entangled with unsuitable girls – they did also have another life, as Princes of the Blood Royal, and this was not something that could be forgotten. 'He was always in trouble with the girls. Scotland Yard chased so many of them out of the country that the Palace stopped counting,' one equerry remembered. Michael Canfield, who later married Laura, Duchess of Marlborough, was believed by David to be George's son.

George was much happier as soon as he left the Navy. At last, he hoped, he could find fulfilment in work. He spent three years with the Foreign Office, but found that too undemanding. He wanted something which related more closely to the people over whom his father reigned. So, after some thought, he was moved in 1932 to the Home Office where he was given the somewhat unlikely job of Home Office Factory Inspector. After the First World War the royal family had begun to pay more attention to the industrial world. Britain needed a stable and prosperous manufacturing base to achieve the regeneration of the country. In the four years preceding the war, Wheeler-Bennett tells us that the King and his sons had visited fewer than twenty factories. That had now changed. Sir Malcolm Delvigne, Permanent Under-Secretary of State, outlined George's duties in a report to the Home Secretary, Sir Herbert Samuel:

As his work will lie in the Metropolitan area we would propose to attach him to three London districts, Southwark, Woolwich and South Essex, in order to give him as interesting a range of work as possible and at the same time allow of some concentration of interest in the more important and live issues of factory administration ... work in the London docks (loading and unloading of ships, which are processes fruitful of accident and are governed by an elaborate code of regulations, and which happen to be, at the moment, the subject of internal discussion); the asbestos industry with its newly discovered dangers to health; different branches of the engineering and woodworking industries; the building industry with its recently amended code of safety regulations, etc. It would also be arranged to let him see interesting developments in health and welfare work ... the actual visiting of factories should be alternated with visits to the Home Office Industrial Museum ... where he would be given some intensive instruction in the principles and practice of the safeguarding of machinery and the prevention of various kinds of accidents; the nature and prevention of industrial diseases and the promotion of industrial health and welfare; the principles of factory ventilation and lights; and so on. This is now part of the ordinary training of recruits to the Factory Inspectorate.

To some this might seem dull, but George had fun enough for this to provide a real and interesting contrast. He became genuinely involved with the problems of the working man, expending much effort on his job and insisting on carrying it out on the same level as others within the department, not as a prince. As was pointed out earlier, this was easier than it would be now, and the Prince could always arrive at, and in many cases leave, a factory anonymously.

The third strand of George's life at this time was of course his royal duties. King George had insisted that, whatever shape his son's Home Office job took, it should not prevent him from his primary work as a member of the royal family. Among the highest-profile jobs he undertook were royal tours with David. In 1927 the two brothers paid an official visit to Spain, then later in the year they went (with Prime Minister Baldwin who irritated both brothers by endlessly cracking his fingers) to Canada to celebrate the Diamond Jubilee of the Confederation. If, as some believed at the time, Baldwin accompanied the Princes to keep an eye on them, especially the Prince of Wales, his mission was not entirely successful. Guests including Baldwin and his wife arrived for dinner at Government House to see the Prince of Wales and Prince George leaving, dressed in shorts for squash. The company was kept waiting while the Princes played their game and then dressed for dinner. On another occasion the brothers left an official function to go to a private party.

In 1930 George represented his father at King Haakon of Norway's twenty-fifth accession celebrations, and in 1931 David and George once again undertook a tour together – this time of Latin America. Their mission was to boost trade with South America, and both worked hard at improving their Spanish on the journey out (George was a good linguist and had already mastered French and Italian). The tour was a mixed success: both the brothers had personal charm enough to win over a whole continent, but neither used it quite consistently enough to escape criticism. Reports from Peru and Chile, the first two stops, spoke highly of the hard work and interest shown by the brothers, although the ambassador in Chile did remark on David's 'extra-curricular activities; baccarat, roulette, double whiskey sodas and ladies with pasts were his favourites'. As the journey continued so the brothers' (and in particular David's) faults were more apparent: in Argentina David turned up two hours late, in the wrong clothes and not entirely sober for one function, in Uruguay his 'tiredness' stood in the way of his work and in Rio de Janeiro both Princes put backs up with their bad timekeeping and casual attitudes. At last they arrived in São Paulo, where matters improved and it was reported that 'the British are intensely proud of the two Princes and with reason, for they have won the good will of everyone with whom they have been in contact'.

His tour of South Africa, Rhodesia, the Belgian Congo and Portuguese West Africa, undertaken in the spring of 1934 was another success – but again Prince George put his own personal touch to the visit. In South Africa he undertook a 5 mile run under the hot African sun alongside Len Richardson, an Olympic champion. The mixture of common touch and sheer machismo appealed tremendously to observers both in Africa and at home.

Prince George's tours were usually successful, but sometimes he failed to carry them out at all. He was to have gone to Australia and New Zealand later in 1934 but did not feel up to a second tour in a year and was replaced by his duller, more conscientious brother Harry.

The time had come for Prince George to find himself a wife. His uncle Alge Athlone told him directly that he should think of getting married, but George did not even bother to answer him. The rumour is that there was the possibility of a paternity suit being brought against him, and it is true to say that more than one young woman had had to be warned off the Prince. He was taking his place in the machinery of the royal family, but he needed to be made secure. If the pressure was being put on him at this time, he was lucky. Marina was at hand, was eminently suitable, and was all the slightly confused young man could have asked for in a wife. To his great good fortune, he fell in love.

This, then, was the Prince Marina was to marry: a young man fond of pleasure but capable of compassion for those less fortunate than himself and willing to work hard in their cause. A man with charm and wit, and alone among his family, an artistic soul. He had had a gilded life but had suffered (with the illness and death of his brother Prince John and with his own drug addiction) and perhaps become a better man as a result. Like Marina, George's family life was important to him: his brother David was his closest confidant and friend and his relationship with his mother was the most satisfactory among her children. Perhaps this was why he alone among his brothers could marry a woman who was in no sense a mother figure to him.

CHAPTER FOUR

The Fairy Tale

It was natural that, given her background and age, Princess Marina's parents should be concerned about finding a husband for their third daughter. Princess Nicholas had spent the early thirties taking her two younger daughters on a round of visits to royal relations in Germany, Italy and Austria in the hope of finding them husbands. Now, by 1934, both Olga and Elizabeth had made love matches, which by a stroke of luck were also suitable. But Marina proved less easy to settle. She stuck by her childhood declaration that she would only marry for love, and she failed to fall in love. And so her parents prepared to continue the rounds in Europe, and hoped.

There was a moment when it looked as though England's Prince of Wales was taking an interest in the young Greek Princess. Hitherto he had only been attracted to married women, but maybe, it was thought, Marina would be the girl to wean him from his wilder ways. Queen Mary had already considered her goddaughter as a future daughter-in-law, inviting her to stay at Windsor just after David's return from India. On that occasion he showed no interest. However, four years later, during the spring of 1927, when Marina was staying with Olga and Paul in London, David paid marked attention to his young Greek cousin, enough to be noticed by both her family (with hope) and his (with equal gratification). Bradford, in her biography of George VI, quotes a friend of the (then) Yorks who witnessed a part of the courtship:

The Yorks were entertaining a woman friend to dinner when the Prince of Wales rang up and asked the three of them round to York House. When they arrived there, there was practically nobody else, except for the beautiful Princess Marina of Greece. 'He danced with her the whole evening,' the Yorks' friend recalled. 'He never danced with anybody else ... the whole time, an hour or two or three. I could see that the Duke and Duchess of York were thrilled. Then Freda Dudley Ward arrived back next day and that was the end of that.'

Chips Channon, the diarist and friend of the Duke and Duchess of Kent, also believed that David and Marina's relationship 'might well have led to marriage and was progressing very well but Freda Dudley Ward, at the last moment, interfered and stopped it'.

Another match suggested for Marina, but one with even less chance of success, was with Prince Louis Ferdinand of Prussia (one of the Kaiser's grandsons). The Prince's father favoured the match but Marina herself did not. In 1934 Marina was still unmarried and nearing twenty-eight. After Elizabeth's wedding in January she perhaps felt at something of a loose end. Her family certainly felt she needed something more, but there was little they could do other than keep her moving around the right circles.

During a stay in London at the end of 1933, Marina re-met her cousin George at a lunch party given by Emerald Cunard, the famous socialite, for Marina's sister Olga and her husband Prince Paul. For the first time their friendship took on a new edge, and when Marina returned to London the following spring to stay with Paul and Olga at Claridge's Prince George was among the first callers. Arriving when Olga and Marina were out shopping, he sat and talked to Prince Paul. When Olga returned without Marina, he waited. When Marina finally returned to the hotel, George showed no signs of leaving in a hurry. During this May visit Chips and Honor Channon entertained Prince Paul, Olga and Marina to lunch. 'They are surely the two most beautiful Princesses, if not women, in the world,' Chips wrote in his diary. 'Princess Marina is very much thinner, and I hope one day she will make a suitable marriage with the House of Windsor.'

The likelihood of such a marriage was increasing daily. For

the rest of Marina's stay she and Prince George spent a great deal of time together. They went walking, dancing, out for drives in the country. George confided to a friend that 'we laugh at the same sort of things. She beats me at most games. And she doesn't care a damn how fast I drive when I take her out in a car.' George, with his eye for the beautiful, found Marina very attractive. And with his own liking of fast cars and derring-do he liked a girl with a bit of spirit about her.

Prince Christopher, Marina's uncle, was sure that it was the very informality of the affair that ensured its success:

I imagine that it was the very fact of her being so unlike the other princesses he had met that appealed to him. Instead of all the solemn ritual of a royal betrothal, the formal introduction, the process of mutual inspection with all the relatives waiting expectantly in the background ready to bestow their blessing, they were able to see one another as often as they wanted.

Prince George's great good luck was that he could have a truly modern courtship with a girl so suitable that a generation earlier she might well have been forced upon him.

Marina was to spend a three-month summer holiday with Olga and Paul at Bohinj, their summer house in the countryside of Yugoslavia. First she and Princess Nicholas visited a health spa in France, where Marina dieted away half a stone and made up for the pleasures of London life with strict exercise and sport. Then, as arranged, the mother and daughter joined the family in Yugoslavia.

George had made no plans to join the Greeks on their holiday (he was going to Cowes Regatta), but on impulse sent a telegram announcing his imminent arrival. Prince Paul immediately sent Prince Christopher a telegram, 'Get into the next train and come to Bohinj. We need your help in some very serious business.' Christopher rang them, worried that there was bad news in the family but Olga, showing a streak of Greek superstition which Christopher certainly shared, explained that George was soon to arrive from England. 'Do you remember you were with us when Elizabeth got engaged to Toto?' she asked. 'They are both so happy that I have an idea you will bring Marina luck too.'

Nothing loath, Christopher arrived the following week, the day before George, who had borrowed a plane from the Prince of Wales. Marina and her friend Madame Ralli were staying at the chalet, Prince and Princess Nicholas were in a rented villa 25 miles away.

The family did not have long to wait. Three days were spent in the idyllically romantic pine-clad mountains which surround Bohinj lake. The couple could shoot, fish, bathe, walk and of course motor their way through the last days of their courtship. Prince Christopher takes up the story of the night of 20 August:

The atmosphere grew more and more electric.

Then one evening we all played backgammon in the sitting-room until we could hardly keep awake. One by one we departed for bed until George and Marina were left sitting alone at opposite ends of the sofa. I had been in my bedroom for about half an hour when I discovered that I had left my cigarette-case on the backgammon table. Putting on my dressing-gown I went in search of it. The door of the sitting-room was open; George and Marina were still seated on the sofa, though no longer, I observed with satisfaction, at the opposite ends of it. I stole back to bed without my case.

The next day their engagement was announced.

Prince Christopher could be satisfied that his luck had worked for another niece, and Marina too was happy at the coincidence that 'we got engaged by the lakes at Bohinj. George proposed to me in the same room that my sister Elizabeth got engaged in exactly a year and a month before – the drawing room of Prince Paul's villa.' Later, when impertinently asked by a friend what had taken place in that drawing room, she just smiled and said, 'I was wearing a blue frock.'

Everyone discovers that as soon as an announcement is made of an engagement they lose all control of their own lives: none more so than royalty. But for George and Marina there were a few more days of peace while they waited for official permission from George's father the King. George sent a naval friend a picture postcard with the message, 'I've done it! I can't tell you how happy I am,' but otherwise, despite rumours (Prince George once answered the telephone, denied there was an engagement and pretended to be the butler), the secret was kept for a few more days.

On 28 August there was an announcement from Balmoral, where the King and Queen were spending their summer holidays. It was in the traditional format: 'It is with the greatest pleasure that the King and Queen announce the betrothal of their dearly beloved son, Prince George, to Princess Marina, daughter of Prince and Princess Nicholas of Greece, to which union the King has gladly given his consent.' But behind the formal wording was real joy that their wayward son had found himself a wife – and one known to the family who could be welcomed wholeheartedly. Both agreed that Marina was 'very pretty and charming and will be a great addition to the family'. The Prince of Wales was more circumspect: 'Brother George was quick on the job, wasn't he?' he said to Godfrey Thomas, a long-time member of his staff. 'So d—d quick that one wonders how long it will last. You know my views on "Royal Marriages", so that unless they really are fond of each other I'm sorry for both. However, marriage of some kind was the only hope for him, giving him some responsibility and a home of his own.'

The English family was delighted with the news, but although some felt that perhaps George was just giving in to family pressure in finding a suitable wife, they were clearly wrong. Freda Dudley Ward, ex-mistress of David and still a friend of George's, told Bruce-Lockhart that 'Prince George is very in love with Princess Marina, although at first, when he was saying that he would have to settle down and marry and Princess Marina's name was suggested to him, he did think ... that she was too "bossy".'

George, Marina, Paul and Olga and Prince and Princess Nicholas were in Salzburg when the news broke in England. They had left Bohinj for a few days' shopping and to see *Don Giovanni* and attend other concerts at the Salzburg Festival. They were staying in the Hotel de l'Europe when the journalists started ringing and arriving from England. Their job was not an easy one. Here was one of the King's sons engaged to a Princess, but one of whom almost nothing was known. Marina's many visits to England had been private, and there were no pictures of her on file. (Her engagement visit to England was to be the first ever recorded in the press.) She was obviously suitable, but who was she? The public wanted to know. Symptomatic of the family's anonymity in England was the resumé of Marina's life published in *The Times* the day after the betrothal was announced from Balmoral. It baldly names her parents and sisters, adding that 'the second daughter, Princess Elizabeth, born in 1904, is unmarried.' *The Times* also, when announcing who were to be the bridesmaids, misinformed the public that Princess Katharine of Greece was Marina's sister.

Prince Nicholas told a newspaper that 'we are both very much attached to England and so is Marina who is delighted at the prospect of going to live there. There is nothing political in the marriage.' And, although he was speaking for the press, everyone who knew George and Marina realised that this was indeed a love match. Meanwhile the photographers took every opportunity to fill up their files with pictures of the Princess – including one of her taken outside, smoking through a cigarette holder which was, in 1934, considered rather racy. Queen Mary was to try in vain to stop this habit: by the end of her life Marina chain-smoked through a gold cigarette holder.

Prince George earned his share of newspaper coverage on his engagement – but unlike the modern approach to royal news (find out as much dirt as you can and then remember it as often as possible), his wild days were left unmentioned. 'Like other members of the Royal Family, the Prince has taken his share devotedly in public ceremonies,' said *The Times*, while a leader column on the same day (29 August) remarked that 'His Majesty is himself an example of the excellence of the training afforded by the Royal Navy, and Prince George's early years were spent in that service.' His 'genial presence' is mentioned and *The Times* sums up that 'by character and personality as well as by training the Prince has amply earned the hearty congratulations and good wishes which will assuredly be offered him in full measure by the millions of his father's loyal subjects.'

The Times was not, however, above printing a masterly piece of non-news in an effort to satisfy public interest in the royal engagement:

Prince George will probably return home from Yugoslavia on Saturday, September 8, making the greater part of the journey by train. He may, however, travel from Paris to London by air. It is not yet certain whether he will make the journey alone. Princess Marina will not come to England until later, but Prince George may be accompanied on the journey by her brother-in-law and sister, Prince and Princess Paul of Yugoslavia, who intend shortly to bring their son to school in this country.

Some things do not change.

From then on the couple was inundated with telegrams from almost every mayor and organisation in Britain. Countries George had visited in the course of duty took an almost pro-prietorial pride in his engagement. The *Ottawa Citizen* recorded the 'modest geniality' he had evinced seven years earlier on his visit with David, while the Greek press filled many column inches with stories about their exiled Princess and her Prince. (Venizelos issued a statement saying, 'I am convinced this wedding has no political significance. It is the most natural thing in the world for two young people to fall in love. If I thought the marriage had any political import I should say more.' But on such an occasion no one was particularly interested in his view.)

George and Marina's holiday lasted a short while longer – long enough for King Alexander and Queen Marie of Yugoslavia to come to lunch at Bohinj to offer their congratulations and for the villagers at Bohinj to give the engaged couple an old-fashioned and picturesque tribute. Led by the mayor, the women in national head-dresses and brightly embroidered linen shirts, the men in feathered hats and waistcoats, they walked up to Prince Paul's chalet and, accompanied by fiddlers and con-certinas, sung their congratulations. Marina was presented with a bouquet of cornflowers and eidelweiss (blue and white for Greece) and George with red roses for England. Prince Paul thanked the villagers and told them he would send down barrels of beer for the couple's health to be drunk. The mayor announced that a street in Bohinj would be named after Prince George in honour of the occasion, and the villagers filed away again.

It was an occasion entirely reminiscent of the Old Europe,

the one in which Marina had grown up but which she was now, finally, to leave. From now on the wedding arrangements were to take priority. After a few days in Munich with Toto and Elizabeth, George accompanied Marina and Princess Nicholas back to Paris and on 12 September returned to England leaving his fiancée and her mother to go shopping.

The Paris to which Marina returned was much more interested in her now than when she had left before her engagement. Marina was no longer yet another exile, she was about to become a Princess of Great Britain. Marina was somebody. It must have seemed as though the whole of Paris was waiting at the station for her return. Suddenly people who had ignored the family welcomed them back, wanted to meet them. After the years of exile they were once again important. Prince Nicholas, a proud man, who had borne his troubles with stoic calm if occasional bitterness, was angry at this volte-face (something he must have experienced before), but Marina was more philosophical, telling her father he should not have expected anything different. Of course she was right. From now on everyone she met would want to be her friend.

Because the family had returned to Paris sooner than expected their flat was still shut up. But as their stay was not to be a long one – they had been invited to join the King and Queen at Balmoral – Marina stayed with friends and her parents put up at a hotel. After some clothes shopping, the family left Paris for England. Once again the railway station was crammed with people hoping for a glimpse of the Greek Princess. This time Marina was less surprised by the crowds: they were something to which she had to become accustomed. So when she saw a group of girls she knew from her dressmaker's, she made her way over to them and thanked them for coming before boarding her train. Marina had always been able to charm, but now her charm was to become a valuable asset. She had always been polite, but from now normal politeness to near-strangers would have a huge effect. Marina had always been royal, and always been aware of her position. But from now on her status would no longer just be a fact of life. It was to be a way of life.

If the Gare du Nord had been crowded, Folkestone on 16

September was even more so. A foreign bride was arriving in England the traditional way – by sea – and the English wanted to be there to see her. Again and again the papers pointed out that the last Princess to cross the seas to marry an English prince had been Alexandra of Denmark, that most beautiful and popular Queen. Marina was her great-niece and as beautiful. Her welcome was as great, and to the slight figure in russet-brown, almost overwhelming. 'The reception was wonderful. I was so touched I could hardly speak. They were all so friendly and they made me feel so at home. All those people who came to meet me,' she later said.

There was one spot of homeliness to greet the future bride. Of course the Mayor of Folkestone was there, backed by a group of civic worthies. Of course members of the royal family were there to greet their new relation. But Marina's old nurse, Miss Fox, was also there to welcome her ex-charge. Marina's delight in seeing the old lady was wholehearted. Here, in the form of the nanny, was a bit of England that seemed unchanging. 'I feel a little dazed,' she confessed to Foxy, before setting off in the train to Victoria. Yet more crowds greeted her with even more enthusiasm in the capital, and George was waiting at the station to take Marina and her parents to York House. When he kissed her in greeting the cheers almost broke windows. At York House, the crowds could not be persuaded to move until they had seen the Prince and Princess. Finally they came to a window and, when someone called out a question about the engagement ring, Marina answered 'It's a sapphire', and held up her hand for the crowd to see. George later wrote to Prince Paul, thanking him for the Yugoslavian holiday which had won him a wife, saying:

I want to thank you a million times for *all* your kindness and for taking me to Salzburg and Munchen which I loved and for letting me see Marina and so get engaged to her! It's all so lovely and I am so happy that I can hardly believe it. Everyone is so delighted with her – the crowd especially – 'cos when she arrived at Victoria Station they expected a dowdy princess – such as unfortunately my family are – but when they saw this lovely chic creature – they could hardly believe it and even the men were interested and shouted 'Don't change – don't let them change you!' Of course she won't be changed – not if I have anything to do with it. My parents were charming and so pleased with M. and me! They couldn't have been nicer and Mama was endlessly making lists and producing jewels and making arrangements – she was sweet. In a short time all the main essentials were fixed, which was indeed clever. As to the bridesmaids, as they would have 8 (it's the custom for royalty here!) I thought much better have all family – that's why they are so assorted and Tim [Irene of Greece] has been asked .... It's not so much fun here in London as it's always full of crowds and it's impossible to go anywhere together but everyone is so pleased that one really shouldn't complain .... We went to see Aunt Toria ... she told M. that she was for David and I was for Tim! But poor old lady she's rather gaga! We saw David last night at midnight – he wouldn't dine – the parents-in-law (mine) he wouldn't see. I mean, he never even mentioned them or asked about them. He *did* send a cable to Salzburg but it got lost. He was very nice but nothing if you know what I mean....

Marina's first introduction to the King and Queen as their future daughter-in-law was to take place at Balmoral, where the royal family was still taking its summer break. (Her cousin ex-King George of Greece had arrived there on 1 September.) Marina and her parents travelled up to Scotland on a sleeper with George. Although she had known the King and Queen all her life, it must have been a daunting prospect, but she was welcomed by them as genuinely as she had been by the London crowds. King George found it easier to get along with women than with men, and had good relationships with all his daughters-in-law (except of course Mrs Simpson, whom he did not wish to know and of whom he certainly did not approve.) Prince Henry's fiancée, Lady Alice Montagu-Douglas-Scott, started out on a bad footing when, on her first visit to Balmoral, she told her host that she intended to accompany Prince Henry out stalking: 'I could not, it seemed, have made a worse *faux pas*. Ladies at Balmoral at that time were not even allowed to watch the grouse shooting, so the idea that I was intending to go out stalking was completely beyond the pale. It later transpired that the King had been so surprised he had not dared say anything.' Despite that beginning the King became genuinely fond of her, as he did of Marina and Bertie's wife Elizabeth. Queen Mary was also approving, telling her lady-in-waiting Mabell Airlie that 'the women of that Danish family make good wives. They have the art of marriage. Look at Queen Alexandra. Could any other wife have managed King Edward as well as she did? No bread-and-butter miss would be of any help to my son, but this girl is sophisticated as well as charming, and she will be. Theirs will be a happy marriage.'

For Marina, going to Scotland 'felt like coming home again', it reminded her so of Greece. Both the landscape and the way of life – with the bagpipes, folklore and old songs – reminded her vividly of her early home. That first official visit to Balmoral was therefore a very happy occasion. The days were spent pleasantly, motoring (George's passion surfacing again), discussing wedding arrangements (the date, 29 November, was announced while Marina and her parents were still staying at Balmoral) and shopping with the Yorks and Princess Elizabeth for tartans, sporting check tweeds, travelling rugs and 'other woollen goods'. George bought Marina some hunting Stuart tartans, which after her marriage she would be entitled to wear. Whether the chic Marina's heart lifted at the sight of all these tweeds history does not relate.

According to Bruce-Lockhart it was on this first visit that Queen Mary looked at Marina's red nails and said, 'I am afraid the King doesn't like painted nails; can you do something about it?' To which Marina replied, 'Your George may not, but mine does.'

It was also announced at this time that George and Marina's wedding would take place in Westminster Abbey but would be followed by a second ceremony conducted by the rites of the Greek Orthodox Church. This was not the first time a British prince had been married by the rites of another church, but was the first time it had happened in England. Prince Alfred, Duke of Edinburgh, Queen Victoria's second son and George's great-uncle had in 1874 married Grand Duchess Marie, Alexander II's daughter and Marina's great-aunt in a joint ceremony held in the Winter Palace at St Petersburg.

Marina's first public ordeal with the royal family was the ghillies' ball, a dance traditionally held at Balmoral and attended by estate workers and house servants as well as the royal family. The Queen and Duchess of York coached her in the steps for several days beforehand, so that by the 19 September Marina could dance such old Scottish favourites as 'The Dashing White Sergeant'. In honour of Marina a Greek national air was included – the only change made to the programme of music at the ball since 1919. There were twelve dances, all of which, according to the *Times* report the next day, were danced by Marina with 'enjoyment and good spirits'. She herself later praised the tradition for its relaxed air. 'I was enchanted by the ghillies' ball. There the servants dance with the royal family without any sense of familiarity, but with the utmost good friendship.' This too was like the Greece of her childhood.

Marina returned to Paris on 1 October: there was the wedding dress to consider and after all Paris was still her home. Marina had wanted to employ Patou, the Paris couturier, to make her dress. He had over the past years been very generous to Marina in the way of arranging discounts for his clothes and she thought it a way to pay him back. However, George pointed out to her that she was marrying a British Prince and so must, out of tact, employ a British dressmaker. Showing a fine sense of compromise Marina agreed to use Edward Molyneux, who was English but based in Paris. And then there was the trousseau to be considered. Marina was torn as to who should make what, but came to a sensible decision. 'When I am a British Princess,' she said, 'I shall adopt my new country, but now I shall divide the work. British employment for the future British Princess, Russian work for those who are my kin and need it badly, and French employment for the country which gave me hospitality in years of exile, and to those who have been kind to me.' No one could or did take offence at such a decision. The wedding cake, after all, was to be made in Edinburgh, iced in London, and its ingredients were guaranteed to be 'of Empire origin'. Marina began playing her role of British Princess well – she even, while preparing for her wedding, made time to send a drawing of a boy's head to an exhibition at Agnew's entitled 'Amateur Art by all Ages'.

England, which is good at such things, continued its rejoicing in the face of a royal wedding, the first since the Duke of York's to Lady Elizabeth Bowes-Lyon eleven years earlier. But not everyone was entirely happy. To the Prince of Wales, George's wedding meant he was not so much gaining a sister-in-law as losing his closest friend. Wallis Simpson had often met Prince George at Fort Belvedere, David's country house, and she knew how close the two men were. She had seen them at their most informal and relaxed but knew 'the princely brothers plainly enjoyed their friends and loved to exchange quips, but there was no mistaking the fact that between them and even the friends with whom they galloped across country in the closest of companionships was a barrier that could never be breached'. So this companionship, the closest of all, was to be interrupted by a third, and however welcome she might be, David could not help but mourn. The Duchess of Windsor wrote in her autobiography,

As I watched the Prince during the weeks preceding [the wedding], it seemed to me that a sadness began to envelop him. He and his younger brother were very close, and the bonds of blood were strengthened by an unusual kinship of spirit.

George and David spent a great deal of time together in the last weeks before the wedding, with George at the Fort almost every weekend. She continued:

I rather suspected that, with Princess Marina still in Paris with her parents, selecting her trousseau, the Prince, who was to be best man at the wedding, thought it was just as well to keep a close eye upon the bridegroom-to-be until he had been safely led to the altar .... We all had great fun together. Prince George was genuinely in love with Princess Marina, a most beautiful woman, whom I had met earlier at the Fort; and he was also delighted at the prospect of at last having his own home.

Princess Nicholas caused problems when the invitations were printed without her full correct title. She declared that unless they were reprinted with 'Her Imperial Highness' she would not go to the wedding. They were reprinted.

The preparations for the wedding were rudely interrupted on 9 October by the assassination of King Alexander of Yugoslavia, who was shot in an open-topped car at Marseilles while on an official visit to France. King Alexander had been a cousin and close friend of Paul, so his death was a family as well as a national tragedy. 'He was the steadiest of them all, the best, the most needed, the most important, the one who counted the most,' wrote his anguished mother-in-law, Queen Marie of Rumania.

Alexander's death gave Prince Paul a new international importance: in the King's will he had named Paul as the chief of three regents who were to govern the country until his eleven-year-old son Peter reached his majority, which would happen in 1941. He and his Queen had been among the first to see and congratulate George and Marina on their engagement and now, only a few months later, he was killed in the same way as Marina's grandfather and so many of her relations, by a political fanatic. It was decided that the wedding preparations were too advanced to be cancelled, but both Marina (with her parents) and George (representing King George) went to the funeral in Belgrade five days later. On his way back to London, Prince George spent a few days in Paris with Marina's family. They lived those days as Marina had always lived in France – anonymously, travelling on public transport, visiting Prince Nicholas's studio and, of course, shopping.

Meanwhile the presents flooded in, and were put on public show at St James's Palace in aid of charity. The Greek colony in London gave a souvenir plate made for the marriage of George I, Marina's grandfather; the Freemasons gave 300 guineas; the Aga Khan gave a ten-foot elephant tusk; the King and Queen gave Marina jewels, as did Princess Nicholas, who gave her daughter a diamond bow which had been given to her by the Tsar. There were cigarette boxes and snuff boxes, clocks, decanters and candlesticks. There were pieces of silver and antique furniture, ostrich feather bedcovers, an ostrich feather and mother-of-pearl fan (from the Greeks in Cape Town) and even a 70 lb cheese.

With Marina in Paris, George took a particular interest in the presents as they arrived. Wallis Simpson recorded 'the joking way in which he estimated the probable worth of the day's deliveries'. One evening he asked Wallis for some help – what was the most expensive kind of fur. 'I'm trying to solve a problem for a very rich friend who wants to give Marina a fur coat for a wedding present.' Wallis told him chinchilla was the best.

'Fine,' he answered, 'I wouldn't want my friend to make a mistake.' 'Damn it, George' interposed the Prince of Wales, 'You're beginning to sound like an auctioneer.'

Marina, on the other hand, had taken a less acquisitive line. Just before leaving England for Paris she had issued a statement:

I would like the people of England to share in some way my great happiness on the occasion of my engagement to Prince George. As you know, my years of exile have taught me how much unhappiness there is in the world. Although I should be happy to think that the preparations for my wedding were in some small measure giving employment to those who need it, I should be more than happy for the unemployed, and particularly their children, to receive any money which has been intended for the purchase of wedding gifts for me.

George was not just checking the wedding presents, though. He worked throughout October and November until the wedding ceremonies began. His appointments included industrial visits – to the Ford Motor Works, the Institute of Fuel, the London Brick Company – and Social Service centres. He was made Patron of the Kent Council of Social Services, an appointment hailed in the press as a significant advance in the way the Social Services were considered.

Once the trousseau, comprising 'three morning ensembles, five afternoon dresses, six evening gowns, two coats' was bought, Marina and her parents left Paris. Her last day was spent among her relations and old friends. She had lunch at home with her mother and sisters, visited M. Grande, her hairdresser, in the afternoon, and gave a small party for her best friends in the evening. Only one woman friend stayed on for supper with the family.

The next day Marina and her family (both sisters, her parents and Toto) and their attendants left Paris in the President's coach and crossed the Channel in an especially chartered boat from Calais to Dover, where they were met by George and various Dover worthies. Once again, this time with a Pullman 'parlour car', first-class coach and dining coach as well as a whole luggage van to themselves, they made the journey by train to Victoria where they were met by, among others, the King and Queen and Prince of Wales. They were all taken to Buckingham Palace, where they were guests in the run-up to the wedding.

King George had arranged for Prince Nicholas to be welcomed to England with a new honour: Knight Grand Cross of the order of the Bath. Prince George was also given a new decoration in time for his wedding: on 9 October he was created Duke of Kent, Earl of St Andrews and Baron Downpatrick (he took his seat on 7 November). The Greeks marked the marriage in similar style bestowing on George the Grand Cross of the Order of the Redeemer.

The last days before the wedding were spent in a round of festivities, except for one quiet moment the evening before the wedding. A verger recognised a couple kneeling in prayer before the High Altar of Westminster Abbey as the Duke and future Duchess of Kent.

The high point of the gala days was the ball given for two thousand people by the King and Queen at Buckingham Palace. Prince Christopher of Greece, who was staying in the palace for the occasion, remembered the wedding and the run-up to it as the most beautiful he had ever seen outside imperial Russia. Every royal house in Europe was represented: the King and Queen of Denmark with Prince Waldemar (George I and Queen Alexandra's last surviving brother), the King and Queen of Norway, Princess Juliana of the Netherlands (who was one of the bridesmaids), and Grand Dukes and Duchesses from Russia, members of the English and Greek royal families.

Among the less grand guests were Mr and Mrs Ernest Simpson, who had been invited at the express insistence of the Prince of Wales. Although Marina, in her dress of white with sapphires and diamonds given her by King George, was at her most beautiful, two men at least found their eyes drawn to Mrs Simpson. Prince Paul of Yugoslavia told her that her violet lamé dress with a vivid green sash was 'the most striking gown in the room' and the Prince of Wales (who had given her the diamonds and emeralds she was also wearing) 'scarcely left her side all that evening' (according to Prince Christopher), 'despite the fact that some of the most beautiful women in Europe were doing their utmost to attract his attention. He appeared never even to notice them. He was in love as it is given to men and women to love only once in a lifetime.'

This ball was the only occasion on which the King and Queen Mary met Wallis Simpson, the woman whom David was to marry, and then it was almost by mistake (at least as far as they were concerned). The Prince of Wales took Mrs Simpson over to them and introduced them. 'It was the briefest of encounters – a few words of perfunctory greeting, an exchange of meaningless pleasantries,' but the thing was done. It was all the bolder in that the King had originally scratched the Simpsons' name from a list of guests David wanted to be invited to the party: the King later expressed his 'fury' that David had 'smuggled ... that woman' into the palace and then dared effect an introduction. The injury was compounded when it was seen that Mr and Mrs Simpson had been given two of the best seats in the Abbey for the actual wedding.

After the banquet George and Marina slipped out of Buckingham Palace to join the crowds in the West End, looking at the decorations and enjoying the general revelry. They were recognised and mobbed by an enormous crowd in Piccadilly Circus.

The decorations had indeed caused some controversy. To the royal family, Marina was a Princess of Greece. To the Greek government, Greece was a republic and Marina was a Princess of Denmark (through her grandfather, who had of course been a Prince of Denmark before becoming King of Greece). In the end the Foreign Office decided that as long as both flags were used, and both country's ministers in London were asked for permission, no offence could be taken at the use of the blue and white Greek flag.

The other complication came when the Royal Horse Guards' Director of Music had the bright idea of writing to Athens for a copy of 'Son of the Eagle', the royalist rallying song. The consul was very nervous at the idea, knowing how offensive it would be to the Greek republicans, and suggested that the Greek music should be limited to 'the harmless traditional songs and country dances which I sent you ... they are sure to give great pleasure to members of the Greek Royal Family.'

On 28 November, the day before the wedding, the Duke and Duchess of York gave a lunch party for the bride and groom at their house in Piccadilly. That evening they delighted West End crowds by going to the theatre with Queen Mary to see *Theatre Royal* starring Laurence Olivier and Marie Tempest. *The Times* reported the way in which the royal party took the theatre by surprise:

The royal party waited until the lights had been dimmed in preparation for the curtain to go up before taking their seats. As the Queen walked to the front of the box she was immediately recognised by the audience, who stood and applauded. When Princess Marina and the Duke of Kent appeared in the second box there was a great burst of cheering and clapping, which the Duke and the Princess acknowledged by waving .... The rising of the curtain was delayed by two minutes owing to the spontaneous welcome of the audience .... The Duke of Kent and his fiancée were cheered by a great crowd when they left the theatre. As their car was driven away thousands surged forward through the police barrier, and women ran to the side of the car waving their handkerchiefs in greeting.

On the day of the wedding Prince Christopher was being amused by his Buckingham Palace valet who told him the joke doing the rounds below stairs: 'Why will Princess Marina be able to smooth life for Prince George? Because for twenty-seven years she has been preserved in Greece.' (The valet was later reprimanded by the King's valet for 'telling dirty stories to visiting royalties'.) While Marina dressed, George wandered out into St James's to cash a cheque and was found by his brothers, Bertie and David (who were his joint supporters) pushing his way back through the crowds towards Buckingham Palace.

The wedding was set for eleven o'clock. Marina was dressed by Miss Fox, the old nanny, whose pride in this turn of events knew no bounds. The Molyneux wedding dress was in silver French brocade woven with English roses. The train and sleeves were lined with plain silver. The dress was medieval in concept, with wide flowing sleeves. Her veil was held in place by a diamond tiara and she wore a bunch of the traditional orange blossoms over each ear. Her other jewels were diamond earrings, necklace and brooch, and the family order given by George V.

Her bouquet was of white lilies, grown at Windsor with a sprig of myrtle from a tree planted for Queen Victoria and included in royal brides' bouquets. The bridesmaids carried white roses.

Marina was attended by eight bridesmaids: Princesses Irene, Eugenie and Katherine of Greece, Lady Iris Mountbatten, Princess Juliana of the Netherlands and Grand Duchess Kira of Russia all dressed in white crepe with silver thread and silver lamé sashes to match Marina. Their headdresses were made of twisted silver lamé and white crepe. The two little girls, wearing dresses of stiffened tulle (which the King had ordered to be shortened so that he could see their 'pretty little knees') were Princess Elizabeth of York and Lady May Cambridge.

The procession was nearly held up by Princess Victoria, old now and fairly feeble, who decided that she did not approve of some of the guests with whom she was to share a carriage and refused to get in with them. Luckily a brave old family friend deliberately misunderstood her and saying, 'Can't get into the carriage, Madam? Oh yes you can, let me help you,' scooped her up and sat her in her seat without further ado.

In fact the procession was one of the fastest royal progresses on record. Scotland Yard had received information that an assassination attempt was to be made on Prince Paul of Yugoslavia, who was due to travel in a coach with Prince and Princess Nicholas and George II of Greece. After extensive searching of all buildings adjoining the route, it was decided that the procession should be speeded up from a walk to a trot. With the royal protection squad the most massive to date, nothing happened to mar the wedding celebrations.

Marina and George's wedding was also unique for another reason: it was the first royal wedding to be broadcast live by wireless. (The BBC had suggested broadcasting Bertie's wedding to Elizabeth Bowes-Lyon in 1923 but although the Dean of Westminster approved the proposal the Chapter, horrified, opposed it.) So that not only were the massive crowds in London in on the event, so also were people all over England. In Denmark, in Belgium, and even in republican Greece families gathered together to listen to the couple exchange their vows.

'Never in history has a marriage been attended by so vast a company of witnesses,' the Archbishop of Canterbury said in his address. 'For, by a new and marvellous invention of science, countless multitudes in every variety of place are joining in this service. The whole nation, nay the whole Empire, are the wedding guests.'

The marriage was conducted by the Archbishop of Canterbury, Dr Cosmo Lang, who reminded Marina that in marrying George she was not taking on just a man, but a country and a new way of life with great responsibilities:

You cannot choose what changes and chances are to befall you in the coming year .... You, Sir, have already and fully taken your place in the service of the community. And you, dear bride, as your husband's comrade, will find a new happiness in sharing the joys and sorrows and in ministering to the needs of the good British folk who have already, with a warmth so swift and spontaneous, taken you into their heart. I am sure that that heart is now speaking through my words as I say – God bless you both. God guide you. God keep you always.

The couple, now married, left the body of the Abbey to sign the register in the Chapel of St Edward the Confessor.

And then back they drove (Marina with an ermine wrap over her dress and a small hot-water bottle wrapped in a white blanket to keep her warm) through the pealing of bells and thunderous cheers of the crowds. 'They were profoundly touching in their wonderful enthusiasm,' wrote Prince Christopher. He went on:

Only in England now, I think, do you find this personal love of the Sovereign and his family, a sentiment that surpasses even fidelity; a perfect understanding that makes even the poorest subject feel that he has a right to share in the joys and sorrows of the Royal Family. Monarchy can never die out in England, whatever its fate in other countries. It is too deeply ingrained in the hearts of the people.

And the *Daily Mail* came out with popular sentimentality: 'For all its lavish pageantry, its impersonal splendour, the royal wedding remains first and foremost the happy ending to a real-life love story as romantic as any in the fairy tales.' As Walter Bagehot wrote in *The English Constitution*, first published during the reign of Victoria, 'A princely marriage is the brilliant edition of a universal fact, and as such it rivets mankind.'

The second ceremony, a joint wedding and betrothal service was held in the private chapel at Buckingham Palace (now the Queen's Gallery) and conducted in Greek by Doctor Strinopoulos. Dr Cosmo Lang was present, as had been Germanos at the Church of England wedding. The British would have liked the double crowns and picturesque traditions of an Orthodox wedding, but at the same time they might well have distrusted it. In any event, this wedding was entirely private. Which was fortunate as the Prince of Wales distinguished himself on the occasion by pulling out a cigarette and 'absentmindedly' lighting it from a candle held by a priest. At this ceremony Marina's ring was moved to her right hand, where it was to remain.

After the wedding breakfast (filet of sole, lamb chops, partridges, pêches melba) and the cutting of the 9-foot high, 800 lb cake, the couple set off on honeymoon, Marina dressed in green tweed (which showed a remarkable lack of superstition for a Greek) and a sable coat. Accompanied by an escort of Lifeguards and followed by the King and Queen in a closed car, they clattered away from Buckingham Palace to Paddington Station, from where they were to go to the Earl of Dudley's house, Himley Hall in Staffordshire, for the first part of the honeymoon.

As they left, London continued to celebrate: English gentlemen rode on the roofs of taxis, others broke limbs in overenthusiastic happiness.

The length of the Kents' journey crowds waited to cheer the passing train: at Aynho Junction they were met with fireworks, and everywhere flags fluttered a welcome. It is said that those waiting at Birmingham Station knew when the train was coming from the noise of the cheers from outlying stations. And as they drove up to Himley Hall, which had been floodlit for their arrival, a hundred firework rockets were lit and estate workers lined the drive with flickering torches.

George and Marina took their honeymoon seriously, travelling for five months before settling into normal life. At Himley Hall they entertained their host and the Prince of Wales at a shooting weekend, and watched film of their wedding in a squash court converted into a cinema. Then, leaving presents of tie pins, cuff links and brooches for the staff who had looked after them, they moved on to Trent Park, Sir Philip Sassoon's house, then spent Christmas with the royal family at Sandringham before moving on for skiing with Elizabeth and Toto (with Princess Nicholas) in Bavaria. Elizabeth's son was born on 11 January, after which the Kents returned to England via Paris.

They cruised the West Indies (Trinidad, San Juan, Haiti, Kingston, Montego Bay). While in Kingston they spent a weekend with the Duke of Gloucester, who had had to miss their wedding as his military duties kept him abroad. George fished in the Bahamas, where the Kents spent two weeks with the Governor and his wife, Sir Bede and Lady Clifford. At the end of March, in Nassau, George and Marina met the American President Roosevelt, who was taking a holiday aboard the yacht *Nourmahal* with the Vincent Astors. Roosevelt was, said his son, 'fascinated by kings and queens, half-amused, half-impressed, by the pomp and pageantry that enveloped royalty'. He and the Kents were drawn to each other and became firm friends.

Finally, in April, they began the journey home via Vigo and Santander, and then by land to Paris and back to London. They arrived in England on 16 April, and went for a few days to Windsor while the final touches were given to their house. Despite the enormous good will of the British towards the young couple, it was felt that their honeymoon had lasted too long and been too extravagant: as a result when Prince Henry, Duke of Gloucester married Lady Alice Montagu-Douglas-Scott (daughter of the Duke of Buccleuch) a year later they were told that their honeymoon should 'be spent quietly in England'.

The Kents, though, had made the most of their five months' holiday and returned to Number 3, Belgrave Square, which was to be their first home.

CHAPTER FIVE

Marriage

And so Marina was married and mistress of her own establishment at last. She had gained in status, not only as a married woman, but as a woman married into one of the most important families in Europe.

'I believe in the family coming at once and close together so that the parents and children can all be friends and enjoy the same things,' Marina once said to her friend Helena von der Hoven, and indeed she was already pregnant when she and George moved into the house they had rented furnished from Lady Juliet Duff. The first months of life in Belgrave Square were therefore taken up with redecoration of her house and the wait for the birth. In fact the Duke, who had always had an eye for colour and interior design, took a large part in the changes made to the house. He put much of Lady Juliet's furniture into store and began to buy antiques to suit his own taste. Marina's bathroom was black and silver, painted by Joseph Sert with shepherds and nymphs frolicking in a classical landscape. Her bedroom, which stretched the whole width of the second floor and was notable for its ceiling-to-floor mirrored alcove, was furnished with a *Directoire* bed overhung by a peach and 'tea-green' striped canopy. The Duke's bedroom was pale green and the hall pale grey with a marble floor while the nursery was prepared in blue and white.

George did not stop at taking control of the interior design of Belgrave Square. It was he who organised the menus of the day, planned dinner parties and ensured that his guests were comfortable. Marina admitted to Lady Airlie after one dinner party that 'I am really a very bad hostess. I must confess that I didn't know what we were going to eat tonight until the food appeared. My husband chose the dinner and the wine – and the flowers and everything else. He enjoys doing it, and so I always leave the household affairs to him.' George also took an active interest in Marina's clothes, but there she needed little help. Marina had always been known for her impeccable dress sense, even in her poorer days, and now that she was Duchess of the blood royal designers were more eager than ever to dress her. As a young woman Marina had been fat: indeed it was not until her engagement that she really acquired the elegant thinness that was to remain with her for the rest of her life. After re-meeting George, Marina had taken a holiday at a spa near Savoie and had lost half a stone. She had lost another stone during her engagement, after which she stayed thin. Even in her middle years Marina was aware of what she ate, and although she loved nothing more than an evening spent playing cards and eating chocolates, she would caution herself against her sweet tooth, fearing that her early plumpness would creep back upon her. Her daughter Alexandra was later to express worry at how little her mother ate and how often she dieted.

The English people had decided to take Marina to their hearts, which meant that from the day of her marriage she was watched. The clothes she wore, her mannerisms, her smile, all became news. And to the great joy of the English it was abundantly clear that at last there was a Princess in the House of Windsor with style, a Princess who could give any Hollywood film star a run for her money. The Duchess of York was much loved, but even in her youth her dress was unexciting and conventional. The Duchess of Kent, with her romantic foreign background, her accented voice and her unrivalled bone structure, had chic. Her impact upon the country was much the same as was the Princess of Wales's on her marriage. As Diana brought knick-erbockers into fashion, so Marina brought a shade called 'Marina Blue'. As Diana patronised English couturiers to help promote the British clothing industry, so Marina took to wearing cotton dresses (unheard of then for an upper-class woman) to help alleviate the depression in the Lancashire cotton industry.

Pill-box hats became a fashion necessity after Marina took to wearing them, while touching up make-up in public stopped after it was noticed that the Duchess of Kent always looked perfect without ever resorting to her compact mirror. Dress designer Captain Molyneux was one of the many to rave about Marina's sense of style: 'She will not let herself be stormed by any whimsical change of fashion, but wears only what suits her. And her guiding principle is understatement, the unobvious and the unshowy.' He said that she would often sketch changes to his designs, showing an unerring eye for design, and added that he believed her to be the greatest influence on fashion since Empress Eugenie set the Empire style throughout Europe.

Before long the Kents had taken their place at the head of fashionable London society. Actors, writers and aristocrats came to their parties. They were fêted and loved.

Marina was eased into her royal duties fairly gently. While on honeymoon, it had been announced that the Kents would visit Glasgow, probably in June. It had also been announced that both Kents had accepted patronage of the Royal Waterloo Hospital, and that George had been made Lord High Commissioner to the General Assembly of the Church of Scotland.

Marina's first public engagement after her marriage was an informal and unannounced visit to the *Daily Mail* Ideal Home Exhibition, a few days after her return from honeymoon. With their new house in mind, and with the inevitable excitement generated by the newlyweds' visit, it was not a difficult beginning.

The year 1935 was that of King George V's silver jubilee, so the excitement of a royal wedding continued into the celebrations for the King. The day of national rejoicing was 6 May, and the procession was described by Henry ('Chips') Channon in his diary. The American Channon had known Marina for some years, and was a best friend of Paul of Yugoslavia (they had met at Oxford and lived together when first coming to London). He was a compulsive diarist, moved in the most glittering of London social circles and, from November 1935, was an MP. Almost everything of importance was put down in his diaries:

After a long wait the first procession, and the Speaker ... passed at a walking pace in a gorgeous coach. Then came the Prime Ministers of the Dominions, led by Ramsay MacDonald, seated with his daughter, Ishbel. He looked grim and she dowdy. No applause ... the minor Royalties – a few cheers .... Then masses of troops, magnificent and virile .... Then thunderous applause for the royal carriages. The Yorks in a large landau with the two tiny pink children. The Duchess of York was charming and gracious .... The next landau carried the Kents, that dazzling pair; Princess Marina wore an enormous platter hat, chic but slightly unsuitable. She was much cheered .... Finally the Prince of Wales smiling his dentist smile.

Marina's large hat, which had in fact drawn criticism from other quarters, had been especially chosen for its large brim, which could be used to hide behind if her pregnancy and the ceremony combined to overcome her. The photographer Cecil Beaton at least approved: 'Princess Marina's picture hats have put Mr Winston Churchill's in the shade and are seriously weighed in comparison with the Duchess of York's smile,' he wrote in *Vogue*.

This was an enormously happy and successful time for the British monarchy, with the nation at its most affectionate and the royal family – despite worries about the King's health and the Prince of Wales's way of life – at its most stable. In November there was another royal wedding, although this was much quieter than Marina and George's extravagant celebration. Prince Henry, now Duke of Gloucester, married Lady Alice Montagu-Douglas-Scott, daughter of the Duke of Buccleuch. Because the Duke had died suddenly a month before the wedding, the ceremony was held quietly in the Chapel of Buckingham Palace rather than in Westminster Abbey. Therefore Henry's wedding was more of a family affair than Marina's had been, but it nevertheless contributed to the general rejoicing which the country shared with the royal family during 1935. George V himself was overwhelmed at his reception as he toured a celebrating London during the jubilee period. 'I'd no idea they felt like that about me,' he said after a visit to the East End. 'I am beginning to think they must like me for myself.'

The only shadow on the royal family was the concern already

felt about David. Walter Bagehot, writing in the time of David's great-grandmother Queen Victoria, described the problem:

The place of a constitutional king has greater temptations than almost any other, and fewer suitable occupations than almost any other. All the world and all the glory of it, whatever is most attractive, whatever is most seductive, has always been offered to the Prince of Wales of the day, and always will be. It is not rational to expect the best virtue where temptation is applied in the most trying form at the frailest time of human life.

David's temptations were enjoyment and women, and as yet there seemed to be no sign of his finding an acceptable wife.

In his early days there had been a few dukes' daughters with whom he had danced and who might have made acceptable brides, but from 1918 for the next fifteen years David was in love with Freda Dudley Ward, a middle-class girl married to a Liberal Member of Parliament. She was nothing but a good influence on him, but of course she could never be his wife. After the first flight of passion, she turned into more of a friend and confidante than a lover, although he remained in love with her for many years.

By 1931 David had found another woman who proved to be more than an easy sexual conquest: Thelma Furness. He was never in love with her as he had been with Freda, but she was a woman with whom he found it easy to spend time. She enjoyed the same things as he, and where Freda had offered some peace in her house with her two small girls Thelma encouraged David in his wilder ways. 'The Prince is more irresponsible than he was,' wrote Bruce-Lockhart in his diary in October 1931. 'They blame Lady Furness who has a bad influence on him. Freda, at any rate, kept him under restraint. She could get him back tomorrow if she wanted to, but apparently she does not want.' Chips Channon later blamed Lady Furness for the 'modernisation' of the Prince which led to his abdication. She 'Americanized him, making him over-democratic, casual and a little common,' claimed Chips. Not only did she do that, but she also introduced him to Wallis Simpson.

The love affair of the British people with their newest Princess continued, and so did the love affair of George and Marina. 'If you want to see two completely happy people, you need only spend a few minutes with my niece Marina and her husband,' Marina's uncle Christopher told a friend a few years after their marriage. Mabell Airlie also recalled being 'impressed not so much by the externals of happiness – the brilliance of the conversation, the beautifully arranged rooms and the perfectly chosen meal – as by the deeper harmony of two temperaments'. Archduchess Ileana also reported favourably on the Kent household: 'I've just been to lunch with Marina and George and they are so wonderfully happy. In spite of the fact that they are now quite "an old married couple" one still feels with them that life is a glorious adventure.'

It was an adventure, but not always glorious. Marina's friends agree that George married Marina loving her, but his was a wild and weak nature and he was not always able to confine himself to the pleasures of domesticity. It was not long before George was unfaithful, and his past as well as his present conduct gave Marina cause for both unhappiness and humiliation. A well-known South American homosexual sidled up to Marina in a London nightclub one night and said, 'You don't know me, but I was your predecessor.' Marina was sophisticated and cosmopolitan, but nothing in her upbringing can have prepared her for such treatment. However, she was strong enough – and her undoubted love was powerful enough – for her to live with this without her spirit breaking. She might occasionally break down in tears in public (among her friends, never while 'on duty'), but she was determined to hold on to George. Both Princess Nicholas and Lilia Ralli were to confide their fears for the future of the marriage, but they underestimated the strength of will concealed under Marina's feminine and superficially pliant exterior.

To the public at least, the Duke of Kent was a reformed character. The playboy image was replaced by that of a loving husband, caring father and hard-working member of the royal family. The work begun before his marriage was continued in earnest, as the Duke travelled the country visiting the industrial areas which were hit so badly by the Depression. He also had other duties than those of the 'Factory Inspector': in 1935 he was given the job of High Commissioner of the Church of Scotland, an ancient honour in which the holder represents the monarch in Scotland (taking precedence even over the monarch's oldest son) during the Assembly. George was at Holyrood for ten days, one of the trips on which he was joined by the Duchess. Again, Marina was let in gently. George undertook a full series of engagements, on many of which he was accompanied by his wife, but she only undertook two solo jobs – presenting prizes to nurses and visiting a children's home.

Gradually Princess Marina began taking on her own share of royal duties and offices; among the first were the patronages of the Elizabeth Garrett Anderson Hospital and the Central School of Speech and Drama; presidencies of the Alexandra Rose Day and Young Women's Christian Association charities followed soon after. From the very beginning Marina was notable for the effort she put into each and every charitable work she undertook: it was a lesson she had learned from her mother in the lean days, and one she did not forget now that times were fatter.

Her first child was born early on 9 October 1935, after a long night in labour. The house was full – Marina's parents and sister Elizabeth were in England for the birth. George and Princess Nicholas were both present at the birth (George, ahead of his time, strongly believed in the importance of attending his wife's labours to the end). There were two nurses, Louie Roberts of Wilmslow and Ethel Smith, who had recently returned to England from Yugoslavia where she had been looking after Olga's children. The Home Secretary Sir John Simon was also there – he was still required to be present at royal births. He was not the only outsider. Journalists spent the night in the secretary's sitting room on the ground floor, waiting for news. Just before midnight the Duke came in to tell them that coffee would be brought in to them, after which the kitchens would be closed until six when they would be brought breakfast. As he left the room he turned back with a smile and said, 'I do hope it'll be over soon. I don't think I could stand much more of this.' This human touch would have made every reader in the land weep with emotion, but not one paper used it.

The baby, the boy so hoped for by Queen Mary, was born on the same day as the son of Sir Henry Channon and his wife Lady Honor (Guiness), who were soon to move into the house next door to the Kents in Belgrave Square. Chips had been a friend of the Greeks as well as of the Duke of Kent, since before the marriage and no one could have been more pleased at the coincidence of the births. A few weeks before the two boys were born, Chips took tea at Claridge's with Prince and Princess Nicholas:

The Duchess of Kent was there in a brown dress and much bejewelled, and rather large, but not so large as Honor. Her curls were faultlessly done at the back. She was sweetness itself, but she has not become in the least English .... At one point the Grand-Duchess [Princess Nicholas] sent her daughter into the next room to fetch her spectacles and the Duchess went meekly. She has been well brought-up in an old-fashioned, affectionate way.

This was the upbringing which had been given Prince Nicholas, and which he had seen that his daughters, despite their peripatetic life, also received. The son shortly to be born to the Duchess would in turn profit from such 'old-fashioned affection'.

Edward George Nicholas Patrick was duly christened by the Archbishop of Canterbury at the private chapel in Buckingham Palace, after which the Kents gave a lunch party at Belgrave Square.

The year 1935 also brought George and Marina a second house. On 3 December George V's sister Victoria died. She left the Kents her house. Princess Victoria had lived a sad life. Both her sisters were married – Maud, the younger, to the King of Norway and Louise to the Duke of Fife – and Victoria had remained the typical Victorian spinster, living at home (Sandringham and Marlborough House) and caring for an increasingly autocratic mother. Once hopes of her own establishment had faded her one solace was her relationship with her brother the King: a relationship carried on to a great extent through endless telephone conversations. (A famous story tells how she answered the telephone one morning, expecting her daily call from her brother. 'Hello you old fool,' she said, to hear the operator saying, 'Beg pardon, Your Royal Highness, His Majesty is not yet on the line.')

Princess Victoria survived her mother by ten years, during which time she indulged her passions for objects and squabbling. The King remained deeply fond of her despite her glaring faults and her consistent hostility to his wife. ('Do try to talk to May at dinner, though one knows she is deadly dull,' she told a guest at Windsor in the early days of her brother's marriage.) Her death was a blow from which the King did not recover.

The home to which Princess Victoria had repaired on her mother's death was Coppins, a Victorian house at Iver in Buckinghamshire. When George inherited it the house reeked of Victoriana. Cluttered with the old Princess's belongings, surrounded by dark trees, it was very different from the sort of house George might have chosen. However, he thoroughly enjoyed the challenge of converting it into something more modern and domestic, decorating and clearing space both indoors and out. Within a year it was a real home to his family and friends. The library was converted into a music room and a ground-floor day nursery was made with doors into the garden. The Kents' London neighbour Chips Channon describes a visit he and his wife paid to Coppins in the following November:

They have modernised and re-decorated it with skill and success. The result is charming, and the rooms now glow with luxe and gaiety. It is entirely Prince George who has transformed it, and he now thinks of little else. We had a massive tea, and then the besotted father carried in the pièce de résistance, the curly-haired, very red, howling Prince Edward. He had fine blue eyes, golden curls, and looks like all four Georges rolled into one. Princess Marina, Honor and I, sat on the floor playing with him.

A happy family picture indeed.

Although Marina was now caught up in her new life, with her new family – her own and the extended one of her husband's relations, the year after her marriage also saw some important changes for her Greek relations. Her cousin King George II of

Greece had, after the break-up of his marriage to the Rumanian Elizabeth, moved to London where he lived in Brown's Hotel waiting for the call to come from his people to return. Perhaps surprisingly, considering how little action he took to further his cause, the call did come. After ten years of bankruptcy, insurrection, military coup, miserable bickering and plain incompetence the Greek leaders decided in 1935 to invite the King home. Once again a plebiscite was held, once again the monarchy was overwhelmingly voted back. And once again a King of Greece packed his bags and returned from exile, this time without a Queen.

The following year the bodies of King Constantine, Queen Sophie and Queen Olga also returned from exile in Florence and, after six day's lying-in-state in Athens were reburied at Tatoi. 'Aunts, uncles, cousins and all one's kith and kin arrived to drive through streets decked with flags and lined by cheering people,' wrote Princess Alexandra of Greece (daughter of the ill-fated King Alexander) of the royal Greeks' return home. A few days later 'dark drapes of mourning' took their place in recognition of the returning bodies. Marina attended a ceremony held to mark the event at the Greek Orthodox cathedral in Bayswater.

There were two causes of discontent in Marina's new life. The first was that despite her impeccable royal credentials, and although she had been a visitor at the royal court since her earliest childhood, she did not at first seem quite at ease with her husband's family. David, of course, was a friend and George's closest ally and the Kents would often spend weekends at Fort Belvedere, with George wielding a scythe in his brother's garden. Fort Belvedere, 'a child's idea of a fort', as Diana Cooper called it, was the place where David was happiest, and therefore the place where his siblings most liked to see him. He had been given the use of the house on the edge of Windsor Great Park by the King in 1929 and had made himself a real home. Here his London friends would come for weekends and cocktails, play games, swim in the new swimming pool or play tennis on the new court. The house was hidden in woods and David loved nothing more than clearing the land. Like his mother in the war years at Badminton, David would dragoon any visiting friends into helping him with the task which was as much therapeutic as anything. David was an obsessive, and gardening became one of his obsessions. 'Prince of Wales has gone mad on gardening,' his golfing companion Bruce-Lockhart wrote in his diary. 'Taken to it 100 per cent like golf. Prince George wanted to bring Marina down. Prince of Wales put him off several times. At last agreed grudgingly, if George would bring a scythe. George had to cut grass all afternoon.'

King George had good relationships with all his daughters-in-law, indeed Princess Nicholas would later affirm that 'the King was a perfect angel to her [Marina] when she arrived in England as a shy bride'. However, there are reports of conflict between Queen Mary and the goddaughter who had married her son. Queen Mary had been delighted to hear that her hitherto wayward son was to marry Marina: 'I am sure we shall like Marina and that she will be a charming addition to the family,' she had written to the King when the engagement was announced.

Marina's relationship with Elizabeth, the Duchess of York, was also a distant one in the early years. The Duchess of York was only six years older than Marina, but she had taken her place in the royal fold eleven years earlier. Marina was royal by birth, whereas Elizabeth was a commoner, but Elizabeth had been a commoner with a court – her family, the Earls of Strathmore, were large Scottish landowners – while Marina had been a Princess in exile. The Yorks' and the Kents' styles were entirely different – the Yorks were homebodies while the Kents were more likely to be seen at smart parties. Marina referred to Elizabeth as 'that common little Scottish girl', which did not help their relationship. Perhaps the main problem was that both women were shy, yet both had their dignity and consciousness of position. And it cannot have failed to hurt the entirely popular Duchess of York to find the new royal Duchess so immediately step ahead in the fashion stakes.

Marina's chief sadness in her new life was the degree to which she missed her family. Telephone bills were one of the few causes of discord between George and Marina, but although she made nominal efforts to spend less time on the line to Europe she found it difficult. She did, however, visit her relations, and they her, regularly. In January 1935 Marina was with Princess Elizabeth in Germany when her son Hans Veit was born, and indeed the Kents often stayed with the Toerrings either in Munich or Winhorring. (While in Germany they could also see her first cousins, Prince Andrew's four daughters, who had all married Germans.) Regular visits to Yugoslavia were also in order – they were there in July 1935 (and moved on with Olga and Paul to Elizabeth and Toto in Munich), and back twice in 1936, once in April to stand godparents to Olga's daughter Elizabeth (when Marina told Olga that she thought she was pregnant again) and again in June, when George and Paul spent hours chopping wood to clear the estate of Paul's new castle Brdo, near Bled. Marina's parents and Elizabeth were in England for the birth of her first son in 1935 and Olga and Paul came from London for three weeks shortly afterwards. Prince and Princess Nicholas visited Marina for an English holiday after the reburial ceremonies in Greece.

Summer holidays at Bohinj (Paul's country retreat) were a regular feature of the Kents' life until the war. After a few weeks with Paul and Olga, they would then move on to stay with other friends, such as the Ivanovics who had a summer house at Cavtat, half an hour from Dubrovnik. 'My parents always gave them their own bedroom,' says Daska, the daughter of the house who was then a young girl and later married Billy Maclean, the swashbuckling politician. 'And I always remember that the first thing they did when they arrived was always to move the little table that separated the two beds and push the beds together. They were not used to being apart. It was a true love match which lasted to the end.'

This life of royal duties interspersed with family holidays could have continued for some years, but the inevitable death of the King was to change everything. In the event it precipitated the crisis which was to change the lives of the entire royal family, as well as the face of the monarchy.

King George's health had not been good for some time, but the death of his sister Victoria on 3 December 1935 seemed to be the final blow from which he could not recover. He who all his life had put his duty before all else cancelled the State Opening of Parliament. He did not cancel his Christmas Broadcast to the Empire, but he read his speech in the weak voice of an old man. 'It was rather a sad Christmas,' said the Duchess of Gloucester, 'with the King ill and the Prince of Wales away ski-ing with Mrs Simpson. Prince Henry and I had also wanted to go ski-ing but were dissuaded because of the embarrassment if we had bumped into Mrs Simpson.' He continued his work with his ministers, but his last days were spent concerning himself with his family: he visited Edward, his Kent grandson, in his bath, wrote to his new daughter-in-law Alice asking if she was comfortable in the house he had loaned her, planted a cedar tree in front of the house at Sandringham. As he grew weaker his family gathered around him. When the Prince of Wales arrived from Windsor on 17 January, his father briefly recognised him, but then slipped into unconsciousness, a state from which he only occasionally and briefly returned. On 20 January a Council of State was set up to deal with the ever-weakening King's business. He was barely able to make his mark on the papers which gave his wife and four sons his powers. For a few hours, on what was to be the last day of the King's life, the five sat together, dealing with his boxes, signing his papers and waiting in sad resignation for his death.

George V was not a young man when he died, but the country – and indeed the royal family itself – seemed unprepared for the arrival of the Prince of Wales as King. Some, who knew him well, were aware of the immense difficulties he would have in squaring up to his destiny. As the King lay dying, with his family gathered around him at Sandringham, Chips Channon wrote in his diary: 'My heart goes out to the Prince of Wales tonight, as he will mind so terribly being King. His loneliness, his seclusion, his isolation will be almost more than his highly-strung and unimaginative nature can bear.'

George V died just before midnight on 20 January, while the Archbishop of Canterbury read the Twenty-Third Psalm and a prayer beginning 'Go forth, O Christian soul'. As her husband died the Queen took her eldest son's hand and kissed it in

homage to the new King. The Duke of Kent immediately followed her example.

The news was broadcast just after midnight: 'Death came
peacefully to the King at 11.55 p.m.' It later became known
that the King's doctor Dawson 'decided to determine the end'
of the King and injected him with morphia and cocaine to help
him to die. This euthanasia was carried out as much to ensure
that *The Times* was the first with the news of the King's death
as for his own sake, but it did mean that the final hours were
less distressing both for him and his watching relations than
they would otherwise have been.

The next day Channon wrote in his diary: 'The King is dead –
Long live the King.' And added, 'The eyes of the world are on
the Prince of Wales, the new King Edward VIII.' For the first
few weeks, though, the family and the country were more
concerned with mourning the old King than worrying about the
new. Not for the royal family a simple burial service with family
and close friends; their grief could not be a private affair.

The day after his death the King's body was taken on a bier
to Sandringham church, led by a piper and followed by his
family and a few courtiers. After three days, during which it
was guarded by estate workers, the coffin was taken by gun
carriage to Wolverton Station, from where it was transported
to London. The carriage was accompanied from Sandringham
to Wolverton by the old King's sons and son-in-law on foot, the
Queen and her daughter and daughters-in-law in carriages.
Behind them followed the estate workers, neighbours and the
small grey shooting pony on which King George had passed
some of his last happy hours around the estate.

The next stage of the King's last journey, from King's Cross
to Westminster Hall, was again made on a gun carriage, with
the four Princes walking solemnly behind. The coffin was draped
with the royal standard, and the imperial crown rested on it. In
a terrible moment of bad portent (even the unsuperstitious new
King noticed 'the flash of light dancing along the pavement' and
'wondered whether it was a bad omen') the Maltese Cross fell
from the crown and lay in the gutter, from where it was retrieved
by a sergeant-major.

Against the wishes of the late King, a short service was held after the arrival of the coffin at Westminster Hall. The Queen chose one hymn, 'Praise my soul, the King of Heaven'. Chips Channon was present, by chance in a good position

nearly on the steps and ... next to the Royal Family; I could have touched the Queen of Spain, fat and smelling slightly of scent, and old Princess Beatrice .... After a little some younger women, heavily draped, came in, and were escorted to the steps. I recognized the Royal Duchesses. Princess Marina, as ever, managed to look infinitely more elegant than the others; she wore violets under her veil and her stockings, if not flesh-coloured, were of black so thin that they seemed so. The great door opened ... the coffin was carried in and placed on the catafalque. It was followed by King Edward, boyish, sad and tired, and the Queen, erect and more magnificent than ever. Behind them were the Royal brothers.

The coffin lay in state for four days, during which hundreds of thousands paid their respects in silence, some queuing for as long as five hours. Various royal relations, including George and Marina, Prince Nicholas, the Gloucesters, the Princess Royal and her husband Lord Harewood, the royalty of Norway, Denmark, Belgium, Italy and Prussia all paid their respects during the course of the lying-in-state.

At midnight on the night of 27 January, a week after the King's death, his four sons (at David's instigation) joined the officers guarding the coffin. All four were in ceremonial uniform: the King wore that of the Welsh Guards, the Duke of York that of the Scots Guards, the Duke of Gloucester that of the 10th Hussars and the Duke of Kent was in naval dress. They stood, bent over swords reversed, for twenty minutes in the silent candlelight, performing the last service they could for their father. Queen Mary was so moved she commissioned a picture of the occasion from F.E. Beresford. Entitled *The Vigil of the Princes*, it was given to David for his birthday in June.

The next day the King's coffin was carried on a gun carriage pulled by sailors from Westminster to Paddington. Once again Channon provides an eye-witness account, this time from the roof of St James's Palace:

It was a long wait in the cold, but at last the procession came .... As it passed, unendingly, a silence fell on the vast crowds ... a feeling of awe came over us as we knew that the gun carriage was approaching and at last, drawn by the Marines at an easy pace, it did. The Monarch of the world lay in that small coffin, draped with the Union Jack, and immediately behind walked his son .... Behind him were his brothers and the Princes, and the Kings .... Slowly the gun carriage went up St James's Street, watched by ten thousand wet eyes. Then the Queen's coach came, magnificent in its red trappings. The Queen sat at the window, all in black, with her sister-in-law, the Queen of Norway.

Five foreign Kings followed the coffin: Christian of Denmark, Haakon of Norway, Carol of Rumania, Boris of Bulgaria and Leopold of the Belgians.

From Windsor Station the carriage was pulled to St George's Chapel. Only after the funeral service, after the new King had sprinkled earth from a silver bowl on to his father's coffin, could the new reign be truly said to begin. Or not, as George V's old friend Dr Lang, Archbishop of Canterbury, noted, 'only a new reign, but a new regime. I can only be most thankful for what has been, and for what is to be, hope for the best. God guide the King!'

It was soon clear to those close to Edward VIII that he had no intention of breaking with his married mistress, Mrs Ernest Simpson. 'Mrs Simpson is bejewelled, eyebrow-plucked, virtuous and wise,' wrote Harold Nicolson on 13 January 1936, a few days before her lover became King. '... She is clearly out to help him .... I have an uneasy feeling that ... in spite of her good intentions [she] is getting him out of touch with the type of person with whom he ought to associate.' Yet Channon's diary entry on 22 January points the dilemma:

We are all riveted by the position of Mrs S——. No man has ever been so in love as the present King; but can she be another Mrs Fitzherbert? [An early reference to the possibility of a morganatic marriage.] If he drops her she will fall – fall – into the nothingness whence she came, but I hope he will not, for she is a good, kindly woman.

Mrs Simpson had been the King's companion (he always denied that she had been his mistress before their marriage) for some years by the time the King died, and it was an alliance that had always caused the family concern. She was an American married to Ernest Simpson, an Englishman, and she had already been divorced once. Mrs Simpson was a woman of marked ambition. She and her current husband first met David at a weekend party in January 1931, at Thelma Furness's house near Melton Mowbray. After the weekend she wrote to her Aunt Bessie Merriman, 'It was quite an experience and as I've had my mind made up to meet him ever since I've been here I feel relieved. I never expected however to accomplish it in such an informal way and Prince George as well.' Reactions to her differed markedly. King George had had strong views about Mrs Simpson and was furious when David introduced her at Buckingham Palace. Chips Channon, on meeting her at Emerald Cunard's in the January before the King died, wrote, 'she is a nice, quiet, well-bred mouse of a woman with large startled eyes and a huge mole. I think she is surprised and rather conscience-stricken by her present position and the limelight which consequently falls upon her.' Cecil Beaton's first impressions were less flattering. Writing in November 1936, when Mrs Simpson was the talk of the town, he recalled the 'great brawny cow or bullock in sapphic blue velvet' whom he had first met at the beginning of the decade: 'To hear her speak was enough. Her voice was raucous and appalling. I though her awful, common, vulgar, strident, a second-rate American with no charm.'

Mrs Simpson took control of the King completely. Under her influence he even dropped all contact with Freda Dudley Ward, with whom he had been in love for so long, and who had been such a wise and good friend to him. One morning in 1934 she telephoned him at York House to be told by the operator that he had been instructed not to put her calls through. And that was the last she heard of her Prince. He even cut off all relations with her daughters, to whom he had been a much loved friend. It was left to his family to pick up the pieces and George Kent in particular was loyal to and kept in touch with his brother's ex-mistress.

By April Channon was aware of Mrs Simpson's importance to the King:

She is a jolly, plain, intelligent, quiet, unpretentious and unprepossessing little woman, but she has already the air of a personage who walks into a room as though she almost expected to be curtsied to. At least she wouldn't be too surprised. She has complete power over the Prince of Wales, who is trying to launch her socially.

And by the summer Beaton was photographing her and finding her 'bright and witty ... enormously improved in looks and chic'. Two years later, he visited her at the Château de Cande where she was waiting for her divorce to become absolute.

In Mrs Simpson's entourage there is no smattering of culture, no appreciation or interest in art of any form. As a diversion it is gay and successful. As a steady diet it would be impossible .... I find she is intelligent within her vast limitations. Politically she may be ignorant, aesthetically she is so, but about life she knows a good deal.

The King's brother George had of course always been the closest to David, and the only one who might have any influence on him. He had already met and was not set against Mrs Simpson, although Marina was at first less at ease meeting her brother-in-law's mistress (the Duchess of York refused outright to do so). Before long it became clear to Channon that some of their friends might be 'trying to poison the Kents against Mrs Simpson and hence the King, and are attempting to drive a wedge between the royal brothers'. Channon himself was in an interesting position: he was an admirer of Mrs Simpson and close friend of the Duke of Kent, but was not particularly friendly with the new King. Indeed, unlike many others who feared or disliked Mrs Simpson's influence over David, Channon believed that she had 'enormously improved the Prince'. By February he was referring to Mrs Simpson and her friends as the 'new Court', 'Mrs Simpson was very charming and gay and vivacious. She said she had not worn black stockings since she gave up the Can-Can.'

While Mrs Simpson was making such diverting comments to her friends, and drinking 'whisky and soda instead of cocktails', the King was enthusiastically (at first) tackling a King's amount of paperwork, meeting his ministers, helping his mother move her possessions from Buckingham Palace, finding ways of saving money, failing to go to church often or have much to do with plans for the coronation, and performing regular royal duties. Parliament voted on the new Civil List. According to Channon, by now a Member of Parliament, the rise of dictatorships in Europe had helped to make even the Socialists come 'tumbling over one another in order to laud the Royal Family'.

The peak of the crisis moved inexorably closer. The King continued to see Mrs Simpson while his mother, who was never able to discuss anything openly with her children, worried in silence. The old King had been more than aware of the trouble that lay ahead with his son and heir. Blanche Lennox, friend of both King George and Queen Mary, told Lady Airlie that only a few weeks before his death the King had declared passionately, 'I pray to God that my eldest son will never marry and have children, and that nothing will come between Bertie and Lilibet [the family's pet name for Princess Elizabeth] and the throne.' She also said that George V had told her that 'Bertie has more guts than the rest of his brothers put together'. On Bertie's marriage he had written to him, saying 'You have always been so sensible & easy to work with & you have always been ready to listen to any advice & to agree with my opinions about people & things, that I feel that we have always got on well together (very different to dear David).'

On another occasion the King had complained to Count Albert Mensdorff (Austrian Ambassador before the First World War and an old friend of Edward VII who had continued to hold his son's ear) that the Prince of Wales 'has not a single friend who is a gentleman. He does not see any decent society. And he is forty-one.' To Mensdorff's mitigating plea in the Prince's favour (charm, mostly), the King replied, 'Yes, certainly. That is the pity. If he were a fool, we would not mind.'

The new King was not entirely a fool. He was just 'Mrs Simpson's absolute slave' (Channon again). To Channon, that was to the good. 'She, clever woman, with her high pitched voice, chic clothes, moles and sense of humour is behaving well. She encourages the King to meet people of importance and to be polite; above all she makes him happy. The Empire ought to be grateful.'

Publicly, and perhaps even privately, there was still no sign that the King intended to give up the throne. He talked 'about traditions and ceremonies which he intends to keep up so long as they do not interfere with ordinary life'. And indeed this insistence on keeping an 'ordinary life' was something of great importance to him:

They must take him as he was – a man different from his father and determined to be himself. He would be available for public business and public occasions when he was wanted, but his private life was to be his own and was, as far as possible, to be lived in the same way as when he was Prince of Wales.

So wrote his great confidant in the crisis (and Attorney-General to the Duchy of Cornwall) Walter Monckton. Queen Marie of Rumania pinpointed the problem when she wrote that 'David kicks against traditions and restrictions, without realising that tradition made him, is his raison d'être.' Nevertheless for a while at least David thought that it would be possible for him to live this dual life of private person and King:

He never spoke to me of any doubt or hesitation about accepting his position as King. It was only later on in the year, when the controversy was upon him, that he would sometimes say that if they were wanting someone exactly reproducing his father, there was the Duke of York.

The King later told Monckton that he had decided to marry Mrs Simpson by 1934 and he had intended to tell the King his father before his death. Both Alan Lascelles, who had been his Private Secretary, and Alec Hardinge (appointed Private Secretary that summer) believed at the time that had the King not died David would have opted out of the succession within six months.

Monckton's loyalty to the King led him to write an account of the abdication which he would not allow to be published during his lifetime. This interesting document is extensively quoted in Lord Birkenhead's biography of him, and it is here that he makes his apologia for the King. It was not, he writes, just 'the intensity and depth of the King's devotion' that was important, nor the fact that the love was not limited to 'the ordinary physical sense of the term. There was an intellectual companionship, and ... his lonely nature found in her a spiritual comradeship'. Monckton believed – and this view is as unpopular now as it was uncredited then – that there was also 'a religious side' to the problem. Monckton continues:

The King had the strongest standards which he set himself of right and wrong. They were often irritatingly unconventional .... It was the cant which he saw on all sides which made him out of touch and out of sympathy with the leaders of the Churches .... He would say that a marriage blessed by the bishops was a marriage in which the two spouses remained one in the eyes of the law while they went their separate ways sub rosa .... He felt that he and Mrs Simpson were made for one another and there was no other honest way of meeting the situation than marrying her. The easy view is that she should have made him give her up. But I never knew any man whom it would have been harder to get rid of.

Despite his real knowledge of the King, and his awareness of the complexity of the problem, Monckton remained sure right until the end that if and when the stark choice faced them between their love and his obligations as King-Emperor, they would in the end each make the sacrifice, 'devastating though it would be.' (The other school of thought is that Mrs Simpson was never really in love with the Prince but was always out for maximum personal gain.)

It was not until the summer of 1936 that the question of the King's affair became a matter for discussion outside his own immediate circle. In May Queen Mary confided her fear that David might ask her to receive Mrs Simpson to Mabell Airlie, and her old friend saw the torment that the whole question was causing her. Until then, although Mrs Simpson was at Fort Belvedere, the King's house, every weekend, often without her husband, the matter of the love affair had been a secret known to everyone in London society, but not to a wider audience. Mr and Mrs Simpson were invited to all the same parties as the King, and sometimes only Wallis accepted. Chips and Honor Channon gave a dinner party in June at which the guests included Wallis without Ernest (who had made his excuses), the King and George and Marina. Always, even at small private dinner parties, the etiquette was adhered to rigidly: first the guests would arrive, then the Duke and Duchess, then the King ('He kissed Princess Marina who curtsied').

By July, Channon was writing in his diary that 'the Simpson

scandal is growing, and she, poor Wallis, looks unhappy. The world is closing in around her, the flatterers, the sycophants and the malice.' For the first time the subject moved out of the purely private arena into something more open with an announcement in the Court Circular. In May the King gave his first official dinner and included among the guests the Simpsons and Emerald Cunard. Nancy Astor, who 'considers Lady Cunard and Chips Channon as "disintegrating influences"', was according to Harold Nicolson prepared to tell the King that 'although Mrs Simpson may appear at Court, she must not appear in the Court Circular.' In July Ramsay MacDonald was still trying to persuade the King not to include Mrs Simpson's name in the circular. 'We smile at the *Court Circular*,' says Bagehot, 'but remember how many people read the *Court Circular*! its use is not in what it says, but in those to whom it speaks.' Among the guests listed at a dinner party given by the King in July were the Duke and Duchess of York and Mrs Ernest Simpson (by now without her husband). It was also in July that Ernest Simpson finally gave up his pretence of a marriage and moved out of the Simpson flat. The King's advisors dreaded the idea of a divorce, which would bring the scandal into the open, but David refused to have anything to do with what he insisted was Mrs Simpson's private business. Mrs Simpson herself insisted that it was her husband who sought a divorce, and that she had no part in it. (Monckton had first heard of the possibility of divorce proceedings begun by Mrs Simpson in April, but old-fashioned courtesy still meant that the woman always divorced the man, not vice versa.) Although the King would do nothing to stop it, he did go so far as to ask Lord Beaverbrook not to cover the divorce in the press and succeeded in making Beaverbrook persuade the other newspaper proprietors to remain similarly silent. However, everyone knew this state of affairs could be guaranteed not to last.

All seemed to be under control until David, never a keeper of tradition for tradition's sake, decided that rather than spend August in Scotland as his father had done he would charter a yacht. He found the *Nahlin*, belonging to a Lady Yule who agreed to let the King have it for the cost of expenses only.

Guests included Duff and Diana Cooper and, of course, Mrs Simpson – without Mr Simpson.

The cruise around the Adriatic took in Belgrade, Ankara and Sofia. And, although much of the holiday was spent carousing, walking through streets bare-chested and drinking from lemonade bottles (not very bad behaviour, but not the sort of thing expected of even a holidaying King), David did spend some time on diplomatic visits. He met the Turkish President Kemal Atatürk in Istanbul; President Miklas and Chancellor Schuschnigg in Vienna; Tzar Boris III, 'a versatile monarch' (David later wrote), in Bulgaria (the leave-taking at the Yugoslav frontier was somewhat perfunctory owing to an argument between the Tzar and his brother as to who should drive the locomotive of the train waiting to take them back to the capital); and Prime Minister Metaxas in Athens. In Corfu David saw King George of Greece, whom he found looking thin and homesick for London.

When I asked him, as one King to another, how he was getting along, he answered almost bitterly that he wasn't getting along at all. He had returned to Greece to find the loyalties of his people divided between innumerable factions and cliques .... 'I am a King in name only ... I might just as well be back at Brown's Hotel ... I hope you have better luck.'

Mrs Simpson caused a change in the King's mood when, during a discussion about King George and his mistress Mrs Jones, she asked why the Greek King did not just marry the woman who was his constant companion. With genuine astonishment one of the other guests on the yacht told her the entirely obvious (to an Englishman) fact that a King could not marry a commoner who was already married. Even David must have drawn a parallel with his own situation.

The King had caused some offence with his lack of interest in Prince Paul's visit to England earlier in the year, but now included Paul on his tour. His party reached Yugoslavia on 9 August and were lent the royal train for the journey across the country to Sibenic on the Dalmation coast, where the *Nahlin* was waiting. On the return journey, three weeks later, the King stopped briefly at Belgrade where they visited the royal palaces. Olga and Paul's loyalties were by now to the royal family in England, not to David and his mistress. Olga refused to treat Mrs Simpson as the King's lady-friend at Brdo, and Paul and Olga both resented being put in the position of having to entertain the King's mistress at all.

The most important repercussion of the cruise was that the affair was now widely discussed all over Europe and America. Everywhere, in fact, but in England where the King's subjects were still kept in blissful ignorance by a compliant press. As Prince of Wales, David had encouraged the press to ignore him for years; as early as November 1929 he 'begged me [Bruce-Lockhart] to use my influence with Beaverbrook to have his name kept out of the papers'. With a matter of such moment the press was willing to play the King's game for a while at least.

While the King was amusing himself with his friends and Mrs Simpson, George and Marina were at Cavtat with the Ivanovics. 'The Duke was terrified at the thought that the King would stop and see them,' said Daska Maclean, 'and horrified that Wallis Simpson was on the yacht too.' If by now even George, the closest of his brothers and the one most likely to condone a bit of self-indulgence, was stepping back from the affair, it is clear that the middle-class morality of the majority of the King's subjects (and indeed of his own family) would have no truck with a Queen Wallis. 'The Duke was completely against the idea of any sort of marriage between Mrs Simpson and the King,' said Daska Maclean. 'He talked about it when the crisis was happening and said the King must abdicate, there could not be a morganatic marriage.'

Be that as it may, George and Marina were both at Balmoral for the last fortnight of the summer holiday at a house party hosted by the King sleeping not in his own quarters but in the dressing room of the best spare room. Mrs Simpson was of course in the best spare room (and mentioned in the *Court Circular*) and her husband was not at Balmoral at all. The King had once again refused to listen to his advisors and, rather than inviting the dignitaries who were traditionally asked to Balmoral, filled the castle with his own friends. The visit also caused bad blood in Scotland, especially when David cancelled a visit to a hospital in Aberdeen and sent the Yorks in his place while he went to Aberdeen Station to meet Mrs Simpson's train.

Cecil Beaton later saw a home film of the Balmoral visit, in which the King was seen playing an Austrian bow and arrow game with his guests, the Duke of Kent and Lord Louis Mountbatten trying without much success to join in. A bevy of Duchesses (Buccleuch, Marlborough, Sunderland) looked 'untidy and relaxed' while 'only the Duchess of Kent looked romantic with her hair untidily blowing and tied with a baby bow of ribbon. Every few feet of film, the King appeared with Wallis. She looked different from the others, neat and towny in smart clothes and a black felt hat.'

George's thank-you letter indicates that a good time was had by all: 'I could never believe that any place could change so much and have such a different atmosphere. It was all so comfortable and everyone seemed so happy – it really was fun.' Yet he told William Dugdale, Prime Minister Baldwin's Parliamentary Private Secretary, that while at Balmoral Mrs Simpson had used him (George) successfully to provoke the King's jealousy, and that by the end of dinner 'the King was beaten into a frenzy of jealousy and desire'. On another occasion, George complained to Baldwin himself that his brother was 'besotted by the woman, one can't get a word of sense out of him'. Even George's instinctive sympathy for his brother was being eroded in the face of Mrs Simpson's influence. All the brothers felt increasingly cut off from David, as he withdrew into a world in which only he and his lover existed. Yet despite the family's reservations George Kent and Harry Gloucester continued to visit the Fort where Mrs Simpson was an almost constant visitor. Even as late as 15 November, only days before the final act in the drama opened (and over a fortnight after Mrs Simpson was granted a decree nisi), George and Marina were entertaining David and Mrs Simpson to Sunday afternoon tea at Coppins. At this stage David had already told Walter Monckton that 'he felt he could not go forward to the Coronation on 12 May 1937 meaning to make the marriage whatever happened and, as he felt, deceiving the

Government and the people into imagining that he had dropped the association or, at any rate, did not intend to marry.'

For a long while David believed, or hoped, that the people of England would support him. But Harold Nicolson was more perceptive than his King when he wrote that 'the upper classes mind her being an American more than they mind her being divorced. The lower classes do not mind her being an American but loathe the idea that she has had two husbands already.'

On 16 November the King told his Prime Minister Baldwin that he had decided he would marry Mrs Simpson, even if that meant he must abdicate. (Baldwin, having told his Cabinet the news, said to his Chief Whip, 'I have heard such things from my King tonight as I never thought to hear. I am going to bed.')

Channon had predicted David's decision in his diary only a fortnight earlier, for 'the King is naturally uxorious, a trait he inherits from his domestic father .... He thinks only of Wallis.' Baldwin, too, took this view, later telling Mabell Airlie that contrary to rumour David had not been drunk through the week of the crisis: 'He was absolutely sober, but certainly in a very exalted state. Just a romantic boy, all for marriage,' However, in November Mrs Simpson told Sibyl Colefax that 'of course' the King had not proposed to her. Eight days later Harold Nicolson wrote in his diary: 'I do not understand the situation. On the one hand you have Mrs Simpson saying that he has never suggested marriage, and on the other hand you have the Privy Council organised for revolt. I believe quite sincerely that the King has proposed to Mr Baldwin and has not proposed to Wallis.'

On the evening of the 16th David dined with his mother at Marlborough House. He arrived to find both his sister and his new sister-in-law, Alice Gloucester ('a newcomer, almost a stranger to the family' he later remarked somewhat coldly) waiting there. Queen Mary had come to depend on her daughter more and more since King George's death, so David was not surprised to see her there. However, David did find it in himself to feel sorry for Alice who had 'all unwittingly sat down at my mother's table only to find herself caught up in the opening scene of one of the most poignant episodes in the annals of the

Royal Family'. After a dinner spent awkwardly discussing the Newmarket sales, Alice excused herself and, curtseying, left. David then broke the news which almost broke the Queen's heart. She could not understand that he should abdicate, not so much the throne, as what she saw as his sole duty. She adamantly refused her son's request that she see Mrs Simpson.

The Kents, most especially Marina, were lucky in having Olga and Paul staying with them during these days of rumour and counter-rumour. Although staying informally at Belgrave Square and week-ending at Coppins, Paul and Olga were in fact in London officially. Paul was astounded to find London buzzing with the story of the King and the divorcee, and he and Chips set to find suitable alternatives to Wallis as Queen. Of course matters had gone far beyond such an easy and old-fashioned solution. But while they waited they had little choice but to attend the cocktail parties and charity concerts given for them. Even now Wallis was mixing easily in royal circles, even joking about herself. 'The conversation got on to tiaras, and Princess Olga said that hers gave her a headache. Wallis Simpson laughingly added, "Well, anyway, a tiara is one of the things I shall never have ...." There was an embarrassed pause.'

On 19 November Chips and Honor Channon gave a party attended by the King who was just back from a tour to distressed parts of Wales. This tour was prompted by his sympathy for the poor which to many was his saving grace although others, among them Marina's friend the journalist Alistair Forbes, say that his 'sympathy was superficial, his empathy non-existent'. Also present were Paul and Olga, Wallis, and George and Marina 'in a trailing black velvet tea gown which half hid her pregnancy'. The evening was a tremendous success, with Chips half mad with happiness at 'a three-handed conversation – two reigning sovereigns and Chips'. However, it was not until a few days later, when rumours were rife beyond imagining, that he commented on George's 'mysterious remark' at dinner that 'in a month or six weeks' time something terrific will happen. I wish I could tell you now.' This may sound a little light-hearted. In fact he was probably more distressed than light-hearted: he later told Chips that the King had told him that evening, just before dinner, that he was going to marry Wallis, and that he had only told him then because he knew he would meet him at the Channon dinner party.

'What will she call herself?' gasped George.

'Call herself? What do you think – Queen of England of course,' answered his brother.

'She is going to be Queen?'

'Yes and Empress of India, the whole bag of tricks.'

George rushed home to change for the dinner party and tell Marina and Olga the astonishing news. So while Chips was congratulating himself on the success of his entertaining, his chief guests were in a turmoil – of excitement on David's part, and embarrassment about how to greet Wallis on George's part.

Channon claims that the Duke of Kent asked Kitty Brownlow what she thought of 'this marriage' and when she, as Channon put it 'tried to nance out, he insisted "After all they are my relations." Then he made an astonishing rejoinder: "I am very discreet." "As discreet as a Chubb safe when you've given away all the keys," Kitty retorted.'

Meanwhile Bertie was preparing himself for what now seemed to be the inevitable. 'If the worst happens & I have to take over,' he wrote to Godfrey Thomas, David's Assistant Private Secretary, 'you can be assured I will do my best to clear up the inevitable mess, if the whole fabric does not crumble under the shock and strain of it all.'

On 2 December, though, the news was bad enough for the Kents to cancel drinks at Kitty Brownlow's house. That morning some provincial papers had quoted a speech made by Bishop Blunt of Bradford, in which the King was criticised. The address ran:

The benefit of the King's Coronation depends, under God, upon two elements, first on the faith, prayer, and self-dedication of the King himself – and on that it would be improper for me to say anything except commend him, and ask you to commend him, to God's grace, which he will so abundantly need, as we all need it – for the King is a man like ourselves – if he is to do his duty faithfully. We hope that he is aware of his need. Some of us wish that he gave more positive signs of his awareness.

Bishop Blunt was referring mostly to David's sporadic attendances at church, but his words were enough to open the discussion throughout England.

The next day the national papers followed the provincials' lead and at last the majority of the British public was let in on the secret that London society had known for months: their King was in love with an American who had two husbands still living. 'The whole world recoils from the shock; but very few know that she is a woman of infinite charm, gentleness, courage and loyalty, whose influence upon the King, until now, has been highly salutary,' wrote an ever-partisan Chips.

He did not find his friends the Kents had taken the news as philosophically. George was 'upset' and Chips 'threw all discretion, all reverence overboard, and ... advised him to go at once to the Queen, to take his brothers with him, to call a family council, and in a body to implore the King to change his mind, so as to gain time'. Chips then went with 'the Yugoslavs', as he called Paul and Olga, to an Admiralty lunch after which, as they were shown around the Admiralty, he begged Olga to find Marina and go with her to the Queen.

At midnight that night George rang Chips who, dressed in lederhosen, was just leaving his house for a fancy dress ball at the Austrian Legation. He went instead next door and told the Kents and Yugoslavs the House of Commons news, that the abdication had not yet happened. He and George then returned to Number 3 where they sat up with Honor and another friend and talked until after four in the morning. 'The Duke of Kent unburdened his heart, said he loved the King more than anyone, how the King ignored him ....'

On 4 December George and Marina went to see Queen Mary, whom they found 'very upset and angry with David'. That evening George rang David, saying he wanted to help him and would love to see him. David was evasive, and finally did not let George go to him. Paul of Yugoslavia, who knew David (from Oxford), Bertie (through his wife) and now George extremely well, found himself shuttling back and forth between Bertie and George, both of whom found him a kind and useful friend. He put off his return home, feeling unable to leave while his friends were in such sore straits. By now, no matter how the country was divided on the subject, the family felt 'he had better go as he can't be trusted to play the game' (as Princess Olga wrote in her diary).

On the 6th, with the King still in self-imposed purdah (Bertie had been ringing daily, but each time his brother had put him off), the Kents and the Yugoslavs went to tea with the Yorks, where they found the Gloucesters.

Meanwhile Mrs Simpson, who had been spirited away to France by David's Lord-in-Waiting Lord Brownlow, issued a 'renunciation' of the King which looked as though it might make it possible for him to stay on the throne:

Mrs Simpson, throughout the last few weeks has invariably wished to avoid any action or proposal which would hurt or damage His Majesty or the Throne. To-day her attitude is unchanged, and she is willing, if such action would solve the problem, to withdraw forthwith from a situation that has been rendered unhappy and untenable.

She had also signed – but never put into effect – a letter instructing her solicitors to withdraw from the divorce proceedings.

Until then Mrs Simpson had been urging David to 'fight for his rights ... maintaining that he was King and that his popularity would carry anything etc ...' (so noted Sir Edward Peacock, Walter Monckton's colleague and Receiver-General of the Duchy of Lancaster). 'The lady persisted in her advice until she saw that that tack was hopeless. Then she apparently began to think of her own unpopularity, and a statement was suggested, which she issued from Cannes. The King approved, well realising that this would to some extent divert criticism from her to him, the very thing he wanted.' England, and the royal family, continued to wait on the King's final decision. In a moment almost of comedy, Marlene Dietrich decided she could persuade the King not to abdicate, and had her chauffeur drive her to the Fort. Despite her many charms and pleadings, she was not allowed past the gates. On the 7th the King finally agreed to see George and a 'miserable' Bertie, who both went to the Fort to try desperately to persuade him to stay. 'I was with him at 7.0pm,' wrote Bertie. 'The awful and ghastly suspense of waiting was over. I found him pacing up & down the room & he told me his decision that he would go.'

With George away at the Fort, the heavily pregnant Marina, 'looking ill and sad', relied greatly on her sister for comfort and Chips for Commons news. The two women sat in Belgrave Square with heavy colds, dining miserably together or with another woman friend, the former Princess Galitzine, a long-standing friend of Marina's, now Mrs James Campbell. George returned on the evening of the 9th (he and Marina were to dine with his mother), saying that nothing could be done to change the King's mind. Even Wallis was begging him from Cannes to stay, but not even for her would he reconsider. George reported that, unlike everyone else, the King was in good spirits and that indeed dinner at the Fort the night before had been 'almost festive'. The King, exhausted, had been determined to show no weakness and not only hosted the dinner (among those there were the Prime Minister and Monckton as well as Bertie and George), but managed to keep talking. Bertie later remembered the King as 'the life & soul of the party, telling the P.M. things I am sure he had never heard before about unemployed centres etc. (referring to his visit in S. Wales). I whispered to W.M. "& this is the man we are going to lose." One couldn't, nobody could, believe it.' As Chips commented, that table was probably the only one in the land at which the likely abdication was not discussed.

For many not directly involved in the trauma, it provided nothing more than something to gossip about. Evelyn Waugh wrote in his diary at the beginning of December that 'The Simpson crisis has been a great delight to everyone. At Maidie's nursing home they report a pronounced turn for the better in all adult patients. There can seldom have been an event that has caused so much general delight and so little pain.' But for those to whom it had more implications than gossip there was a great deal of pain. When Bertie told his mother that nothing would change David's mind he 'broke down & sobbed like a child'.

Journalists, once they were allowed to discuss the matter, thoroughly enjoyed themselves. Among their suggestions was the idea that George should succeed, as Bertie was ill and unwilling and Harry was clearly not up to the job (George of course also had a royal wife and a son). It was also suggested that Princess Elizabeth should succeed, with Queen Mary as her regent. However, these were idle speculations: the Cabinet and royal family knew that the position of monarch could only fall to Bertie.

After lunch on the 9th the royal family gathered together at the Yorks' house, Royal Lodge. Queen Mary arrived first with her daughter and her brother Alge Athlone. She and David were alone together for a while. Then came the Dukes of York and Gloucester and, last as always, Kent. Queen Mary had refused to go to the Fort so for the first time in six days David left his haven and arrived at Royal Lodge just before four. After dinner that night David went to Marlborough House to see his mother and the Duke of York with the draft Instrument of Abdication ('because he wishes to marry Mrs Simpson!!!!!' wrote Queen Mary in her diary).

On 10 December, George returned to the Fort while Marina rang Chips to tell him that it was all over. David was waiting for his three brothers to witness his Instrument of Abdication and Message to the Parliaments of the Empire: the Dukes of York and Gloucester arrived at 9.30 a.m., Kent at 10.00 a.m. 'George *would* be late,' the King said with a laugh. The brothers sat together in the drawing room and the deed was done. 'It was a dreadful moment & one never to be forgotten by those present,' wrote the new King, although David, in signing, was 'perfectly calm'.

Chips and Honor were among the many who crowded into a tearful House of Commons to hear the Speaker read a simple and moving message from the King followed by a speech from Baldwin. 'I have never known in any assemblage', wrote Nicolson, 'such accumulation of pity and terror.'

The following day they were back at the Commons again, where they met 'Mikey and David Lyon who were waiting to hear their sister made Queen of England. They were simple, charming and bored as ever.' Then the Abdication Bill was moved and passed into law. 'The Clerk bowed "Le Roi le veult" and Edward, the beautiful boy King with his gaiety and honesty, his American accent and nervous twitching, his flair

'Princess Marina, Duchess of Kent, whose nobility was printed on features of the utmost refinement . . .' Harold Acton

Noel Coward, for a long time a close friend of both the Kents, escorts Marina to the races

Chips Channon was a neighbour and friend of Marina in Belgrave Square. He combined his interest in high society with his political career

Marina and Princess Elizabeth are godmothers at the christening of the infant son of
Philip and Margaret Hay at St. Michael's Church, Chester Square, 23 March 1950,
Philip Hay was private secretary to Marina and his wife was a lady in waiting to
Princess Elizabeth. Steven Runciman was a godfather

Marina brought a stunning elegance to
whatever she wore. Here she is seen as the
Commandant of the Wrens and presenting
awards to members of the St John's
Ambulance Brigade

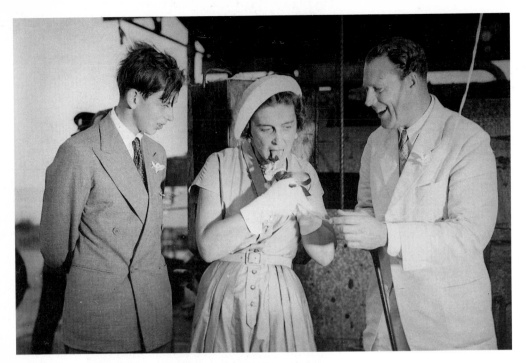

Eddie learns strange habits from his mother in Brunei on their first major royal tour. She sips champagne from a broken bottle which moments before had been used to open the Marina oil well. September 1952

Even the humidity of Singapore does not dampen Marina's elegance when receiving the freedom of the city. October 1952

The Kents are greeted by the Duke of Norfolk at Westminster Abbey for the Queen's coronation in 1953

Together yet apart. Marina and her two younger children on the edge of the Queen's coronation group

Eddie comes of age. 1956

The Ghanian Prime Minister quick-steps away from the Empire during independence celebrations

The first step for African freedom. Ghana 1957. Princess Marina as royal representative of the Imperial power cedes independence to the Gold Coast. African chiefs shield her from the sun at the Accra races

A family outing to the theatre with
Marina's successor as Duchess of
Kent. Kate Worsley faces the camera
as Eddie's future bride. 14 April
1961

The Princess many remember:
Marina asked to see the steel
racquet with which Billy Jean King
had just won her third successive
Wimbledon crown

*The paparazzi move in ... From holidays in the palaces of the Tsars to a lonely walk
in Kensington Palace Gardens, Marina's life saw many changes*

and glamour was part of history. It was 1.52.' 'Thus ends the reign of King Edward VIII,' wrote Nicolson, another witness to the event. 'Back to my steak-and-kidney pie. Down to Sissinghurst.'

On the night of the 11th the family – David, Harry, George, Mary and Queen Mary, Princess Alice and Lord Athlone – all dined together at Royal Lodge. Elizabeth was ill in bed in London, Alice and Marina also stayed at their respective homes. 'Dinner passed pleasantly enough under the circumstances. I hope I was a good guest but I rather doubt it,' David later wrote. After dinner David left for Windsor Castle from where 'His Royal Highness, Prince Edward' broadcast his farewell speech to the nation. While he was on the way there the new King gave his two younger brothers a talking-to. 'If *You Two* think that, now that I have taken this job on, you can go on behaving just as you like, in the same old way, you're very much mistaken! You Two have got to pull yourselves together.'

Then came the ex-King's last address to his people: 'You must believe me when I tell you that I have found it impossible to carry the heavy burden of responsibility and to discharge my duty as King as I would wish to do, without the help and support of the woman I love,' he said, and referred to his brother's 'matchless blessing . . . a happy home with his wife and children . . . . God bless you all. God Save the King.' And a nation bowed its head. 'I wept, and I murmured a prayer for he who had once been King Edward VIII,' noted Channon, adding, 'Then we played bridge.'

After the broadcast David – King no longer – returned to his family at Royal Lodge, for the final farewells. Queen Mary and the Princess Royal soon left, David bowing to his mother as she was driven away. The brothers and Monckton remained together for three quarters of an hour, chatting inconsequentially until George suddenly burst out with 'This is quite mad.' As David left he kissed Bertie as his brother, parted from him as a Freemason, and bowed to him as his King, saying 'God bless you, Sir. I hope you will be happier than your predecessor.' Then he was driven to Portsmouth where he joined the destroyer HMS *Fury* which was to take him to France. From there he

went to Austria, where he stayed at Baron Eugene de Roths-
child's country house, Schloss Enzesfeld.

After it was all over, George wrote to Paul to thank him for
his support:

It was lovely having you and I miss you now ... and wish you could have
stayed longer ... I was glad I was able to be with David a little and try
to be a little help but there was nothing to be done and he had made up
his mind. He was very calm about it all – except about her. But he never
broke down and wouldn't think either of the future or of what he was
giving up – only of her. One can only pray for his future happiness which
one doubts of. It's all been horrible and I'm so miserable about it all. I
feel rotten, cold and nervy and altogether bloody. I wish Olga wasn't
going as she's been an enormous help to Marina, but luckily Lilia is
coming to stop for a little.

This shows a different and more concerned George than that of
Chip's gossip.

Royal families around Europe closed ranks against the erring
King and his adventuress (as they saw it) lover. 'Personally I am
too royal not to look upon David as a deserter,' wrote Marie
of Rumania, echoing Queen Mary's sentiments precisely. She
continued:

Also I can work up no feelings for Mrs Simpson .... She has too much
to do with cocktails and night-clubs .... Do you think David will never
hanker back to all he kicked aside? Do you think Mrs Simpson in great
spoonfuls will replace all he gave up? He is forty-two. Is it luck at that
age to have no duties, no work, no obligations, no outlook – only
nightclubs, bars, rowdy society, sport .... Is this a career, an end for the
golden-headed prince? I could weep over him and my feelings towards
Mrs Simpson are none too charitable.

Channon, old supporter of Mrs Simpson, thought that the
new court went too far in its hatred 'to the point of hysteria'
and persecution of her. George and Marina, who had mixed
with David and his circle, were asked by Bertie not to see David's
friends, in particular Emerald Cunard, again. George agreed,
and Queen Mary wrote to Prince Paul asking him too to drop
his old friend. 'I am hoping that George and Marina will no
longer see certain people who alas were friends of Mrs S and
Lady Cunard's and also David's,' the old Queen wrote to Paul

of Yugoslavia. The royal family, especially Queen Mary and the new King, felt very strongly that such 'friends' as Lady Cunard had done nothing but harm to the King with her patronage of the American divorcee, and hoped that they could freeze her out of polite society. Lady Cunard herself was fearful of the results of having backed the losing side. Soon after the abdication she said to a friend, Mrs Greville, 'Maggie, darling, do tell me about this Mrs Simpson – I've only just met her.' Other friends of the ex-King's rode the storm – but they were friends who could prove useful to the new regime, notably Duff and Diana Cooper who had actually been on the *Nahlin* with David and Mrs Simpson, and Winston Churchill who had supported Edward VIII until the bitter end.

Lady Cunard never regained royal favour. Invited to the Duchess of Sutherland's Coronation Ball, she was, however, told that she must not come until after the King and Queen left. Lady Cunard was kept in the undignified position of having to sit and wait for a telephone call which would give her the all clear. However, Alistair Forbes, a regular visitor at Coppins after the war, says that neither the Kents, nor the Yugoslavs, nor Princess Nicholas, did drop Emerald Cunard, because they all knew she had only befriended Mrs Simpson because she was what Noël Coward called the King's 'cutie'.

David himself was not cast into total darkness on leaving England. His mother wrote regularly to him and he kept in close touch with Bertie, ringing him with advice on how to be a King. George also rang him often. He was even visited, in February, by the Princess Royal and her husband the Earl of Harewood.

George had wanted to go and see his brother, and had tried to arrange a visit at the beginning of January. He was stopped in his plans by his brother the King, who was worried about such a visit reviving newspaper interest in the Duke of Windsor;

It is too soon after what happened to take any risks in this way, and we both want David's future life settled in April [when Mrs Simpson's divorce became absolute. Under law at the time Mrs Simpson's divorce would not go through if it were thought that she were colluding in the proceedings.] The best chance for him to marry Mrs Simpson is by lying low.

George obeyed his brother, and waited until after Mary came back from Austria before going himself.

The family had to bow to the King again in June when David finally married Mrs Simpson. The Duke of Windsor had hoped that some members of his family – perhaps even his mother – would come to the ceremony, but he was cruelly disappointed to be told by Bertie that 'I can't treat this as just a private family matter, however much I want to ... the vast majority of people in this country are undoubtedly as strongly as ever opposed to a marriage which caused a King of England to renounce the throne.' George, too, wrote to his brother: 'You have always been a wonderful friend to me and you know (I hope) my great affection and regard for you, and so I am very *sincerely* sad at not being with you on June 3.'

David's bitterness at his family's refusal to attend the wedding, to grant Wallis the title of HRH after her marriage, and at the arguments about a financial settlement for him, grew so great that he was even angry with his favourite brother. George and Marina sent the Duke a Fabergé box as a wedding present, but the Duke sent it back with the message 'The only boxes I happen to be collecting now are those that can be delivered on the ears.' His answer to a congratulatory telegram from the Kents (everyone in the family sent a telegram on the wedding day) was as reproachful (although he was more friendly to the Channons, whose telegram was answered on the day of the ceremony). To the Kents, David wrote that he believed they were sincere in their good wishes, but that they were 'not at all in tune with the attitude that has been taken by Mama, by Bertie, and by the rest of the family .... I tell you, here and now, that I will never forgive or forget the lead Bertie has given you all in your behaviour to me ever since I left England.' David later told the actress Lili Palmer that the only person he missed in England was his mother, and that his 'tragedy is that I couldn't stand England from the start. But the first time I set foot on American soil ... I knew at a stroke that this was the place for me.' His second tragedy was perhaps that because of Mrs Simpson's insistence and his own unwillingness to pay high taxes, he could not settle in America.

The country (and the royal family) was meanwhile taken up with preparations for Bertie (to be known as George VI) and Elizabeth's coronation, which was to take place on the day which had been set for Edward VIII's coronation. George and Marina were pleased to have Prince Paul to stay for the occasion, and he spent his time between official functions, 'family dinners' and banquets at 'B.P.' and quieter weekends at Coppins.

With the 'Year of Three Kings' behind them, the family hoped it could look forward to quieter times, although of course the vexed questions of David's financial settlements and the date of his return to England remained. There had been one happy event in that year of death and tribulation: the birth at 11.30 a.m. on Christmas morning of a daughter to George and Marina ('the only nice thing to have happened this year,' said Queen Mary). The baby was given a string of family names: Alexandra Helen Elizabeth Olga and finally (because of the date of the birth) Christabel. With the rest of the royal family celebrating Christmas at Sandringham, the Kents were alone in Belgrave Square with Prince and Princess Nicholas. The Duke of Windsor, who had not yet taken such mortal offence with his family, was among those to send a telegram of congratulation to the parents.

George was not entirely on holiday over Christmas. On 28 December he made an Empire Broadcast to commemorate the arrival of the first colonists at Kangaroo Island and the hundred years' anniversary of the proclamation of the Province of South Australia. It was a speech ringing with imperialist values, in which no mention was made either of the family's recent troubles or of the birth of his own daughter. It was the kind of speech the Empire still liked.

Princess Alexandra was christened in the private chapel of Buckingham Palace on 9 February, and she and her older brother Eddie cried throughout the ceremony. Her godparents by proxy were Princess Beatrice (Queen Victoria's youngest surviving daughter), Princess Nicholas, Princess Olga, Queen Maud of Norway and Toto Toerring. The godparents at the font were the King and Queen and the Earl of Athlone. That evening Marina (in black velvet and a silver fox stole) and George went dancing at the Dorchester and a few days later left for a six-week motoring holiday on the continent, without their children.

The coronation on 12 May brought a semblance of family unity and normality back to the Windsors. Queen Mary broke with the tradition that no Queen Dowager attends the coronation of the new monarch, and accompanied by her favourite sister-in-law Queen Maud of Norway, made the journey to the Abbey in the glass coach. The country was with the new King, and enormously proud of the old Queen. 'The regime seems overnight popular,' wrote Channon on the eve of the coronation. Every procession was met with huge and reassuring cheers, 'the tiny Princesses excited by their coronets and trains, and the two Royal Duchesses looking staggering. The Duchess of Gloucester looked so lovely that for a moment I thought she was Princess Marina,' Channon remembered. After it all the family could set off for its summer holiday at Balmoral with some relief.

On 3 June, George V's birthday, David and Mrs Simpson (who had changed her name back to Warfield on her divorce) were married at the Château de Cande. Constance Spry arranged the flowers and Cecil Beaton took the pictures on the day before the wedding. The Duke 'had tears running down his face when he came down into the salon after the ceremony,' wrote Lady Alexandra Metcalfe, whose husband, Fruity, was best man. '... If she occasionally showed a glimmer of softness, took his arm, looked at him as though she loved him one would warm towards her. The effect is of a woman unmoved by the infatuated love of a younger man. Let's hope that she lets up in private with him otherwise it must be grim.' Yet even for those who hated all that Mrs Simpson represented, it was sometimes hard to hate the woman herself. 'He sees through Wallis' eyes, hears through her ears and speaks through her mouth .... Nevertheless, although I loathe her for what she has done, I am unable to dislike her when I see her,' said Lady Alexandra.

Beaton's view of the couple was as depressing; he wrote that Mrs Simpson was 'today especially unlovable, hard and calculating and showing an anxiety but no feeling of emotion'. Her face, he said, was 'broken out in spots and not looking her best'. Of the Duke he wrote that 'his expression though intent was essentially sad. Tragic eyes belied by impertinent tilt of nose.' On his visit earlier in the year Beaton had also decided that Mrs Simpson was 'determined to love him, though I feel she is not in love with him. She has a great responsibility in looking after someone who, so essentially different, entirely relies upon her.'

The English newspapers – except *The Times* – ran leaders wishing the Windsors good luck in their marriage. The House of Commons collectively began to feel some embarrassment at the treatment of the ex-King, but the new King was sure that the best way forward was to wipe out the memory of the recent past as quickly as possible.

Memories and affections cannot, however, be banished to order. When Cecil Beaton returned from the Château de Candé he took the photographs first to the Channons, then next door to the Kents. They could not go to the wedding, but they wanted to know as much as possible about it.

In July Marina was involved in a car accident while driving with the children to Sandwich in Kent. Alexandra was covered in broken glass and Marina lost her engagement ring in a ditch, but no one was hurt and the ring was finally found. The incident did, however, bring Marina into the public eye again, and in a most satisfactory light: what could be more pleasing after all than royal babies being taken on an English seaside holiday?

The Kents' own holiday after the coronation was a motoring tour through Europe. They drove through Germany to Poland, where they were to stay with Agnes de Stoeckl's daughter, Marina's old friend Zoia. Although they were travelling privately, the Kents were met at the Polish border with a fervour they could not have expected. They were the first members of the British royal family to go to Poland, and their visit fuelled hopes that perhaps George might become that country's King. However, flattered though they were by the attention, to the Kents this had never been more than a holiday with an old friend.

There was another holiday the following autumn. First they cruised, then they stayed with Paul and Olga at Brdo (where the Channons joined the party). Chips found Marina 'lovely, dark and more glamorous and gentler than ever', both she and George brown from the sun. Only a few hours away from the Windsors, who were now at Wasserleonburg in Carinthia (southern Austria), George wrote to his brother saying he and Paul would like to come and see him for a couple of nights. When George rang to make the arrangements, there was a pause during which George thought David was consulting his wife, then David asked, 'Are you coming with your wives?' George said that as they had just arrived and Princess Nicholas was also staying, it would not be 'convenient at the moment' for Marina and Olga to come as well. In fact, George told Paul that 'I have strong instructions from Mama that Marina (being a foreigner by birth) shouldn't be the first female member of the family to call on her [the new Duchess of Windsor].' 'In that case, it's No,' said David, and hung up. His outrage was such that the rules were changed. The King decided that George should visit David, even if it meant Marina also went. The Duke was triumphant, but Marina was very unwilling to go, and in England Queen Mary was trying to change the order from the King, who finally capitulated. The Kents cancelled the Duke with the feeble apology that they would not after all be able to come back from a yachting trip in time to make the journey to Austria. It was another blow for the bitter Duke.

It was during the troubled times of the Abdication Crisis, and the days that followed, that Marina first truly showed her mettle. The whole royal family had been seriously worried that the abdication would unsettle the throne, perhaps terminally. The family had decided before even David that he would have to go – that if he stayed as King, even if he did not marry Mrs Simpson, the monarchy might well not survive. So, after David had left and while he and Mrs Simpson were pining for each other in their separate retreats, the family went to work to repair the damage he had done. 'I am new to the job,' George VI wrote to the Prime Minister on New Year's Eve 1936, 'but I hope that time will be allowed to me to make amends for what has happened.' Baldwin answered with comforting words, 'you need have no fear for the future, so far as you are concerned. The whole country is behind you with a deep and understanding sympathy.' Nevertheless for a long time after his accession

George VI remained aware of having a predecessor who was not only alive but was infinitely more charming and had been much more popular. Sir Ronald Lindsay, the British Ambassador to Washington, wrote after a visit to Balmoral that 'really the King does not yet feel safe on his throne, and up to a point he is like a medieval monarch who has a hated rival claimant living in exile.'

George Kent's Empire Speech just after Christmas 1936 was immensely popular with the public. Then Marina's reluctance, which amounted to a refusal, to call on the Duchess of Windsor at Wasserleonburg, earned her the approval and gratitude of both Queen Mary and Queen Elizabeth. The King's whole attitude in dealing with his older brother was to take the line which would involve the least press interest in the ex-King, and although George longed to see David again both he and Marina closed ranks with the royal family against him. Marina had come from a troubled monarchy: she knew the signs, she knew the dangers, and she knew the price that had to be paid to keep the monarchy stable.

The whole family worked harder than ever before to regain their people's trust. And Marina was prepared not only to work hard at her official engagements, but to take the first steps towards letting the people of England closer to the royal family.

Cecil Beaton had wanted to photograph Marina since her first arrival in England as the future bride of Prince George. She, shy despite her astounding beauty, had held him at bay. Finally, in the coronation summer she agreed that he should take a portrait. Beaton wrote:

The Duchess looked excessively beautiful in a huge brown tulle crinoline, ruched like a Queen Anne window blind, or a lampshade, with old-fashioned jewellery, a bow knot, large drop earrings. She looked like a Winterhalter painting and it was thus that she was photographed, slightly nervous at first and very Royal, with her deep, clipped, accented voice, but soon she was as pliable as any sitter I have ever had and we made many jokes and got along splendidly.

As so often, Marina's shyness soon gave way to warmth and humour. Then the Duke arrived in a bad temper 'and there is no one bloodier than he in a bad mood'. A few days later Beaton was back with the pictures. 'Oh!' said Marina, 'I hate to be in *Sketch* and *Tatler* and *Vogue* ... but *Vogue*'s a fashion magazine,' 'Well, what about it?' answered the Duke with a laugh, 'Aren't we fashionable?' Indeed they were.

Beaton, as successful a social climber as he was a photographer, longed to mix with such as the Kents – as early as January 1933 Beaton confessed to his diary that he had 'realised my ... ambitions of the winter ... I get a charming letter from Prince George calling me by my first name. My life is sensibly planned and he is definitely in my plan of campaign.' He never became a particular intimate of George's, but this picture session with Marina was the beginning of a long friendship with his wife.

In January 1938 the Kents went together to Athens for the wedding of Prince Paul, George II's brother and heir, to Princess Frederika of Brunswick. From Athens they went to St Anton for a skiing holiday with the Toerrings. One day George found a gold cigarette case in the snow, and was rewarded a hundred francs by the owner. Delighted, he gave the money to a local charity. That day, the family heard the news that Prince Nicholas was dying. He had been ill almost since his return to Greece in November 1936, and his daughters had been worried about him for some time. All four immediately left to travel to the bedside. Unfortunately, Marina's fear of flying – it was one interest she could not share with her husband – meant that they travelled by train, rather than by air. At Belgrade station Prince Paul met their train and told them the sad news that Prince Nicholas had died on 8 February, with Olga and his wife beside him. His last words before losing consciousness had been, 'I am happy to die in my own beloved country.' Channon, who had known him for many years, wrote when he heard the news,

a gentle, dreamy gentleman, he tasted many of the vicissitudes of fortune .... He was bald and brown and wore the eye-glass which is traditional in the Greek branch of the Glucksberg family. When his daughter, Princess Marina, married ... his paternal pride was a pleasure to see. Prince Nicholas spoke every language, wrote endless letters to his royal relations, and was particularly devoted to the late George V.

The Prince was buried at Tatoi, and after his death Princess Nicholas settled in the suburbs of Athens, where she lived until her own death in 1957.

For Marina and George 1938 was the last year of normality. Marina and George's trip to Greece for Prince Paul's wedding was the first time Marina had been able to take her husband to her birthplace (the royal family had been forbidden to visit Greece during the ten years of republicanism). George had already taken on Marina's family as his own (as indeed they were, distantly) and was always welcoming to those friends from her past who had not survived the troubles of their countries as well as she. Now he could see for himself the country which had shaped her life, and he fell in love all over again. 'Although Athens is not home, it is the next best thing,' he said. A pretty compliment perhaps, but one which pleased the Greeks as much as it did his wife. Even more valued by her was the comment he made to some Athenians during the visit: 'Greece has given me a wife, the full extent of whose influence over me I shall probably never know ... her influence is as incalculable as the Hellenic influence over civilisation.'

Then in July George was in Rumania for Queen Marie's funeral, and in December he represented the King at the Oslo funeral of their aunt Queen Maud. There was the usual round of dinner parties – with the Channons, the Buccleuchs, Noël Coward – and official work. The summer holiday that year was spent cruising with Marina's old friend Lilia Ralli, after which the Kents stayed with Paul and Olga in Yugoslavia. George and Paul took day trips to shop in Munich and swam in the river together – a breakthrough for Paul who had not swum since his mad cousin had tried to drown him in Lake Geneva. The Kents then moved on to stay with the Toerrings in Bavaria where the Yugoslavs joined them and they were entertained by the local wine festival.

Then in October came the news that would change their lives. George was appointed Governor-General of Australia, and would take the job up the following November (1939). It would mean an uprooting even more violent than that from Greece, or that which had taken Marina from Paris to London as George's wife. Further than ever from her family and friends, she would have to face an entirely new world and way of life. For the first time she would, as wife of the King's representative, be entirely on show. For a woman who had admitted to being 'shy at the idea' of a weekend with her husband's friends, the prospect was daunting. 'I suppose I do "vegetate" and one gets used to it,' she had added. In Australia she would have no time to vegetate.

When Paul and Olga came to stay in England at the end of the year (first at Buckingham Palace, then after Paul's departure Olga moved to Belgrave Square) Marina must have felt a sense of impending loss. There would be few such visits in her future home.

CHAPTER SIX

War and Death

The royal family had continued its round of work and play during the years since King Edward VIII had abdicated from the throne, but by the end of 1938 the most ill-informed of the new King's subjects was aware of the threat of war.

England itself might be at peace after its unsettled recent past, but everywhere else in Europe seemed to be facing trouble. English thinkers raced to fight in the Spanish Civil War, and in Germany Hitler was already making clear the extent of his ambition. In Italy too the Fascist dictator Mussolini was posturing and strutting.

The question of appeasement divided King George's government. Prime Minister Chamberlain was convinced that the surest way of keeping peace in Europe was by weakening the Axis (Germany–Italy) powers, if need be by making an agreement with Italy. Anthony Eden, the Foreign Secretary, was set against any dealings with Italy. The rift led to Eden's resignation, a resignation of which in the heat of the moment the King was not informed; he learned about it only from the press.

On 12 March 1938 the Nazis took over Austria. Then, despite protestations to the contrary, it became increasingly clear that Hitler had his eyes on Czechoslovakia too. When Czechoslovakia turned to France for reiteration of her promise of defence should the Nazis invade, France turned to England where Chamberlain continued to believe that Hitler would not occupy Prague. A speech by Alan Lennox-Boyd in the House of Commons voiced the not unpopular view that there would be no sense or merit in promising to defend Czechoslovakia.

In the face of increasing pressure, Chamberlain foolishly or bravely continued to hold firm to his policy of appeasement. On 14 September, by which time even he was aware of the very real dangers ahead, he flew to Germany to meet Hitler in person. It was an act which fired the imagination of the country and the King, but not one which would make any difference to Hitler. On his return Chamberlain told the Cabinet and then the King that Hitler would surely invade Czechoslovakia. His visit had bought a week's grace, but nothing else had been achieved. The French must be made to face up to their obligations, and the Czechs to agree to self-rule in the Sudetenland (the part of Czechoslovakia over which Germany claimed rights).

On 22 September Chamberlain was back in Germany with Hitler, this time with no ground gained at all. On the 27th he broadcast a message telling the British of his attempts to keep the peace, now his hopes were almost at an end, and about Britain's defence. The country was prepared for inevitable war.

With such gloom pervading every sitting room in England the relief with which the news (on 28th) of Hitler's invitation to a Four-Power Conference in Munich was almost hysterical. Chamberlain had been in full flow in the House of Commons when the message was brought that seemed to change the future. That morning the Prime Minister had telegrammed Hitler and Mussolini in a last-ditch attempt to keep the peace: Hitler had responded with his invitation to talk. The scenes in the House of Commons – watched by Marina, George, and Queen Mary making what was believed to be her first appearance in the Commons – were riotous. There was still hope for peace.

When Chamberlain returned from Munich two days later with an Agreement for Anglo-German Friendship everyone saw him as a peace-preserving hero. The King could return to his interrupted summer holiday at Balmoral and the nation could breathe again. Never mind the sacrifices that Czechoslovakia had made in Europe's interest: war was averted.

In December France and Germany signed a similar Agreement of Friendship to that already in existence between England and Germany. It was felt that maybe it would now be appropriate to reopen negotiations with Italy, and to this end Chamberlain and Lord Halifax, who had succeeded Eden as Foreign Secretary, visited Italy in January. Chamberlain wrote to the King:

Both Halifax and I were favourably impressed with Mussolini. Talking with him is a much pleasanter affair than with Hitler. You feel you are dealing with a reasonable man, not a fanatic, and he struck us both as straightforward and sincere in what he said. Moreover he has a sense of humour which occasionally breaks out in an attractive smile, whereas it would take a long surgical operation to get a joke into Hitler's head.

They also believed that he wanted peace.

The English felt safe enough to agree to the King and Queen making a state visit to Canada, followed by a brief stay with the Roosevelts in America (at Hyde Park, their country house). This visit, designed partly to show Commonwealth solidarity, partly to display Anglo-American friendship, and partly motivated by the King's long-standing wish to revisit Canada, took place in May–June 1939, despite the deterioration of European stability which took place before then. It was the first time a reigning monarch had been to America.

While they were at sea the Duke of Windsor re-entered public life for the first time for two and a half years with a broadcast he made on the American airwaves from Verdun. It was an appeal for peace, an appeal to avert the possibility of the mayhem that had happened during the First World War, and a plea not to listen to propaganda and not to use 'terms such as "encirclement" and "aggression"'. The British did not broadcast the speech and the timing, with the King away, was not well received. 'What a fool he is and how badly advised; and everyone is furious he should have done it just after you left,' George wrote to Bertie. 'If he had mentioned you in it, it wouldn't have been so bad, and why he broadcast such a peace talk only to America, where they have no intention of fighting, I don't know.' Whatever his loyalty to his brother David personally, in such matters George took the royal party line.

The British people's wish for peace was so great that their eyes were in part blinded by their desires. On 15 March Hitler had forced the Czech President to place his country 'under German protection', and was in Prague, declaring that 'Czechoslovakia has ceased to exist'. Shortly afterwards he tore up the Munich Agreement, making at last clear the depths of his perfidy. At the end of the month the British made an unconditional guarantee to help Poland if the need arose, then in April the Italians took over Albania, with King Zog, Queen Geraldine and their two-day-old baby son fleeing the country.

Yugoslavia, a friend of Britain's, was in an increasingly difficult position. Paul had been looking forward to the end of his regency, and planned to retire to England where he had spent so much of his youth and where most of his dearest friends were still to be found. As the British Mininster, Ronald Campbell, reported,

There is nothing to endear him to his present life; his days are spent in granting audiences – most of them tedious, and many of them disagreeable – while his only relaxation is a short walk in the afternoon, with Princess Olga, on the same stretch of road, surrounded by a small army of plain clothes detectives.

Paul's instincts were entirely with the British, but when it came to the war he had to look at the geography of his country, and take into account Hitler's stamping about, before coming to any decisions. Italy's invasion of Albania meant that Yugoslavia shared two borders with Italy. With division in his own country, Paul could not be sure that the Croats would fight the Germans, and Germany itself was very close. Although the friendship with Britain was strong, and although Campbell repeatedly asked the Foreign Office to assist Yugoslavia in her troubles, Paul knew that such help could not be relied upon. The best he could do was to stay neutral. And he was being courted. There was a state visit with Olga to Italy in May 1939, and another to Berlin in June. Hitler was determined the visit should be a success, and did all he could to please not only Paul but Olga, by making sure her many German friends and relations were included in the banquets and receptions. Despite Hitler's generosity, his wheedling and his thinly veiled threats, Paul left Germany without having committed himself to the Axis. 'Prince Paul's attitude', said Winston Churchill, 'looks like that of an unfortunate man in a cage with a tiger, hoping not to provoke him, while dinner time steadily approaches.'

Britain too wooed its old friend. In July Paul and Olga were on a state visit to England, staying at Buckingham Palace, being feted in magnificent style, and Paul was even made a Knight of the Garter. After an enjoyable fortnight, Paul and Olga returned to Yugoslavia where, after three state visits in as many months, they prepared to enjoy a much-needed holiday. Once again they entertained the Kents and Toerrings at their summer residence in Brdo. The summer holiday was soon to be disrupted. On 22 August the news came that Germany and Russia had signed a pact of non-aggression, and George and Toto both immediately left Brdo for their respective homes. The three royal brothers – Bertie, Harry and George – were drawn closer together in the face of the European threat. 'Harry and George have dined with me nearly every night. I have seen more of them in the last week than I have during the year,' the King wrote to his mother on 28 August. The three brothers had also gone to morning service together at Westminster Abbey – quietly and without any show. Then George sent for Marina, who returned to England with Olga's two sons, leaving Princess Nicholas, Olga and Elizabeth with a truncated and lonely holiday. Their farewells were much more painful than normally: each wondered when they might meet again. Once more the threat of war seemed very real and very near.

Hitler was now exercised by the question of his relations with Poland – England had signed an Anglo-Polish Alliance on 26 August, and Hitler was keen to split the Anglo-French-Polish friendship. When this proved impossible to achieve, he invaded Poland at dawn on 1 September. The British set a time limit for the withdrawal of troops, a time limit that was not met. From eleven in the morning on Sunday 3 September Great Britain and France were officially at war with Germany. 'Today we are at war again, and I am no longer a midshipman in the Royal Navy,' the King wrote in his diary, remembering how he had been in the North Sea serving on HMS *Collingwood* when he had heard of the outbreak of the First World War.

Marina and George had spent the last year in making plans for their move to Australia. These included inviting visiting Australians to Coppins to learn more about their country and studying the plans of Government House, Canberra where they were to live. George was particularly involved in choosing the furniture and furnishings for their new home. Chips, judging by the 'houseful of treasures' in Belgrave Square, told George that the governorship would save him £500,000 a year, the amount he must spend in London shops. The Duke, happily spending while he waited for the move, laughed. The lease on the house in Belgrave Square had been dropped, and some of the Kents' possessions had already been sent out to Australia. In September Channon took tea with Marina and found her

sadly lovely with her amber eyes, and I wondered once whether they were tear stained? We sat in what was once her little private sitting room, but today there were two chairs only and a tea tray. The house had been completely dismantled and there were only a few packing cases and dust sheets about, and few traces of its former gaiety and happiness. All the Duke's expensive toys, his Panninis, his Meissen, all had been removed, mostly to the Pantechnicon. They now have no London home at all. We had a sad conversation about poor Prince Paul struggling and hoping for peace in his mountain fastness of Brdo .... It was a sad little talk and I think we both felt a touch like Ruth amid the alien corn, aliens in this incredibly lovely and lovable England.

The family was to have left in November, but as soon as war was declared it was decided that George should remain at home, returning to the Admiralty with a desk job. Lord Gowrie continued to hold the Australian appointment. George was promoted to Rear-Admiral, but once again wanted to leave the navy (this time because he did not want to spend the war in an office job). He found the early stages of hostilities frustrating and depressing in the extreme, writing to Paul of Yugoslavia in March 1940 that 'the war drags on – everyone seems to be talking – but I cannot see any result from it.' The next month he wrote,

I have been at the Admiralty (awful waste of time) and so I went to see Chamberlain weeks ago and asked him if he could find me something which I could do which, being what I am, would be really useful to the country – you see – we are used for anything and everything in peace but when war comes no one wants us as we don't know enough of any particular subject which seems unfair.

Once war was declared and under way, Marina's official work became more important to her than it had been up until now. In February 1940 she became Commandant of the Women's Royal Naval Service (the Wrens), a job which took her all over England on tours of inspection and encouragement. Marina found her new role more stimulating than anything she had yet undertaken. Like her sister-in-law the Queen dressing in uniform was not something Marina was used to or particularly warmed to, but where the Queen was allowed to remain out of uniform, Marina was given no choice but told by Churchill to comply. When she first visited the Charing Cross headquarters she had on the wrong gloves and too low a collar. She at first displayed a fetching inability to salute correctly, and was sent a diagram of details of the art of saluting by senior Wrens. She would often wear high heels and jewellery with her uniform, but was always forgiven. Despite these minor drawbacks Dame Vera Laughton Matthews, Director of the Wrens during the war, spoke warmly of Marina's genuine interest and kindness. She later said,

The Duchess's sense of duty was invincible. She never cut her programme, no matter how heavy it might be or how behind-time events might make her. Her view was that a lot of people had taken a lot of trouble to prepare things and she was not going to disappoint them no matter how late it made her. She started a tour of one Naval station at 9 a.m. one day and finished that night at a civic function in Glasgow at 11 p.m. No time even for half an hour's rest.

(Yet she could, or would, not remember not to call the galley the kitchen or the cabins the bedrooms.)

This sense of duty had been instilled in her by her parents from her earliest days and now it was being called to the fore. And her work gave her a sense of purpose. The royal duties she had undertaken up until the war had not after all been very serious – she had taken part in state banquets and entertaining other royal visitors, she had visited hospitals, but her interests and passions had really lain with her husband and children, and her clothes. With George running their two homes, she had not even been occupied with the daily cares of household management.

Her sense of style came in useful in her work with the Wrens. She was closely involved in the choice of the new uniform hat, trying on several of the prototypes herself. This may sound frivolous, but Marina's instinct was right. As she said, 'No woman wants to wear a hat which makes her look unattractive, war or no war. The right sort of hat is most important if we're to get recruits.'

Marina's greatest success was at recruiting. She was photographed looking as beautiful as ever in uniform ('Marina only had to pull on a scarf and you were astounded again at how beautiful she was,' said Daska Maclean) and, on 20 January 1941, broadcast an appeal for recruits. In the speech she emphasised the 'spirit of friendship' she had found as she toured the Wren bases. She pointed out how much opportunity there was in an organisation where women were promoted from the ranks. 'I feel sure that there are still many women who would like to do their bit by helping the Royal Navy, the traditional service of the Empire,' she said. She also pointed out the possibilities for training: 'Many Wren cooks are being trained at the Royal Naval cookery schools. If you like household duties, the Wrens can make you a first-class steward.' The speech ended with praise for the serving Wrens. 'We admire your courage and we know that danger is met unflinchingly, because the future happiness of our families and homes depends on victory. If you join the Wrens, you will know that you have done your share and are worthy of your country.'

The speech was a resounding success: over three thousand women applied to join up the next day. 'Whatever you do, don't on any account let the Duchess broadcast again,' begged an Admiralty official swamped with paperwork.

The first months of the phoney war passed comparatively peacefully. 'Everything goes on here the same – and it seems years since war started – and the boredom is immense – three months without anything really happening,' George wrote to Paul in December 1939. Indeed, life was so 'normal' that Marina asked Olga to stay for Easter 1940 (Paul and Olga's two sons were at school in England). Denmark and Norway were invaded just before her departure for England, and while she was there

Paul wrote saying he had decided to send their daughter Elizabeth (aged four) to Switzerland with her nanny, Miss Ede, for
safety. From there they made their way to England.

European monarchs were living in fear of kidnap or death.
Queen Wilhelmina of the Netherlands waited for as long as
possible before leaving her country, bombarding George VI
with calls for help from Britain. 'It is not often one is rung up
at that hour, and especially by a Queen,' Bertie noted after a
five o'clock in the morning call. 'But in these days anything may
happen, & far worse things too.' Crown Princess Juliana arrived
with her husband and two baby daughters, and a few days later
Queen Wilhelmina followed, carrying her jewels and a tin hat
given her by the commander of the destroyer on which she had
fled, but no clothes (and being a lady of ample proportions her
royal hosts found it at first very difficult to find clothes to fit
her). Soon after the Dutch arrivals King Haakon and Crown
Prince Olav of Norway were also forced to flee their country,
and also met with a warm welcome from the British royal
family. With Europe every day in greater disarray, Olga found
herself more or less stranded in England. The day it was
finally deemed safe for her to leave, 17 May, all flights were
stopped. The Germans were now in Belgium. Finally George
organised for her to leave the country in the King's new private
bomber.

Marina also worked as a volunteer at the Iver and Denham
Cottage Hospital, and later at University College Hospital as
a nursing auxiliary. While at University College Hospital she
worked anonymously, using the name Nurse Kay. Not even the
other nurses knew who their new recruit really was, so it was
somewhat embarrassing one day when the staff was told that
the Duke of Kent, President of the hospital, was to pay a visit.
Marina went to the sister on the ward and suggested she slip
away, sure that if the patients saw her and George together they
would guess the truth. The sister told her she should stay, as a
sudden disappearance would be more noticeable. In the event
George toured the ward, was introduced to the nurses, and gave
nothing away as his wife dipped a curtsy to him. Of course
Marina's cover did not last for long; a patient who was a

dressmaker's assistant recognised 'Nurse Kay' as the elegant Princess.

One of the major effects of the war all over Europe was to split up families, and none more so than Marina's. Within the British royal family matters were comparatively simple: Queen Mary's brother Lord Athlone went to Canada as Governor-General (where he stayed for six successful years), and although it was suggested both that the little Princesses and Queen Mary should go to safety across the Atlantic, Queen Elizabeth would not allow her daughters to leave and Queen Mary refused on her own account. (Princess Juliana and her family did eventually seek shelter with the Athlones.) The old Queen was finally persuaded to leave London, and went to stay for the duration of the war with her niece, the Duchess of Beaufort, at Badminton. She took with her seventy pieces of luggage and sixty-three members of staff (accompanied by their families). Among her entourage were the Kent children, Eddie and Alexandra, who were to spend long stretches of time at Badminton under their grandmother's care. While they were there their mother visited them every week. The Duke of Windsor was of course in France, and although he visited England immediately after the outbreak of war, it became clear that he would not be offered any serious work in Britain, as he would have wished. His attitude was still causing too many problems. When, on the outbreak of the war, he said he wanted to come to England to discuss his role, Bertie at once offered to send a private aeroplane for him. David said he would accept the offer only if his wife were treated as a proper member of the family. (He had continued to agitate for his wife to be given the title 'Her Royal Highness' and would refer to her as such himself.) So the Windsors travelled to England by sea. While he was in England David saw the King only once, for about an hour, and Bertie reported to George that his mood was his 'usual swaggering one, laying down the law about everything'. David looked well but, as Bertie wrote to the Prime Minister, he seemed 'not a bit worried as to the effects he left on people's minds as to his behaviour in 1936. He has forgotten all about it.'

David was given the job of liaison officer with the British

Military Mission to General Gamelin. The Princess Royal and Duke of Gloucester were home-bound, Mary nursing and Henry continuing his career in the army.

Marina's own family, though, was split up dreadfully. Her mother and Aunt Alice (Princess Andrew) were living in Greece, which was neutral. Elizabeth was married to a German soldier, and thus was suddenly the Enemy, as were Marina's close friends Prince Andrew's three surviving daughters (in 1937 Princess Cecilie had been killed in an air accident with her husband the Grand Duke of Hesse and by Rhine and their children). Marina had to write to them via Queen Louise of Sweden, Lord Mountbatten's sister. Their younger brother Prince Philip, was the only member of the family in Britain – after Gordonstoun he had joined the Royal Navy. With Paul and Olga feeling their country ever more threatened, and fighting to remain neutral, there seemed little chance of seeing them again in the near future. George and Marina wrote every week, but letters could not replace the close contact the couples had shared before.

By the summer of 1940 the effects of war were beginning to be felt. 'What days we are living in and what changes,' George commented. This was the first year that the Kents could not visit Yugoslavia for their summer holiday. George sent a letter to Paul via his sons, Alexander and Nicky, who were returning to Yugoslavia from their English schools on the advice of Paul's Foreign Minister (England feared invasion by the Germans at this time).

This is just one line for the boys to take with them. It's sad they are leaving – but I can imagine how you must feel about leaving them here and it is an added worry for you in a very difficult time with wild beasts all round you – and liable to fight each other over the morsels – what a hell of a world we live in – with evil pushing its way everywhere .... It's horrible to think that in only a week's time in ordinary years we should be leaving to see you all, and here we are stuck for ever.

In October 1940 Mussolini, angered by Hitler's dealings behind his back, decided to prove that he too was a power to be reckoned with and moved his troops stationed in Albania into Greece. For both Marina and Olga this was a new worry:

until then they had hoped that their mother and other relations in Greece would be safe. Paul was in a position to help, and the Yugoslav government provided the Greeks with armaments, food and horses as well as (using their position of neutrality) blocking German supplies to the Italians in Albania.

George would have liked to have been more closely involved with military matters than was allowed, but he worked hard during the early war years. Much of the work was no different from the tasks he had undertaken pre-war: inspecting factories, visiting RAF bases. He also spent a great deal of time in the bomb sites of the East End. He waited in air-raid shelters with thousands of others as the bombs blasted London apart and once was nearly blown up himself when a time bomb exploded within yards of his car. The royal family was touched by bombing when Buckingham Palace was hit in September and October 1940. 'A magnificent piece of bombing, Ma'am, if you'll pardon me saying so,' said a policeman to the Queen.

George was also trusted with more sensitive work. In late June 1940 he led the British delegation at the Portuguese celebrations of eight hundred years of independence. Portugal was neutral in the war, but England needed it to be seen that her position was strong, and that she was in no danger of being overrun by the Nazis. George visited the Portuguese Prime Minister, Dr Salazar, and exercised his full diplomatic charm. This was at the same time as the Duke of Windsor, who had just fled from France before its fall to the Germans, was looking for a way back to England (while once again slowing the arrangements with arguments about his wife's status). He and his wife had arrived in Madrid, and Churchill's plan had been that they should proceed to Lisbon, until Salazar told the British Ambassador that it would be 'inconvenient and undesirable' to have the Duke of Windsor in his country at the same time as his brother. David was thus put in the humiliating position of having to wait while his younger brother carried out his duties with great success before he could take the next step home.

Later in the war George was transferred to the RAF and made Chief Welfare Officer with the rank of Air Vice-Marshal, which he dropped for the working title of Air Commodore so that he should not be superior to his immediate colleagues. The new job entailed more tours of inspection, but also brought with it another opportunity to do more positive work. In July 1941 George was to visit Canada to inspect air training schools, and he suggested that he should break the Canadian visit with a trip to America to see President Roosevelt, whom he and Marina had met while on honeymoon in the West Indies. The President approved the plan, adding that while George was in America he might like to inspect a dockyard where a British warship was being repaired, and maybe also a factory which produced aircraft for Great Britain. George flew to Canada in a Liberator (which made him the first member of the royal family to fly the Atlantic). He toured thousands of miles in Canada, then flew on to America where he addressed thirteen thousand aircraft factory workers, telling them about the realities of the war in England, what it meant to the ordinary people of the country, how it affected their lives. 'Every hour you work', he said, 'saves the lives of women and children. The more you give us the quicker we shall win.' It was an extraordinarily successful speech, appreciated for its directness, its warmth and its humanity.

At the end of the tour the Duke spent a few days with the Roosevelts at their country house, Hyde Park, where he relaxed, eating oranges and bananas with the enthusiasm of deprivation.

By chance, his presence in America had the same element of bad timing as far as David was concerned as had his visit to Portugal earlier in the war. Once again David had to be kept waiting for his younger brother before he was allowed to enter America. Meanwhile in Yugoslavia Paul was facing very real difficulties in his attempts to keep faith both with the Allies, with whom his sympathies lay, and with his people. He saw his first duty as protecting the unity of Yugoslavia, a job that had proved difficult enough before outside pressures from the Axis and Allied powers put more strain on the cracks. Between March and June 1940 Yugoslavia restored diplomatic relations with Russia, in the hope that she would provide protection against an Italian invasion. When Hitler decided to attack Russia and Greece he wanted to keep a right of travel through Yugoslavia (including use of her railway line) so he would not sign the pact of non-aggression Paul offered him in December 1940.

England, hard hit by the fall of France (although Bertie had written to his mother 'Personally I feel happier now that we have no allies to be polite to & to pamper'), still offered no arms or help and in February 1941 asked Yugoslavia to fight – whether or not she was invaded. Paul could and would not offer up his country – he knew she had neither the strength nor the power to do anything more than be destroyed – but he realised that neutrality was no longer an option open to him. Finally, in March, after months of real torment and misery, Yugoslavia signed a tripartite agreement with Germany and Italy, in which German troops and arms were given the right to travel through Yugoslavia in exchange for a promise that she would not be attacked herself. Paul's friends in England were amazed and horrified, even those who trusted him asking themselves whether he had gone mad. Indeed, the stress had brought him very close to breakdown, but at all times he had the aim of keeping Yugoslavia intact as his priority. He knew without needing to be told so by a Serb member of the Opposition, that 'if you accept the pact we shall accuse you of being pro-German. If you go to war we shall accuse you of dragging us into the war because of your wife.'

Within days of the signing Paul was ousted by a *coup d'état*. Peter, the young King, was put on the throne (after a fake proclamation read without Peter's knowledge on the wireless by someone claiming to be the King) and Paul and his family, now declared to be traitors to the Allies, were sent into exile. Paul and Olga, with their sons and daughter, all wept as they said farewell to the King. And he, suddenly faced with the realities from which Paul had protected him for so long, wept too. The family left in dignity and comfort for Greece. 'Poor little Peter tried to be brave and sensible, it was heartrending to leave him alone. As we parted he cried and begged to go with us,' Olga wrote in her diary.

The Foreign Office heard the news of the coup first, and Channon rang Marina to break the news to her. The next few days were grim for all Paul's family and friends: no one was sure he would not be killed by an assassin's bullet. British radio wrongly reported that the family had fled to Germany: they were by then in Greece, hoping to be allowed to go from there to England. The English had no intention of allowing them into the country: Marina, at lunch at Chequers with the Prime Minister, was told by Churchill that 'of course Prince Paul could not possibly come here', so for a while they waited, surrounded by Olga's family. In a gesture of solidarity the whole Greek royal family had collected at the station to meet the Regent and his family on their arrival from Belgrade. 'Mummy the only one to greet Paul very stiffly,' Olga recorded. 'Mummy, Paul & I retired to her salon to talk quietly and for him to explain his point. She listened, then turned on him terribly, implying our country could be sacrificed to save Greece!'

George of Greece, whose country had been so injured by Paul's signing of the agreement with Germany, was more forgiving, and told the British he was willing for Paul and his family to stay on in Greece. However, even this was too near home for either the new Yugoslav government or the British to stomach. After considering India and South America as places to keep Paul, it was decided to send him on to Cairo, then Kenya as a 'privileged prisoner'. The family had suffered further at the news of the German invasion and destruction of Yugoslavia: a week after they had left the country seventeen thousand people were killed in Belgrade by German bombers. On 14 April the troops had marched in. King Peter escaped to Greece and from there to England, where George Kent met him at Poole. On 28 April, Paul's birthday (although they had all forgotten it), he and Olga and their children arrived at their new home near Lake Naivasha, 70 miles from Nairobi. The house had belonged to the murdered Lord Erroll. It was a welcome they could have done without.

Peter meanwhile was welcomed in England by the rest of the British royal family. Bertie, as the boy's godfather, felt particularly responsible for him, writing in his diary 'I must look after him here. Perhaps it was destiny.' Peter's mother Queen Marie was already in England, living near Cambridge. The King encouraged Peter to join the RAF and to go to Cambridge

University, believing that he should become as Anglicised as possible.

The news of the coup and its after-effects was particularly hard for Marina. While Yugoslavia had remained neutral, Paul an official 'Friend' of the Allies, there had always been the possibility of communicating with her sister and the hope of seeing her. Now both Olga and Elizabeth were officially enemies (Toto was indeed pro-Hitler), while other members of her family and close friends including Lilia Ralli were living in a Greece occupied by the Germans.

On the credit side was the fact that, with work to occupy themselves, George and Marina were much happier than they had been for some time. Marina's love for George never wavered, but she could not but be crushed by the humiliations she had endured before the war. Now she found a new strength and George too, with other matters to concern him, was an easier man to live with. Coppins was more than ever a refuge, a place where the family could be together with friends and, temporarily at least, forget the troubles in the outside world. The Duke loved Coppins and his children, and would send away the nurse and give them their baths himself. Alexandra would, to the delight of her father, sometimes wear Marina's childhood uniform of the Greek Evzoni Guards – white kilt and stockings, pompom shoes and red hat.

Chips Channon reports a visit he made in the winter of 1940:

Tea ended in tragedy as little Edward became bumptious, and knocked over a table, spilling a kettle of hot water over his little pink legs, and he bellowed. The Duke lost his temper, the Duchess was in a flurry, nannies rushed in, but little Alexandra, delightfully unconcerned, turned round, and as if to change the subject said, 'I love soldiers, do you?' ... We had a lovely evening. I played backgammon with Princess Marina, whilst the Duke strummed Debussy. He is extremely intelligent, well-informed, but sometimes very nervous and irritable. She, on the other hand, is perfect, and it is touching to see her pride and pleasure in the Greek victories.

(Italy had attacked Greece in October 1940 but was surprised by the brave and determined resistance of that small country. Greece finally fell in April 1941 and King George escaped first to Crete and, when that too was taken, to Cairo.)

Noël Coward was another friend who would drive down to see the Kents at Coppins, and his diary also mentions happy visits. 'Found the Duke on the lawn sunning himself,' he wrote in the summer of 1941, 'Kents knitting and talking. Air raid and a certain amount of gun fire.'

Baroness de Stoeckl, who lived in a cottage belonging to the Kents at Iver, was another intimate who recorded her memories of the family:

I can still see the picture of those evenings when the Duke would be at home. We used to go over at about a quarter to nine, the Duchess looking a dream of beauty in an evening gown – always punctual. He would come in a little late, looking so sleek, so *soigné*, so good-looking. We would have a cocktail, and walk into the dining-room, the only light was from four long candles on the table ... we used to sit at the table until a quarter to eleven o'clock. I would long to get up, but that was his special hour of relaxation. He would talk and discuss and drink several cups of coffee. After dinner we used to walk towards the Music room. After a few minutes he would seat himself before one of the pianos and play endlessly.

The months of the war rolled on, filled with the often monotonous war work, with the details of daily life, and with waiting for a brighter future. George did not give up his collecting, nor did he give up on the work about which he felt most passionately – his attempts to clear Paul of Yugoslavia and open the path for him to return to England. George's loyalty was one of his finest qualities, and it was not in him to forget or forsake an old friend when times were hard. His work was two-fold: to try and keep Paul, who isolated in Kenya with all the time in the world on his hands was beginning to brood, sane and cheerful, and to try and persuade the government that Paul was not indeed a traitor, but a friend to England.

'No words can express ... our deep gratitude for your unfailing friendship and understanding,' Paul wrote to George in August 1941, five months into his exile. He continued,

You, who know me, will understand what it means to me to be considered as an enemy of England ... let me add that nothing can ever diminish our love for your dear country or change our feelings. We only live for the day when we can see the white cliffs and you all again. I know that that moment is far off and that it would be madness to suggest such a thing at present.

He goes on to say that no one in Yugoslavia knew as George did how much he hated his job

and that the last thing I wish is to have anything to do again with Yugoslav politics! I was longing for Peter's majority to release me from a dog's existence and I was at the end of my physical strength when the March events took place.

His description of their isolation and boredom is pitiful to read, and his admiration for his strong, loyal wife, is deeply moving. George resolved to do everything in his power to bring them both home to England. But by the time he presented his view of Paul – showing the letter quoted above and repeating facts told to Marina by Olga – the British government had decided against the Regent. George wrote to Paul that 'I know you were misjudged here at the time – but since then with the collapse of your country in three days – it was obvious that what you did was for the best – and to save the country for Peter,' but for the moment it was only obvious to Paul's oldest and loyalest friends. Winston Churchill, to whom George talked on Paul's behalf, was not at all forthcoming, 'he said it would be much better if you stayed where you were ... he is so busy with today and tomorrow that what happened yesterday or last week is of no interest.'

Cecil Beaton complained that 'the Duke of Kent refused to take the war more seriously than a tiresome interruption to his life,' but he did continue valiantly with his efforts on Paul's behalf. He succeeded in making the Yugoslav government agree to pay Paul's allowance (although the money did not come through regularly), in giving their son Alexander a place in the RAF, and in getting Olga and Marina's great friend Lilia Ralli to Kenya to be a companion to Olga.

After the collapse of Yugoslavia King Peter had arrived in England, where he was kept in the countryside with his mother (who had lived in England since 1937). He was not allowed to see any of his uncle's friends whom he had known for so many years – not the Kents, nor Channon, nor any of the others who had passed so often through Yugoslavia – and, weak as he was, he was easily brainwashed against his former guardian.

The Duke of Kent also found time to visit his mother as often as possible in her temporary home at Badminton. Queen Mary and her son discussed the ivy-clearance which had become her own private war (helped or more likely hindered by the Kent grandchildren) and visited nearby Bath, where they could share their common interest in antiques, and talk with an ease the old Queen did not feel with many. She complained to George of her frustration at 'not doing more publicly' for the war effort, and each night she drank half a bottle of hock, a habit threatened as the length of the war reduced the stocks in England.

In the summer of 1941 the children returned to Coppins. Bath having been bombed by the Germans in the Baedeker raids, Badminton no longer seemed the safest place for them. The most important family event during the early war years was the birth of a new baby in 1942. Miss Fox, Marina's childhood nurse, made the journey from London for the birth of Prince Michael, who was born at Coppins on 4 July and christened a month later at Windsor Castle. The American President, Franklin D. Roosevelt, was asked to stand godfather and accepted, sending 'his affectionate greetings' to the new Prince. 'Tell the Duchess that I count on seeing him as soon as the going is good,' added the President. 'The Duke seems to love this tiny infant,' Agnes de Stoeckl wrote in her diary. 'Every evening, instead of sitting late as usual, he leaves the table shortly after ten o'clock and carries his youngest son to the nursery and lays him in his cot and stands watching and watching. Nannie told me that each night she discreetly leaves the room, but she can hear the Duke talking softly to him.'

The baby was christened Michael George Charles Franklin in Windsor Chapel on 4 August. His other godfathers were George II of Greece and Haakon of Norway.

These were the last few weeks of the Duke of Kent's life. The family was at Coppins, which Beaton visited for a photographic session. The Duke was with his wife and children, carefree and at his best. His mother visited for an afternoon, and the family spent a pleasant day walking in the garden, playing with the

babies, George showing his mother some of his latest acqui-
sitions. 'He looked so happy with his lovely wife & the dear
baby,' Queen Mary wrote in her diary. His future engagements
included a tour of inspection of RAF bases in Finland, and
George left Coppins on 24 August for London, from where he
was to take the train to Scotland.

It should have been a tour like any other – and by now the
Duke was used to such tours. He had travelled 60,000 miles in
the preceding year, working hard but never seemingly in any
line of danger. This latest tour took place as a result of a
conversation George had had earlier in the year with his friend
of ten years' standing, Douglas Fairbanks Jnr. George, still at
heart dissatisfied with his war work, asked Fairbanks (who was
serving in the US Navy) if he could not manipulate the American
Air Force to use him as a liaison officer. Fairbanks arranged a
meeting between George and US Air Force General 'Tooey'
Spaatz, and Spaatz suggested that George fly to the RAF station
in Iceland. Once he was there, Spaatz would invite him to the
US base nearby and then ask officially for his services as a
liaison between the two bases. George agreed to the plan.

The Duke set off from the RAF station at Invergordon, in
Scotland on 25 August. He lunched with Group Captain Francis
while the experienced crew of the Sunderland flying boat which
was to take him to Iceland was briefed. The Duke himself
boarded the aircraft at just after one o'clock, and almost at once
the Sunderland was making its way across the calm waters of
the Cromarty Firth for its take-off. There were fourteen men
aboard apart from the Duke. Flight Lieutenant Frank Goyen,
an Australian with nearly a thousand hours' experience of flying
ocean patrols, was the captain, and all of the crew were experienced men. However, the four leading airmen – captain, first
and second pilots and first navigator – had only flown one short
flight together before.

For some reason never officially explained the plane flew far
too low, at only 700 feet in dense mist, and the inevitable
happened. Only Flight Sergeant Andrew Jack, the rear gunner,
survived the crash as his gun turret broke off and threw him
clear to the ground. He was badly burned pulling seven bodies,

including George's, from the plane, then passed out. He survived until 1978, but died without ever disclosing what had happened on the flight. His sister, Nancy Blows, says the only people Jack told the whole story to were Goyen's parents, and that they had been comforted by what he said. In 1955 he was on duty on a plane carrying Marina, who spent some time talking to him.

Sir Archibald Sinclair's report to the House of Commons, after the official inquiry had taken place, went as follows:

Before departure, the correct procedure for briefing the captain as to the exact route to be followed and for providing full information about the weather conditions likely to be encountered, was complied with. Local weather conditions were not good at the time of take-off, but the general indications showed a likelihood of improvement to the westward. The captain of the aircraft was a flying-boat pilot of long experience on the particular type of aircraft which he was flying that day, and of exceptional ability .... The Court found: First, that the accident occurred because the aircraft was flown on a track other than that indicated in the flight plan given to the pilot, and at too low an altitude to clear the rising ground on the track. Secondly, that the responsibility for this serious mistake in airmanship lies with the captain of the aircraft. Thirdly, that the examination of the propellers showed that the engines were under power when the aircraft struck the ground.

Despite this official closing of the subject, rumours persisted about the crash. It was claimed that the aircraft had been sabotaged, and even that the Duke of Kent himself had been at the controls, making the pilot error not so much Goyen's as his.

A more recent commentator, aviation expert Roy C. Nesbit, discussed the event in the magazine *Aeroplane Monthly*. He believes that the crash was simply caused by instrument error, probably the new gyro-magnetic compass. He thinks that the reading was misread or even altered during a demonstration and that 'the crash was caused by a failure of communication, coupled with very bad luck'. This explanation seems much more likely than the theory that British Intelligence killed him (based on the fact that before the war both he and Marina were widely thought to be pro-German). After all, beside the Duke of Windsor, George Kent was a minor liability.

At about twenty to two a shepherd, David Morrison, and his

son Hugh heard the sound of an aircraft coming through the mist towards them from the sea. Then came the noise of an enormous explosion as the aircraft smashed into the hillside and two and a half thousand gallons of aviation fuel exploded. The shepherd's son raised the alarm, taking his motorcycle first to the little hamlet of Braemore, where he alerted the inhabitants, and then on to Dunbeath, where there was a doctor and police. Search parties set out from Braemore and nearby Berriedale. The remains of the plane and bodies were not discovered until later that afternoon, when the doctor recognised the Duke of Kent's body, dressed in his flying suit. There was a deep cut in his head, but the face was recognisable and round the wrist was an identity bracelet, confirming that these were indeed the mortal remains of 'His Royal Highness the Duke of Kent, "The Coppins", Iver, Buckinghamshire'.

That evening the King was summoned from dinner at Balmoral by a telephone call from the Secretary of State for Air, Sir Archibald Sinclair. 'We were all left in silence at the table, each one of us, and particularly Queen Elizabeth, suspecting something awful had happened,' Alice, Duchess of Gloucester, recalls in her memoirs. 'The King came back and sat in silence. I could feel he was in deep distress and soon the Queen caught my eye, signalling me to rise with her and lead the ladies from the room. In the drawing-room we all assumed the news must be of Queen Mary's death .... Then the Queen left us and came back with the King who told us that it was the Duke of Kent who had been killed.' 'The news came as a great shock to me, and I had to break it to Elizabeth, & Harry & Alice who were staying with us .... We left Balmoral in the evening for London,' the King wrote in his diary that night, but it was his mother who was very much in his thoughts as he knew how much the old Queen had loved her youngest surviving son. She too was told the news over the telephone after dinner. 'I felt so stunned by the shock I could hardly believe it,' she wrote in her diary, and later mourned, 'He often used to say I looked nice. Nobody else ever did.' Cynthia Colville, her lady-in-waiting, wrote that 'the blow to Her Majesty was catastrophic, but I have never had more cause to admire wholeheartedly the Queen's courage and unselfish thought for others. "I must go to Marina tomorrow," she said.'

Whatever his faults, George was sincerely mourned by those who knew him. Even the steady, reliable King, who had had reason in his time to rebuke his wilder younger brother, missed not only George's presence, but his by now very real help. 'The war had brought him out in so many ways,' he wrote in his diary, 'Always charming to people in every walk of life . . . .' To Louis Greig he wrote, 'I shall miss him & his help terribly', and to Edwina Mountbatten, 'It really is a tragedy that [George] of all people, just when he was coming into his own, should have been taken from us. I shall miss him terribly.'

The tributes came in, official ones from foreign governments and unofficial ones from friends. Roosevelt sent telegrams to Marina, and to the King and Queen Mary. To Marina he wrote: 'I am shocked beyond measure at hearing of the tragic accident and I want you to know that I feel the loss very deeply and personally. He has given his life for his Nation and in a great cause. I am thinking much of you and the babies.' Marina's answer was simple, but not devoid of a personal touch: 'Am deeply touched by your kind and understanding sympathy and your appreciation of my beloved husband. Am heartbroken.' The letters poured in, but there was one notable silence. The Duke of Windsor, bitter in his exile, did not write to Marina to commiserate with her for the loss of her husband, his favourite brother. (If he did write, as some aver, Marina did not receive the letter. He did write to his mother, saying that he had written to Marina and he also penned a crabbed letter to Bertie.) The Duchess of Windsor meanwhile wrote to her aunt, 'it is a most tragic death, and I think his services will be greatly missed by Great Britain. He was the one with the most charm left at the job – and they made a couple more up with the advances of this world – in spite of the "turncoat" to us. We are both greatly shocked and distressed.'

For Marina the blow was heavy beyond imagining. Her youngest child was only seven weeks old and would never know his father. For the older two he would be just a vague memory. The news was broken to Marina by Miss Fox, who was still at

Coppins helping with the infant Prince, and for the first few days Marina was too numb to do more than weep and stare at the wall.

The following day Queen Mary, next to Marina possibly the person who had most loved George in his life, left Badminton for Coppins to be with her daughter-in-law. There the old Queen told Marina some home truths. Marina must not, she said, give in to self-pity and allow her grief to overcome her. Marina was a Princess and a royal Duchess. She had a new duty now, a duty to the thousands of other women whose husbands had died on active service. She must rise above her grief and be seen to be carrying out her work as normal.

Such advice may seem harsh, but it had the desired effect. 'How everything can utterly change ... I feel so stunned – it's all so unbelievable, yet day follows day and one goes on doing, mechanically, the same things,' Marina wrote to a friend. Marina, too, knew her duty. She had been trained to it long before she married George and had watched her parents fight against their feelings as their own circumstances worsened.

George's body was brought from Scotland to London in one of the long, mournful processions that had dogged Marina's family. The body had been guarded overnight by aircraftmen at Dunrobin Castle, and from there was taken to the local railway station where it, with the remains of other victims of the crash, made the journey back to London. From London the coffin was driven to the Albert Memorial Chapel at Windsor. Soon after it was in place Marina went to Windsor and spent a quarter of an hour alone with her husband's remains. She did the same again the following day.

George's funeral was held at St George's Chapel, Windsor. 'I have attended very many family funerals in the Chapel, but none have moved me in the same way .... Everybody there I knew well, but I did not dare look at any of them for fear of breaking down,' wrote the King. It was not a large funeral ('short and explicit' noted Bertie), but five monarchs came to pay their respects: King Haakon of Norway, King George of Greece, King Peter of Yugoslavia, Queen Wilhelmina of the Netherlands and of course King George of England. There were no representatives of the King's government, but some of George's staff were there, among them Lala Bill, the nanny who had looked after all six of George V's children, and Frederick Field, who had been George's chauffeur for thirteen years. Marina stood between her mother-in-law and sister-in-law, the two Queens. After the funeral cortège had entered the chapel – the Duke's body, preceded by his insignia carried by two of his equerries, was borne by four air vice-marshals and two air marshals – Marina sank to her knees, where she spent most of the rest of the service.

The coffin carried George's Air Force cap and was decorated with two bouquets: a bunch of flowers picked from the garden at Coppins by Marina and a wreath from the King and Queen. The service was kept simple and the mourners were few, led by the King in Royal Air Force uniform. Beside him were the Duke of Gloucester and Admiral Sir Lionel Halsey, representing the Duke of Windsor (who had recently taken up the governorship of the Bahamas, much to George's disgust – 'to accept to be the governor of a small place like that is fantastic!' he had written). The Duke of Windsor, at the memorial service in Nassau Cathedral, wept like a child throughout.

Noël Coward, an old friend of the Duke's and by now a friend of Marina's too, drove to Windsor for the funeral. 'Was given a seat in the choir very close to everything – almost too close to be borne,' he recorded in his diary. He continued,

The service was impressive and supremely dignified. I tried hard not to cry, but it was useless. When the Duchess came in with the Queen and Queen Mary I broke a bit, and when the coffin passed with flowers from the garden at Coppins and Prince George's cap on it I was finished. I then gave up all pretence and just stood with the tears splashing down my face. I was relieved and heartened to see that both Dickie [Mountbatten] and the King were doing the same thing. The thought that I shall never see him again is terribly painful.

After it was all over and the King had sprinkled the earth and the Royalties had gone away, we all went up one by one to the vault and bowed and secretly said goodbye to him. Then we went out into very strong sunlight. Margot Oxford came up to me and said, 'Very well done, wasn't it?' as though she had been at a successful first night. I thought this offensive and unforgivable.

George's death was not only a personal loss to the royal family, but was also felt as a loss on a wider scale. After Buckingham Palace was bombed Queen Elizabeth said, 'I'm glad we've been bombed. It makes me feel I can look the East End in the face.' It had been seen that the royal family could be touched by the bombing (Kensington Palace had also been hit), it was now seen that it too could be tragically bereaved.

Prime Minister Winston Churchill spoke in the House of Commons of the Duke of Kent, and as was usual with him the speech rang with eloquence:

The loss of this gallant and handsome Prince in the prime of his life has been a shock to all the people of the British Empire .... I knew the late Duke of Kent ... his overpowering desire to render useful service to his King and Country in this period when we are all of us on trial. The Duke of Kent was ready to waive his rank, to put aside all ceremony, to undergo any amount of discomfort and danger in order to feel that he was making a real contribution to our national struggle for life and honour .... There is something about death on active service which makes it different from common or ordinary death in the normal course. It is accepted without question by the fighting men. Those they leave behind them are also conscious of a light of sacrifice and honour which plays around the grave or the tomb of the warrior. They are, for the time being, uplifted. This adds to their fortitude but it does not in any way lessen their pain. Nothing can fill the awful gap, nothing assuage or comfort the loneliness and deprivation which fall on the wife and children when the prop and centre of their home is suddenly snatched away. Only faith in a life after death, in a brighter world where dear ones will meet again – only that and the measured tramp of time can give consolation. The Duke of Kent had a joyous union and a happy family ... and I say, without hesitation, that all our thoughts go out in sympathy to H.R.H. The Duchess of Kent, the beautiful and stricken Princess, who, in her turn, tastes the bitter tribulation which war brings to so many.

Of course Marina had tasted this 'bitter tribulation' before, but never quite so harshly as now.

A more bizarre tribute, published in *The Times* on 2 September, came from the diary of Air Marshal H. Edwards, who had met George during his visit to Canada in 1941:

In the course of my time in this, the forty-ninth year of my life, I have seen and met many dear and sweet people. In all these long years I have known characters strange, strong, and weak; men kind and cruel; men of supreme intelligence and others of lesser wit.

I have felt the warmth of friendship and the delight of battle. I have seen a good part of this world, aground and from the air in many places.

I have felt the keen sense of something done. I have felt the bitterness, the disappointment of things unfathomable.

But in my 49 years I have not felt the warmth I do to-night, for I have seen and felt something I have never seen or felt before. A new character distinct and certain has been added to my memories; a character so fine and delicate; a character so gentle, so superb: a character not now entirely strange to me. Always mindful of duty and of the thoughts of others. A calm spirit in a world of tears.

Perhaps I shall be forgotten before this day is out, but I shall not forget.

Three weeks after George's death the King drove to Berriedale, from where he walked to see for himself where the accident had happened. He met those who had helped in the search and found the bodies. 'The remains of the aircraft had been removed, but the ground for 200 yds long & 100 yds wide had been scored and scorched by its trail & by flame,' he wrote on returning to Balmoral. 'It hit one side of the slope, turned over in the air & slid down the other side on its back. The impact must have been terrific as the aircraft as an aircraft was unrecognisable when found. I felt I had to do this pilgrimage.' If there was any comfort to be gleaned, it was that the Duke and his companions must have died at once.

Such a violent and sudden death, even in war time, jarred everybody who had known the carefree young Duke. On the day after George's death, Noël Coward wrote in his diary:

I can hardly believe it, but of course that is nonsense because I believe it only too well. It is never difficult to believe that someone young and charming and kind is dead. They are always dying. The Duke of Windsor ... etc., remain alive but Prince George has to die by accident. Well, there goes a friendship of nineteen years. I shall miss him most horribly. He may have had his faults, but he was kind always and I feel absolutely miserable. Years ago I stopped being impressed by him being Prince George, especially in the last years when I have seen him so much. I talked to him on Sunday .... And now, suddenly, I must know that I shall never see him again. I am taking this resentfully and personally. I am so deeply sorry for the poor Duchess. I wrote to her this morning, of course, a rather inarticulate letter. It is a beastly tragedy. In memoriam I say, 'Thank you for your friendship for me over all these years and I shall never forget you.'

After the funeral, Marina was alone again at Coppins. Despite her mother-in-law's stern words, she was totally bereft and the family was in despair as to how to help her. It was Bertie who, knowing how important Marina's family was to her, realised that only one of her close relations could help her through the immediate trauma of her widowhood. There was no question of Elizabeth being allowed into the country, or of Princess Nicholas being able to leave occupied Greece, but Bertie persuaded Churchill (who had been so adamant on the subject of Paul and Olga's coming to live in England) to allow him to send for Olga. As soon as the Prime Minister had cleared it, he sent a telegram to Olga in Kenya and she and Lilia Ralli left Nairobi together on 10 September, arriving at Coppins a week later.

Olga had intended to stay only a month, but she found that Marina's need for her was even greater than Paul's, and so put off her return. Although the Duchess of Kent was a much loved figure in England, Paul was not, and before long questions began to be asked in the House as to what Olga was doing in England. One Conservative MP, Captain Alec Cunningham-Reid, seemed particularly vengeful, determined to stir up anti-Paul propaganda in the press and to have Olga deported from the country. He pointed out that her mother was Russian, that she was a loyal wife to a 'dangerous traitor', and called her a 'sinister woman'. 'If you are a quisling and you happen to be royalty, it appears that you are automatically trusted and forgiven,' he said. And a month later he still had not allowed the subject to drop: 'Has not this lady been allowed to be in a position whereby if she return to Kenya she will be able to convey information to her quisling husband which might be invaluable to the Axis?' he asked in December, when Olga was still in England. The government answer from Anthony Eden was brisk: 'The circumstances are well known. Princess Olga was the only sister of the Duchess of Kent who could come to this country at all, and it was with the government's full authority and with their approval and I have no apology to make for it.' His speech was met with cheers: but for Cunningham-Reid it appeared the House was behind Marina and, by implication, in favour of Olga's staying in the country.

Finally it became apparent that Paul's need was greater than Marina's. He was sinking deep into a depression from which the doctors began to fear he would not recover, so on 31 December, four months after George's death, Olga finally returned to her husband in Kenya. Now Marina was truly left alone with her children to face up to her widowhood.

CHAPTER SEVEN

A Princess Alone

Despite her overwhelming grief, Marina took Queen Mary's words to heart. Soon after George's death she wrote to a friend and her letter shows how she was building up her strength. 'I know that I have many tasks ahead and I pray for strength and courage to carry on as he would wish me to – for his dear sake and our children's and the country's. I try not to think of the lonely future. I know he is always very near me – but oh, the aching of one's heart and mind.'

It was only ten weeks after her husband's death that Marina put on her uniform and returned to work. Her first job, on 4 November, was a visit to a Wrens' training centre in London. To work was her duty, and Marina never shirked her duty. Of course the realisation that life must go on comes to every widow, and the presence of small children makes that realisation the more acute. Add to that the family, the war and Marina's upbringing and it was inevitable that she would hide her private sorrow as soon as she could and re-enter public life.

Marina kept her grief private, but she did not allow it to dim for a long, long time. It was months before she gave up her almost weekly visits to pray by George's tomb. On his fortieth birthday, four months after his death, she put a wreath of clover carnations, his favourite flowers, on the crypt. Both James Wentworth Day and Stella King, who wrote early biographies of Princess Marina, say that for years after George's death all mention of his name was forbidden, all photographs and por-traits of him removed before any public engagement for fear the Duchess's grief would overwhelm her. King quotes an unnamed 'royal relation' who said, 'She [Marina] was lost without him. Her whole life revolved around him and she had no one else.' While this is certainly true, Steven Runciman, who became a close friend of Marina's only after the war, says that she never mentioned her husband's name to him. He believes that while he is sure she never stopped loving George, Marina began to question whether she should have loved him as much as she did. Only with the passage of time did she distance herself enough from her love for her husband to question why he had treated her as badly as had sometimes been the case.

The King's instinct to bring Olga to Marina was as successful as it was kind. By the time Olga left for Kenya, Marina's recovery was under way. She had taken over many of George's patronages, thus increasing her own workload, and her old friends were picking up the habit of driving down to Coppins for tea or a night. Mrs Roosevelt was one of the first visitors, and brought with her a crate of oranges for her husband's godson, perhaps remembering how his father had enjoyed the same luxury when staying at her country house in America. Queen Wilhelmina of the Netherlands visited her godson Michael and his family in early November, while Chips came for a night later in the same month:

The Duchess has rearranged her sitting room, kept the Duke's just as it was, and has shut up the music room .... We went up to bed about midnight, and I was haunted by the spirit of the Duke. Every room and object is so inspired by him, the house, in fact, is him .... The house still vibrates with his vivacious personality.

If her sister's love and concern had helped Marina through the first months of her widowhood, concern for her sister and brother-in-law later helped Marina in her adjustment to daily life. While Olga had been in England Marina had done her best to hide the newspapers with reports of Cunningham-Reid's behaviour from her. She had someone other than herself to consider. Her own tragedy had, in a sense, now happened. Her sister's might yet be ahead of her.

Olga's return to Kenya did not have the effect on Prince Paul that the doctors had hoped. Cunningham-Reid's attacks on Olga had been relayed in Kenya and Paul could not bring himself to enter the narrow social circle available to him. He lay in bed with a gun under his pillow, occasionally drinking hot chocolate. At the end of January Olga wrote in her diary:

Pulled through another day – the same eternal discussions on our future. Sh. [Major Sharpe, the retired officer who kept Paul under surveillance] told P that the Gov had a second wire from Oliver [Oliver Stanley, Secretary of State for the Colonies] instructing him to look for a house nearer Nairobi. P can talk of nothing but the subject of his treatment – he doesn't care any more where he lives: only that he will die if he stays here. Eats less than ever and smokes all day – it wears one out and I can't keep Marina in the know each day: even when I do I know the wires are copied.

The bereaved will know how useful it is to have someone else to worry about, and Marina was clearly worried about Paul.

Finally, after the Governor of Kenya had telegraphed Oliver Stanley with the results of a second medical opinion, stating that if Paul's 'present state of acute depression is allowed to persist, the development of insanity in the form of melancholia is definitely to be feared', it became apparent that Paul and Olga must be moved. Only Winston Churchill, who had for so long been so opposed to Paul's coming to England, continued to fight against any improvement in the ex-regent's lot. 'I really do not see why we should worry about this man who did so much harm to his country .... Considering the terrible things that are going on in Yugoslavia, I should think Prince Paul is very lucky to be confined under such easy conditions,' he noted in a memo to Stanley. However, Churchill was, on this occasion, overruled and in June 1943 Paul, Olga and their three children left Kenya for South Africa, where their conditions improved immediately.

Marina's own conditions, however, were not as good as might have been hoped. Marina, presumably assuming that she would not need it, refused the RAF pension for an air commodore's widow (which would have brought her £398 a year). With George's death his income from the Civil List (£25,000 a year) stopped, and there was no provision made for widows of sons of the King. It was an oversight due to the fact that when George VI's Civil List was drawn up at the beginning of his reign there were no such widows in the family. It was nevertheless an oversight that was at first to cost Marina. Parliament could have rectified the position, but it was felt tactless to apply for money during the war and after the war, with England in the grip of post-war austerity, it would have been no better. Marina was of course not poor by the standards of most people living in Britain – not even by the standards she had known in exile in Paris with her family. But all her friends agree that after George's death Marina was, if not exactly impoverished, 'hard-up'. The Duke of Kent had been left three quarters of a million pounds by his father, an enormous sum of money in 1936. George was rich, and had assumed that he would always be so. He spent money with ease, especially on beautifying Coppins. Just before George's death Channon, on a visit to Iver, had remarked to his diary again on the glories of the house: 'How *gemutlich* Coppins is, and how full of rich treasures, and gold boxes, *étuis* and pretty expensive objects always being exchanged or moved about. The Duke adores his possessions.' Rich himself, and married to a vastly rich Guinness, Channon was not a man easily impressed by the spending of great sums of money – in 1935 he had remarked, 'it is very difficult to spend less than £200 a morning when one goes out shopping,' and he knew of himself that he 'loved money for its spending sake'. His own house in Belgrave Square was stunning in its luxury. His friend Marina's house, then, must have been full of magnificent treasures indeed for Channon to remark upon them quite so regularly.

The problem, though, lay not so much in how George had spent his money, but in how he had bequeathed it. Everything, including Coppins, was in trust for his children, which left Marina with almost nothing to live on. Marina realised as soon as 1943 that something must be done to raise money and in November – just over a year after George's death – there was a sale. George's great-aunt, Louise, Duchess of Argyle, had left him some furniture which raised £20,000 for Marina and her children and put off any immediate financial hardship.

Marina had, of course, had good training in the art of thrift. Her years in Paris had given her habits which she had never fully broken and which she now found only too easy to resurrect completely. Her clothes were not always couture – she was the first member of the royal family to wear off-the-peg items, but her elegance was such that no one ever guessed. Marina was notorious for paying low wages to her staff, and for keeping fewer staff than she really needed (of course none of the royal family is said to be generous with salaries). Marina would borrow dresses from designers, wear then for one evening, and return them – and which designer would refuse to dress the most stylish member of the royal family, even without payment? It is said that once she even passed on a bunch of flowers sent her by her friend Sir Malcolm Sargent – she replaced his card with one of her own and sent the roses on to Princess Marie Louise.

Neither the sale nor the thrift was enough to ensure Marina's future, though, and other sales were to follow. In March 1947 there was another auction of Marina's possessions. This one was much larger, and Marina had to part with more than one great-aunt's legacy this time. Furniture, silver, pictures and porcelain all went under the hammer to raise £92,341 for the Duchess. (It is interesting to note that a Queen Anne sofa raised 1,700 guineas; when sold on in 1965 by R.F. Heathcote Amory's estate it only fetched 700 guineas. Presumably the fact that Marina was selling had inflated the value.) Another £12,426 was raised in June 1962 by the sale of various *objets d'art*, mostly pieces of Fabergé which went to the leading dealer, Wartskis.

Rumours abounded about the Duchess's future plans. It was said that she was to go to Hollywood, that she was going to America to make a living. Finally the British Ambassador in Washington issued an official denial that the Duchess had any plans to leave England. The truth was that although poorer than before, Marina certainly had no need to become a Hollywood actress or take any other such extreme measure to earn money. George VI and Queen Mary both gave her an allowance and, even with three children to educate and Coppins to keep up, there was never any danger of real poverty.

Marina no longer had a London house – she and George had left Belgrave Square expecting to go to Australia, but Marina needed a base from which to fulfil her London engagements.

Queen Mary, ever a partisan of her goddaughter, gave her some rooms in Marlborough House, but Coppins remained the family's home. Marina's greatest comfort was of course the three children. As we have seen, family – immediate and extended – had always been one of the most important influences in Marina's life, and when George was killed every instinct told her to draw her children closer. At George's death they were aged only seven, six and seven weeks, and as the years went by Marina found herself making important decisions on her own. A comical moment in 1949 came with the publication in a socialist propaganda feature of a bouncing baby, to illustrate how healthcare in England was better than ever before. 'The prams of Britain are filled with the bonniest babies in living memory,' ran the caption. The baby in question turned out to be Eddie Kent who, now thirteen, was far too large for prams. The picture had been taken in June 1936. An apology was issued.

The year after his father's death Edward (always known as Eddie) was sent to prep school at Ludgrove in Berkshire, the school that the present Prince of Wales's sons were later to attend. From there he went to Eton, but despite having a holiday tutor he did not finish the course. In 1951 Eddie was taken away from Eton and sent for a year to Le Rosey in Switzerland (where Crown Prince Alexander of Yugoslavia was later to follow him). The reason given for this change of plan was 'ill health': he had been a victim of hay fever since his early childhood and it was thought that the pure Swiss air might cure him. A royal Prince had little choice, even by the fifties, of anything other than a service career and both Edward and later Michael (who had also been sent to Eton) went to Sandhurst from where Edward joined the Royal Scots Dragoon Guards and Michael the 11th Hussars. (It is very unlikely that George would have put his sons through the same bizarre education as his, and Marina was not tempted to commit her boys to a naval education in memory of their father.)

After seven years with a Scottish governess, Miss Katherine Peebles (who, after teaching the Kent children went on to teach the Queen's four children), Princess Alexandra was also educated away from home, becoming the first English Princess to go to boarding school. The decision had not been Marina's alone: in this as in all things related to her British family the King's views were important, and it was he who encouraged the idea of giving Alexandra the chance to become an 'ordinary' child. She went sent first to Heathfield in Ascot, Berkshire and from there she went to live in Paris for a while with the Comte de Paris, the Pretender to the French throne. The Comte's sister had married Marina's uncle Christopher (after his first wife, Nancy Leeds, died), so there was a family connection to explain this choice of temporary home for the girl. Nevertheless, that Alexandra was there, and not with her aunt Olga and uncle Paul, who were also living in Paris at the time, points the fact that Marina did not want Alexandra too much under the young Elizabeth's influence. While living with the Parises (who had eleven children), Alexandra went to a finishing school and also took extra piano lessons.

By the end of 1943 Marina was back at work full-time, and working harder than ever. She had taken over nearly thirty of George's patronages, and added more of her own. She even, in deference to George's years as the 'factory inspector' of the family, unofficially took on the same chore. A few times a month Marina would make time for an informal visit to some factory whose work was aiding the war effort, and after the war the visits continued, again to her enduring popularity. In one factory, Sankey at Wellington, Shropshire, one of the aisles between the machines had to be widened to make room for the buggy which, because of her lameness, had been made to carry her around the factory. For years afterwards the widened aisle was affectionately known as 'The Old Kent Road' in memory of the visit.

Another of the jobs Marina took over from George – but this officially – was the presidency of the All England Lawn Tennis and Croquet Club. The year 1949 was the first in which she presented the Wimbledon cup to the men's single's winner (Ted Schroeder), and Marina came never to miss a day of Wimbledon during the great tournament each year. (Her involvement was not just seasonal, either: Marina visited the club and took an active interest throughout the winter months as well.) For many people this is their chief memory of the Duchess of Kent – a slim elegant figure in the front of the Royal Box, eagerly watching each Centre Court match, then with that very faint, only just discernible limp, making her way to present the winner's plate to such as Little Mo and Billy Jean King.

Even with the children away at boarding school and no host there, Coppins continued to be a lively and welcoming house to Marina's many friends. The Duchess was one of those people who kept her friendships from different areas of her life very separate. Daska Maclean never met the 'theatrical' friends of Marina, the likes of Noël Coward, Cecil Beaton and Danny Kaye who provided her with so much of the fun in her life. But while Marina kept her friends separate, she never lost any of them. Indeed, all her women friends – those closest to her – came from her past. George had welcomed them into his house, had visited them on their continental holidays, and now that Marina was alone again they were more than ever needed. Apart from her sisters, there were of course her many cousins. Some of them (such as Prince Philip's four sisters) were separated from her by the war, others had already settled in England. Victoria Milford Haven (the Tsarina's sister who was in large part responsible for bringing up Philip of Greece) was of course much older than Marina, but until her death in 1950 they often met and her son David was a close friend. Poppy Baring, with whom both George and Bertie had been in love, was a good friend, while Princess Lilia Ralli was perhaps her closest friend, a cruising companion of the happy pre-war holidays and the woman who had come with Olga to comfort Marina in her first days of widowhood. Daska Maclean, with whose parents Marina and George had often stayed outside Dubrovnik, was now married to an Englishman and she and Marina remained in close touch. Turia Campbell, with whom Marina and Olga had sat together on the long evenings during the Abdication Crisis, remained close, as did Lady Zia Wernher, another Russian friend. Natasha Johnston, a Russian Princess married to Sir Charles Johnston, was another friend from Marina's childhood to whom she gave active help when Lady Johnston fell upon hard times. Agnes de Stoeckl, the mother of another friend, Zoia Paklevsky, was given a house on the Coppins estate by George and Marina when she had nowhere to go and no money. All Marina's friends emphasise again and again her generosity and loyalty.

Without George, Marina saw less of her sisters-in-law than before. There was never any outright break, but the fact remained that Alice Gloucester and the Queen would never naturally be friends of Marina. George had been their link and, with him dead, there was nothing else to draw them together. She was always, however subliminally, aware of her own royal blood and however hard her sisters-in-law worked at their jobs there was always the feeling that they had learned their trade. By inclination, too, they were very different. Marina was shy, but she enjoyed the social life that smart London had to offer. She enjoyed theatres and parties and bright talk, while her sisters-in-law were both happiest at home. Queen Elizabeth and the Duchess of Gloucester were happy to join in the family traditions, and would willingly spend a cold wet Norfolk day outside with the guns, while Marina preferred the warmth of a Sandringham fire. Marina loved her children, and her family was the central fact and *raison d'être* of her life. This did not mean that she did not want to enjoy a more frivolous life away from home. As Princess Margaret's friend Peter Townsend wrote 'I longed to know this gifted woman better, but felt too shy to insist in face of the sophisticated company with which she often surrounded herself. I believe that wit and brilliance were more effective at buoying up her spirits than the searching, nostalgic conversations I had with her.'

Many of Prince George's racier set had become close and genuine friends to Marina, and his death did not sever these friendships. Chips continued to call at Coppins and to entertain Marina when she was in London. Cecil Beaton, who so long before had crowed with delight at his burgeoning acquaintance with George, became in the end one of Marina's closest friends. She would go with him to his theatrical productions, and they would take holidays together. In the summer of 1949 Marina went to Paris for a charity ball, and Beaton took her and Lilia Ralli on a tour of the Paris nightclubs. Noël Coward was disapproved of by Queen Mary, but although he too had a soft spot for the aristocracy there is no doubt that his feelings for the Duchess of Kent were sincere. Douglas Fairbanks Jnr, who lived in London, was another of the showbusiness circle as was Danny Kaye. Some believe both Coward and Fairbanks to have been Marina's lovers and gossip at the time even claimed Beaton as a flame. The last is certainly untrue. Christopher Warwick, in his biography of Marina, hints without any evidence that Kaye became Marina's lover. They certainly went to the same parties – for instance one given by Georgia Sitwell in February 1948, and a supper party for fifty given by Channon the following month. Marina was as loyal to her English friends as she was to her childhood friends. In 1948 she broke royal protocol by attending a non-royal memorial service for Laura Corrigan, the London 'hostess' who was so popular among the Channon set. (George V had gone to Kitchener's memorial service during the First World War, so Marina was not the first to break that tradition as is sometimes claimed.) She was later (1967) to do the same for Malcolm Sergeant, another close friend.

As well as the old Russian–Greek–Yugoslav circle and the showbusiness circle, Marina visited the old aristocracy of England. She stayed at Antony House, Sir John Carew-Pole's Cornish estate, with the Duke and Duchess of Buccleuch at Boughton. These friends were the ones most approved of and encouraged by the old Queen, and indeed were those most to be expected of a sister-in-law to the King. Marina naturally felt totally at ease in such surroundings, where the sorts of word-games at which she excelled were played (not just in English) until the early hours of the morning.

Any member of the public who had anything to do with Marina fell under her spell. There was something about the combination of her kindness, her curiosity about other people and their lives ('Tell me, what *is* an El-san?' she once asked Princess Alexandra's dancing teacher, Stephanie Tanner) and the aura of royalty that won hearts. Squadron Leader Jimson Parsons's own personal experience of Marina's kindness was typical. In August 1944 he was travelling with secret papers from King's Cross to Scotland, where they were to be delivered to Group Captain the Duke of Hamilton. When he arrived at the station, he found that apart from his compartment the whole of the rest of the sleeper had been reserved for Marina, her children and party, who were on their way to Balmoral:

Soon after leaving King's Cross, an aide arrived in my compartment to tell me that the Duchess was asking if I would like to share her party's picnic. I needed no persuasion as I had only managed to buy a Spam sandwich at King's Cross. As I consumed fresh salmon, followed by fresh peaches (all 'off season', of course), washed down by hock, the Duchess appeared at my door and came and sat on my bed – perhaps because, as you know, she had only one good leg. I have no memory at all of what we talked about for ten minutes or so, but her immense beauty and charm and, perhaps most of all, her great kindness and thoughtfulness, made an impact on me which has never faded .... [My] only other memory of the journey is of the liveliness and energy which the present Duke of Kent displayed in the corridor of the train before he retired to his bed.

This kind of behaviour was typical of Marina, even off duty.

The year after George's death Marina asked a friend to visit the scene of the accident and pray for her husband. It was not until four years later that Marina felt able to make the journey herself, although as we know she had been at Balmoral during the intervening years. In 1946, accompanied by the doctor who had been there on the day of the crash and some friends, Marina walked to the long black scar which still remained in the hill. It was a pilgrimage she was not to repeat for another six years. The next time she visited the site of the crash was in August 1952 when she took her children with her from Balmoral during the summer holiday. By then a granite cross had been raised to the memory of George and the men who had died with him in the Sunderland.

Meanwhile, as always for Marina, family affairs took a high priority. Coppins was more than once used as a haven for royal lovers, who needed somewhere to court and be courted away from the (even then) avid public eye. Princess Aspasia, widow of the unfortunate King Alexander (he who had died of a monkey bite) was openly ambitious for her anorexic daughter Alexandra. The war had brought them both to England too and she rung Daska Maclean, thinking that as a Yugoslav she might have access to the young King Peter, and invited herself and her daughter to lunch. Mrs Maclean was honoured by the self-invitation, but puzzled until she realised the motive. As soon as

Madame Aspasia discovered that Mrs Maclean did not know the King, she made her excuses and she and her daughter left. She sent Alexandra to work for the Red Cross in Cambridge, as Peter was at the university, and there she had more luck. He left the university after a few months and pursued some of his courtship under Marina's wing at Coppins. Alexandra later said that Marina had been the first person she had confided in over the love affair, and told Peter that Marina had helped them enormously by talking to Bertie and making him see their point of view. As 'Koom' (or godfather) it was actually one of Bertie's duties to give advice on both education and marriage, so his consent was very important to the couple. Both Queen Marie and the Yugoslav government in exile were against the match as Peter was two and half years younger than Alexandra and it was felt that because of his youth and his unsettled position the marriage should not take place. The couple was to marry at the Yugoslav Embassy in London in March 1944, without Marie's blessing (she stayed away, claiming toothache). But with the King of England as best man and many royal guests including Marina present it was official, not an elopement.

Another romance Marina helped further was that of Princess Katherine of Greece, King Constantine's daughter. She brought her commoner lover Major Richard Brandram to Coppins after she had met him on shipboard from Greece in 1946. (They married in Athens in 1947, Katherine being given the rank of duke's daughter by George VI.)

Historically speaking the most important of all the matches Marina was instrumental in bringing about was that between her young first cousin, Prince Philip of Greece, and her husband's niece, Princess Elizabeth. While at school at Gordonstoun and throughout the war Philip, separated from the rest of his immediate family, had had a second home at Coppins and it was there, at a small private party, that Philip and Elizabeth first danced together. Channon had remarked to his diary as early as January 1941 that the 'extraordinarily handsome' Philip 'is to be our Prince Consort, and that is why he is serving in our Navy. He is charming, but I deplore such a marriage; he and Princess Elizabeth are too inter-related.' By January 1944 he had forgotten his earlier certainty, writing that 'I do believe a marriage may well be arranged one day between Princess Elizabeth and Prince Philip of Greece,' and by October of that year he noticed that the Coppins visitors' book was full of Philip's signature. 'It is at Coppins that he sees Princess Elizabeth. I think she will marry him.' Marina's part in the romance drew her niece closer to her and it was with this marriage that she really returned to the bosom of the family.

The marriage did not, in fact, take place until 20 November 1947. Alexandra and Michael were bridesmaid and page, and Marina and Queen Frederika of Greece later made what Channon called 'a secret visit to the affronted German relations, to tell them about the Wedding'. Nor had the Duke and Duchess of Windsor been invited to the wedding, Queen Mary in particular feeling that the Duchess was not fit to be invited to witness a holy sacrament: she did, however, write to David describing the event. The Princess Royal did not go to the wedding, giving a 'chill' as the excuse. Many thought she boycotted it in support of David, whom she felt should have been asked. Six months later there was another party at Coppins, in honour of the young Edinburghs. Princess Elizabeth wore black lace, dressed as an infanta, and danced until five in the morning. Prince Philip, looking tired, was a great success in his policeman's uniform. 'He and Princess Elizabeth seemed supremely happy and often danced together ... and the Duchess in her shimmering white dress looked as lovely as the blue dawn itself,' wrote Channon, who of course was at the ball. There is no doubt that Marina was at times lonely, but she never lost the ability to have fun and to enable others to enjoy themselves with her. As Princess Alexandra was later to say, 'Mother always makes fun out of everything, both for herself and for us.' Marina continued to enjoy dancing, and used to take young men out with her. There was one Oxford undergraduate often seen walking around the town with his coat collar turned up because he had been too busy dancing with Marina to pick up his laundry.

Steven Runciman remembers having her to stay in his Scottish house. He says that she always enjoyed the isolation of his home, and the fact that she could just put on a headscarf and take herself for a walk on her own. 'I always did my own cooking, and I can't bear anyone coming into the kitchen, but she would love to come in and see what was happening.' He went to the lengths of locking the door, but still the Duchess found her way into the kitchen. Presumably few of her friends did their own cooking, and she found Sir Steven's work a diversion.

Perhaps one of the most important events of Marina's post-war life was the appointment in 1948 of Philip Hay as her Personal Private Secretary. Educated at Harrow and Cambridge, Hay had learned the horrors of life on the Burma Railway during the war. He recuperated in Italy, joined the picture department of Spinks, and married Lady Margaret Seymour, later a lady-in-waiting to Princess Elizabeth. Hay was a civilised and cultured man, who was to become much more than a courtier to Marina, a close and trusted friend and, in Steven Runciman's words, 'the pivot of her life'. Channon described him a 'the handsome Comptroller to the Duchess of Kent, who looks like a policeman and is well-meaning but, like all courtiers, slowly becoming pompous'. Pompous or not, he provided an essential emotional rock for the Duchess for the rest of her life, and became a father-figure to Marina's three children. It is undisputed that Hay was Marina's lover, but it was a relationship conducted with the utmost discretion throughout. Hay's surviving relations attest to the fact of there having been a love affair. The true depth of the relationship between Marina and her 'handsome Comptroller' was, and remains, a private affair. On the public level Hay's contribution to Marina and her children was enormous: it was he who arranged their foreign tours and his *Times* obituary in 1986 gives him much of the credit for their success. Later Hay was to become Comptroller to Marina, and after her death he continued to provide a wise and friendly ear to her children. Indeed his influence continued as he looked after Prince Michael's financial affairs. He was a brilliant financial advisor, and in that position alone would have proved of use to the family. As public relations officer he was sometimes brusque, but always respected. He was an old fashioned courtier and a loyal and discreet friend.

After the war the normal routines of family life were reinstated – without, of course, the presence of the children's father. There were holidays at Sandringham, the Kents went to Bexhill-on-Sea for an out of season holiday. The children visited Jersey and Sussex, Marina wishing to emulate the English seaside holidays that she herself had enjoyed as a child. In 1951 Marina took all three children to France for the summer to visit Paris and stay in a converted mill near Grasse in Provence.

The war years had seen more changes in Marina's family life. George II's return to Greece had not been easy nor had it lasted very long. The Greeks under George fought off an Italian invasion, but the Germans were more successful. When they invaded Greece the royal court fled the mainland in an RAF Sunderland flying boat for Crete. Then, when that island was also taken over (at the end of May 1941) the court and government in exile moved between Egypt, South Africa and London. Unlike Paul of Yugoslavia, George II was hailed as a hero in England, and was awarded the DSO in recognition of his courage in the face of the enemy in Crete. He was the only reigning monarch to be so decorated. In December 1944, while the King was in London, the factional fighting in Greece had reached the point where he was forced by Eden and Churchill, for the sake of peace, to agree not to return to his country without another plebiscite. The British government presumably did not know that the King's enemies were not so much anti-monarchist as Communist. After the British had liberated Athens Communist guerrillas attacked the capital: by the time Churchill sanctioned the use of force by the British troops and the Communists were routed, they had killed twenty thousand people in Athens alone.

Despite the British government, royalist feelings were once again aroused. The Greek monarchy had of course lived through all this before, and had recovered their lost position. In September 1946 a plebiscite voted 65 per cent to 30 per cent in favour of bringing the King home. George II read the results on a tape-machine in Claridges, his official home during his four years of waiting. When he saw that in one village of three hundred and three inhabitants, three hundred and one had voted for him to come home, he lost his impassive dignity for the first time and wept. King George returned to Greece once more, and survived as King until his sudden death the following year.

While he was in England George II had almost lived at Coppins. Sixteen years older than Marina, he was nevertheless one of the most important links with her past and one of the few relations with whom she was regularly in contact during the difficult war years. For a while after the war the Greek monarchy seemed comparatively stable: George II was succeeded by his younger brother Paul (all King Constantine's sons therefore taking their turn at kingship), who was married to Frederika, daughter of the Duke of Brunswick-Luneburg, head of the House of Hanover. The new King and Queen worked hard to rebuild Greece's fortunes, travelling all over the country to encourage the Greeks in their return to prosperity, and helping them not only to recover after the Communist warfare, but also after the floods and earthquakes which followed.

Although by now Greece was a safe place to visit, Marina went there comparatively little after the death of her mother in 1957. According to Steven Runciman, none of the family was very fond of Queen Frederika and under the circumstances it was easier to stay at home. As long as her mother was alive there was of course good reason to return to her childhood home. In the summer of 1952, after the coronation celebrations, Marina took Alexandra and Michael to Greece for the first time to see their grandmother and also to be shown a part of their history. They went to Tatoi and spent a week at Mon Repos in Corfu, recreating the summers Marina had enjoyed while her grandfather was alive.

Paul and Olga stayed in South Africa for some years after the war. In 1946 Tito, supported by the British who believed that the Communists had been more effective in the war against the Nazis than the monarchists, gained control of Yugoslavia. General Smuts, who had been instrumental in bringing Paul to South Africa, believed Paul had been treated badly, but public opinion was still against the ex-regent. His re-admission to all that he cared about began in the first half of 1947 when Bertie and Elizabeth made a state visit to South Africa and insisted, against protocol and Foreign Office advice, on seeing Paul and Olga. Like George and Marina (but not David) Elizabeth and Bertie were fiercely loyal to their friends.

At the end of October 1948 Paul and Olga were at last given permission to return to Europe and went, with Lilia, Elizabeth and her nanny to Switzerland. The next year it was made clear that he would not be unwelcome in France and so, while Olga was staying with her mother in Athens, he took himself house-hunting in Paris, where he saw King Peter again. That summer Elizabeth was sent to stay with Marina in England. In July Marina, on an official visit to Paris, was able to see her brother-in-law again at last (Olga was still in Athens). That same year (1949) Marina was also at last able publicly to see her sister Elizabeth, who during the war and in its immediate aftermath, was a public enemy by virtue of her marriage to Toto. When Paul saw her first (in 1950) he was horrified by what the intervening years had done to his formerly beautiful sister-in-law: 'I found [her] looking old and haggard. It is so depressing to see a lovely creature grow old prematurely.'

On 6 February 1952, almost ten years after the death of George, his brother Bertie, King George VI, died at Sandringham after a day spent hare shooting. Bertie had been in poor health for some time, having to cancel a tour of New Zealand and Australia: the tour was rescheduled for 1952, but then he fell ill again and a lung was removed. He died while Elizabeth and Philip were on tour in Kenya, and had last been seen in public waving them off at London Airport. 'I longed for him to have some peace of mind. He was so young to die, and was becoming so wise in kingship. He was so kind too, and had a natural nobility of thought and life,' wrote his wife to a friend after his death. Philip Ziegler quotes a young workman who summed up the feelings of so many on the King's death: 'I think we all liked the King a great deal. Never wanted to be King. Sacrificed practically everything for his country. I think if anybody died for his country it was the King.' For Queen Mary it was the loss of a third son in her lifetime – first John, then George and now Bertie. Only Mary and the estranged David were left. Lady Airlie thought that Queen Mary never really recovered from the death of George, and this death was yet another cruel blow. Her lady-in-waiting Cynthia Colville baulked at telling the Queen: 'Oh dear!' she said to Private Secretary Edward Ford, who had brought the news: 'It's very difficult.

Queen Mary's never forgiven me for telling her without any adornments that the Duke of Kent had been killed.' Later the old Queen said to her friend Lady Shaftesbury, 'I suppose one must force oneself to go on until the end?' 'I am sure that Your Majesty will,' came the reply.

Bertie had always been kind to Marina – especially in the matter of bringing Olga to England in 1942, and in paying her an allowance out of his own income. But his death of course meant much more than the loss of a brother-in-law. When he died Marina was in Munich with Elizabeth, Eddie was at school in Switzerland and the new Queen was at Treetops in Kenya. Marina's first cousin Philip was now consort to the Queen of England. Lord Mountbatten is well known to have been delighted at the dynastic success he had achieved with the marriage of his nephew to the heir to the throne. Marina took such matches more for granted, but she cannot but have been pleased at the royal Greeks having a foothold in Europe's most successful monarchy.

Before the new reign began, the King must be buried. The Duke of Windsor came home from Paris without the Duchess (and saw Bertie's wife Elizabeth for the first time since 1936) and he, along with Harry Gloucester, Philip Edinburgh and Eddie Kent, followed the gun carriage which bore the King's body in the funeral procession through the streets of London. Paul of Yugoslavia also came to the funeral – the first time since the war that he had been back to England. Both the Queen and the Queen Mother invited him, and there was no doubt left that he was reinstated in the bosom of the royal family, even if public opinion was still somewhat mixed. All his children were now living in England – Nicky was at Oxford, Alexander had left the RAF and was now, somewhat to his father's disapproval, an airline pilot, and Elizabeth was at boarding school. Elizabeth became slightly wild as she grew older and Marina, worried that she might influence her own daughter Alexandra, tried to keep the two girls apart.

From then on Paul and Olga regularly visited England and were always made as welcome by the Queen Mother and their other old friends as they were by Marina at Coppins. Public opinion never swung enough in their favour for them to move to England as Paul had for so long hoped to do, but if he was not entirely vindicated by the world he knew he was by those for whom he cared. He and Olga were invited to Queen Elizabeth's coronation and that year (1953) the entire family spent Christmas at Coppins with Marina and her children. To that extent at least the family was reunited. There was one last tragedy in store for Paul and Olga: in April 1954 their favourite son, Nicky, was killed aged twenty-five in a car accident at Datchet, near Windsor. The funeral was held from Coppins. Nicky had been his father's favourite, successful, clever and popular, and his loss was felt deeply by his entire family.

Just over a year after the death of the King, and before the coronation of the new Queen, Queen Mary finally came to the end of her long life. 'Beside her, all royalties, except the Kents, look second-rate,' Channon had written many years before. He was not alone in that feeling. For the old guard she represented the correct style of monarchy, and it is a tribute to her character that she, whose perception of monarchy was influenced by the awareness of her own morganatic blood, had become its figurehead. Edward VIII had blotted not only his copybook but that of the whole family. George VI had, with Elizabeth's help, overcome his difficulties, his stutter and his shyness, but to many remained a much loved dull dog. George of course had style and verve, while the Princess Royal worked hard but lacked both glamour and presence. Queen Mary was the strongest character in her family and her death was a tremendous loss to the children who had so relied on her unswerving views and unending loyalty. 'There had not been a word of criticism of the grand old lady .... The world will be poorer,' wrote Channon.

While the Duke of Windsor was in England for his mother's funeral he was told that he and his wife would not be receiving invitations to the forthcoming coronation. Even with Queen Mary dead, there was to be no place for Wallis Simpson alongside her undoubtedly better-behaved royal sisters-in-law. On the night of the old Queen's funeral, the Duchess scandalised even hard-bitten New Yorkers when she was seen dining and dancing with her long-time companion, homosexual Woolworth's heir

Jimmy Donahue at a Manhattan nightclub. It was unlikely that Marina, Alice or Elizabeth would welcome the American into the family, nor that their niece, the new Queen, would go against their feelings in the matter. While David was in England for the funeral, though, there was some feeling of personal *rapprochement* between him and his surviving siblings. He stayed with the Gloucesters at York House and one night he, Harry and Mary sat up until the early hours discussing the past and old friends. 'It was particularly moving listening to the Duke because he was so obviously pleased to be talking with his own family again,' wrote Alice Gloucester in her memoirs.

A few months after Queen Mary's death Queen Elizabeth II was crowned. Once again England could revel in its pageantry, and once again Marina was acclaimed as the most beautiful of the royal women. Marina and Alexandra – nearly sixteen – were dressed by Norman Hartnell. Marina's train was carried by her lady-in-waiting of long-standing, Lady Rachel Davidson, and her coronet was carried by Philip Hay. 'The Duchess of Kent was fairy-like,' wrote Channon, 'and there was a well-bred gasp as she walked in with the children.' Beaton also remarked upon Marina in his diary: 'The Duchess of Kent has the dignity of a carved wooden effigy,' he wrote. Marina, Michael and Alexandra sat in the Royal Gallery, watching as the Queen was crowned and as Eddie, third in family precedence, knelt in homage to the new Queen.

Beaton took the photographs after the ceremony, and wrote of the Kents:

PM, romantically beautiful and remarkably distinguished but sad, and incapable of keeping her children in a vein of seriousness: they all joked, and made staccato noises. It was difficult not to get exasperated with my delightful friends, but they, poor things, were at the end of a long, tiring, possibly unnerving day; they confessed their feet hurt.

The weekend after the coronation the family was back at work, and Marina was in Llandudno launching a lifeboat. She stayed with Michael Duff at his nearby house, Vaynol. Beaton was another guest. 'The weekend ... ended with the inevitable practical jokes, and "ghost figures" found elaborately bedecked in the royal bedroom. But the wholesale jollity, the wild exuberance of youth, was missing,' he wrote. Perhaps Marina wondered where her future lay under her niece's reign.

The advent of a new monarch meant that the Civil List was reviewed and a new scale of payments worked out. Marina was not given a direct payment from the list, but the Queen was given £25,000 from which she could help any royal relations who were not on the list but who undertook public duties. Not only Marina, but by now Alexandra and Eddie, qualified for financial help under those terms. The Queen allocated Marina £5,000 a year, which, together with a small annuity left her by Queen Mary the following year, made a difference to her financial security, without really making her rich again.

In the years since George's death Marina had adapted her life to her new situation: it was not, after all, the first time she had been called upon to be adaptable. Even her closest friends and family noticed how she changed as a widow. Had George not died she might well have continued the old round of royal duty – visits, smiles, pageantry – with her own added ingredient of inexpressible chic. Marina was in many ways an old-fashioned woman. She had gained independence in exile in Paris, but once married she relied utterly on her husband, through thick and thin. Thrown upon herself, with her children to look after and her position to live up to, Marina grew stronger and more independent. She learned to make decisions – George had not even given her much say in the cloth of a curtain – and to think for herself. Those who knew her well might have guessed at the strength of character that lay behind her womanliness and shyness: not many people dared to stand up to Queen Mary and Marina did – over nail varnish and smoking – without ever losing the old Queen's respect or affection.

It may not have been surprising to see how Marina developed privately, but her increasing role in public life, her aptitude and her dedication, did astound many who remembered her as the inherently unpunctual style-setter of the thirties.

As the old reign drew to its close and the new one began, Marina started to take an increasingly important role in the shaping of the modern monarchy.

CHAPTER EIGHT

A Modern Princess

Gradually Marina's ties with the past were broken by death. Prince Christopher of Greece died in Rome in 1940 and was buried in Athens. In 1949 Kate Fox, the nurse who had a lifetime before tied three Greek princesses to a tree to stop them straying, died at Iver hospital, where Marina had moved her after she became too frail to live alone in her flat in Belsize Park. Elizabeth von Toerring died in 1955 of cancer. Princess Nicholas died two years later in Athens.

But although the past and those connected with it were slipping out of Marina's reach, she was not a woman to repine. Neither was she, despite her own feelings of shyness, one to evade her duty. With Princess Elizabeth now Queen, the royal family had no Prince of Wales, no second generation which could yet begin to take its place in the royal round of engagements. Of the older generation only the Princess Royal and the Duke of Gloucester were left. The Duchess of Gloucester played her part well. For just over two years from 1944 the Duke had undertaken the Governor-Generalship of Australia, the job that was to have been George's. The Duke, however, though well-meaning and dependable, was weak and over-fond of the whisky bottle. All King George and Queen Mary's sons had married strong women, and Harry was no exception. The Duchess of Gloucester, scion of one of Scotland's noblest houses, was no more a 'bread-and-butter miss' than Marina or Elizabeth (or, indeed, Mrs Simpson).

It is not to be forgotten that from 1942 until 1953 Marina was not paid by the government for her increasing burden of work, and indeed after that she was paid only at the Queen's discretion. Marina's sense of duty went far beyond a question of earning a pay packet. As her mother in exile had continued to shoulder royal responsibilities, so Marina accepted without question her role in life. Like her mother, Marina was tremendously popular. Post-war Britain adored the Duchess, loved the romance of her story, admired the simple elegance which was so rare in the House of Windsor. Only the Duchess of Windsor could rival Marina in style, and she was a little too flashy, as well as still enormously unpopular (and absent).

The real change in Marina's position in the royal family came with her first foreign tour. She had always been present for the standard royal events, the banquets for foreign royalty and other dignitaries, the line-ups at stations and airports to greet or wave off the same worthies. She had continued to fulfil her share of the domestic chores, the factory visits, Alexandra Rose Day, various hospitals, the RNLI. There was also the more light-hearted side of the royal year, August at Balmoral, Christmas at Sandringham, Royal Ascot, from which Marina was never excluded. However, gradually Marina's role began to take on more importance. She was, after all, so very *good* at her job.

One of Marina's presidencies in England was of the National Association for the Prevention of Tuberculosis, and it was in this capacity that she was invited to open a new clinic in Singapore by their Anti-Tuberculosis Association. Once she had accepted that invitation it made sense to include other engagements: a visit to the Wrens in Singapore was fixed and then one to the 1st Battalion, The Queen's Own Royal West Kent Regiment (based in Malaya) of which she was Colonel-in-Chief. From these beginnings grew the basis for a major tour, with nearly seventy official engagements in Singapore, Malaya, Sarawak, North Borneo and Hong Kong.

It was decided that Marina should take Eddie, the young Duke of Kent, with her. One of Marina's triumphs was how she brought up her three children to become totally professional members of the royal family, and on this occasion the company of the other must have been a comfort and help to each.

After months of planning, Marina and Eddie (accompanied

by Philip, Lady Rachel Davidson and Viscount Althorp, whose daughter Diana was later to marry Elizabeth's son Charles) finally left England on 27 September 1952, on the same aeroplane that had taken Princess Elizabeth to Kenya in February.

The tour lasted five weeks, and was an admitted triumph. As always Marina won hearts wherever she went, and as always she showed no signs of flagging spirits or interest.

The journey to Singapore took three days, with stops at Cyprus and Colombo. Marina and Eddie, the first royal visitors for nearly twenty-five years, were greeted at Singapore by a twenty-one gun salute. Marina, dressed in gold silk with a gold pillbox hat and carrying a small black fan, looked as elegant as always: that was her character and it had become part of her job.

What was not part of her job was the way she met the public. Overcoming her diffidence she walked among the crowds, shook hands with countless strangers, smiling all the while. More to her liking were the shopping outings: whether buying groceries in the market or trying on Chinese slippers and jackets for Christmas presents it was an adventure.

Every day was fully planned: visits to hospitals, barracks, RAF and naval stations, a ball at Government House. Presents were received, smiles were smiled, gratitude was shown. (One present was recycled twelve years later: when Marina opened an army museum in Kent she presented it with a parang given her in Malaya during this tour.) Royal tours such as these are very hard work; they more than compensate for the months at Balmoral or Sandringham, the visits to relations all over Europe. And Marina was one of the first to learn the truth of this.

On 5 October the royal party flew on to Kuala Lumpur, where Marina and Eddie stayed in different houses (Marina in King's House, Eddie with the Deputy High Commissioner). As they arrived the RAF was bombing the roadside jungle to frighten away bandits – they did indeed find a machine-gun ambush put in place to destroy the royal convoy. From Kuala Lumpur they went to Malacca, where they visited a rubber plantation and were given a feast of local food. On the route to Kuala Kubu Bahru, where the Queen's Own Royal West Kent Regiment was waiting to be reviewed by Marina, another ambush was discovered. While Marina was inspecting the regiment Eddie practised on the rifle range.

They returned to Singapore in time for Eddie's seventeenth birthday. The governor gave him a birthday dinner which included Shui Pi Nan Shan (May you Live as Long as the Southern Mountain) soup, thousand-year-old eggs and almond chicken. There was a special Malay cake, and Eddie was given a *kris*, a wavy-bladed dagger, with which to cut it. Waving the dagger around his head in approved Malay style, he managed to cut his mother's eye so that blood poured down the front of her dress. The wound was in fact a minor one, and with a clean dress and a plaster on her eye Marina returned to the party.

On 14 October, after two garden parties, a youth rally and more visits, the Kents finally flew from Singapore for Sarawak. There, the Sunderland flying boat was met by a barge which took the Kents to the palace of the Brookes, the 'White Rajahs' who had ruled the state until after the war when, having been almost destroyed by the Japanese, Sir Charles Brooke decided to cede the state to the Crown.

Once again there were garden parties to attend, barracks to visit, presents of spears, daggers, even a straw hat to receive with gratitude and sincerity. Marina met headhunters (one showed her a lock of hair he wore in his sword belt: it had come from the head of a Japanese officer) and officials. She opened a Marina Barracks and a Duchess of Kent Hospital. In Brunei Marina and Eddie were carried in a litter through the streets and given chicken curry and warm champagne. Here an oil well was named after her, and she opened it as if it were a ship, with a bottle of champagne smashed against its side.

There followed another weekend at Singapore and then a visit to Hong Kong, which was just beginning its massive post-war regeneration. Here again there were foundation stones to lay, dinners to attend, visits and inspections.

Eddie and Marina set out from Hong Kong on 9 November, leaving behind then an enormous legacy of good will towards Britain and a crop of babies called Mirian (the closest the Malays could get to Marina). They came home to a huge welcome. At

Heathrow Airport the Queen and Duke of Edinburgh, Alexandra and Michael and the Queen Mother and Princess Margaret were all waiting to receive them. The success of the trip was immediately clear to Britain, to the royal family and to the politicians. On 16 November a lunch was given at the Mansion House in Marina's honour. The guests included Churchill, Attlee, the High Commissioners for Australia, South Africa, Pakistan and Southern Rhodesia and was hosted by the Secretary of State for the Colonies, Oliver Lyttelton (later Viscount Chandos). Lyttelton proposed a toast to Marina, thanking her not only for carrying out the tour but for doing so with enthusiasm, energy and serenity. Marina's reply was elegant and to the point:

Mr Lyttelton has said something of the affection which peoples of all races throughout the Commonwealth feel towards the Queen, and I would like to confirm that this loyalty and devotion to the Crown, and to the great family of nations which it represents, was what impressed me most profoundly wherever I went – one was very conscious of a great tide of feeling everywhere spontaneously expressed – and that was something which I found deeply moving, and indeed, remarkable, at this time of material change and spiritual unrest.

After so successful a tour it was inevitable that Marina would be called upon to represent the Queen abroad again. In 1954 Marina, this time accompanied by seventeen-year-old Alexandra, was sent to Canada. Once again the tour was an unqualified success for all concerned, although of course there were a few dissident voices among the press. Why, asked the *Daily Mirror*, did Marina and Alexandra need two ladies-in-waiting, one aide de camp, three maids and one secretary for their Canadian tour. Was it not all a huge waste of money? The same paper was also furious at the rules imposed on the press during the visit: no photographers within 15 feet of Marina and Alexandra; no 'surprise pictures; and no press conferences or conversations with either of the two royal women. 'The security arrangements for the tour are obnoxious and absurd. One might gather from the proclamation that no one will be allowed within 15ft. of the Royal couple because this is the city of untouchables with a penchant for going berserk.'

This was Princess Alexandra's first major royal tour and Marina's job was therefore twofold: to carry out her own engagements and to keep an eye on her daughter. The royal party arrived in Quebec in a Royal Canadian Air Force plane and was met by the Governor General, Vincent Massey, who took them up to the Citadel. Both Marina and Alexandra proved popular: the Duchess for her elegance and her ease at her job, Alexandra for her very youth and enthusiasm. Marina's jobs were of the usual category: she unveiled Montreal University's new war memorial, opened a new generating station at Niagara Falls and opened the National Exhibition in Toronto. Alexandra had a few engagements on her own, involving the Junior Red Cross of which she had been patron for two years.

While in Canada Marina made one private visit, to someone who drew her back to her past. Grand Duchess Olga Alexandrovna, Princess Nicholas's cousin, now lived in Cooksville near Toronto. Marina had last seen the Grand Duchess in Tsarskoe Selo, and could not remember her cousin from those childhood visits. But her coming meant a great deal to the old lady who had survived a revolution and moved from a palace in the Old World to a four-roomed red-brick cottage in the New. 'Marina is really a lovely person and so friendly and sweet. She looked in our little house and ate some sandwiches in the kitchen.' Marina's good manners prevented her giving anything away, but she later admitted she had been somewhat horrified at the conditions in which a Tsar's sister was living.

After Toronto the Kents visited Halifax, St John's Fredericton and then returned to Montreal and finally to New York for a holiday. They sailed home on the *Queen Mary*, Marina having proved yet again how well she combined the roles of private mother and public princess.

For the rest of her life, with or without one of her children, Princess Marina continued to work as the Queen's representative abroad. In 1959 she and Alexandra (with a party which included Philip Hay and Lady Rachel Davidson) visited South America, another long and arduous tour, covering Mexico, Peru, Chile and Brazil.

British and local press followed their every move and wrote nothing but praise. They were called 'unassuming' and their 'quiet charm endeared them more and more to those who have met them and to the Mexican public in general. The Press', wrote *The Times*, 'has been unanimous in their praise, and the leading articles have commented on the Duchess's delicately worded offer of economic aid, made, they say, without any taint of coercion or suspect motives.'

There was work to be done, but of course tours like this offer something in return. As well as the tremendous response from the crowd – and nobody could fail to be moved by such appreciation – Marina had always enjoyed travelling abroad and now she could visit parts of the world she might never have seen. As well as wreath-laying and charity balls and visits to industrial centres there were rodeos, temples carved with flowers and hands, the ruins of a city sacred to a religion that no longer existed. Marina slept in modern hotels and in an Inca city 2,000 feet above sea level. She dined in Government Houses and picnicked in Brazil. In her few hours off in Mexico she and Alexandra, dressed in cotton frocks, sandals and scarves, went to the national museum of anthropology and history and then to the shrine of Our Lady of Guadalupe.

Marina's popularity was as much for her impromptu touches as for the ease with which she carried out the more formal parts of her engagements. Taken to a paper factory in Chile, she showed as much interest in the workmen's kitchens and dining rooms (much as she did in Steven Runciman's Scottish kitchen) as she did in the works. It was her innate curiosity that endeared her to the ordinary people. Taken side by side with her aura of royalty which everyone, from a man who shook her hand on a walkabout to the most seasoned member of the British aristocracy, comments on and admires, Marina could not but win friends wherever she went.

Again and again the papers echo the same sentiment: 'By their graciousness and friendliness it is clear that they have already won the hearts of all those with whom they have come in contact.' Another newspaper commented that 'the tireless Kents have done their part of the job. Now it's up to the City and to

British businessmen to follow up the advantages they have created. The keys are in the doors.'

Marina was now at ease in this role of royal visitor, but the South American trip was a curtain-raiser for Alexandra, who a few months later was to perform her first solo tour, going to Australia as the Queen's representative at the Centenary Celebrations of Queensland. Alexandra set off in August 1959 with her lady-in-waiting Moyra Hamilton and accompanied by Philip Hay for moral and practical support.

It was then that Marina's training really showed. Without her mother to overshadow her – for Alexandra was not yet as good-looking or as elegant as she was to become – and with her own schedule of engagements to keep to, Alexandra proved herself worthy of her descent. Princess Alexandra has more royal blood in her than any other Princess in Europe. On both parents' side her pedigree is impeccable. She combines the blood of the Tsars with that of the Danes, the Stuarts with that of the Hanovers. She is, by birth, more royal than the Queen herself. Her breeding and her upbringing combined to help her through what must have been an awesome task, and the success of her Australian tour proved her mettle.

For six weeks she toured the cities and outback of Australia, showing spontaneity (an attribute loved by the Australians), a sense of humour, and a tireless energy. On her return she stayed with the King and Queen of Siam and went to New Delhi. Before going to Australia Alexandra had already begun to fulfil royal engagements, but this was really the beginning of her career. A year later she was once again the Queen's representative abroad, when she went to Nigeria for its independence celebrations.

The Duchess was also sent by the Queen to represent her in African independence celebrations. The first country to gain independence was Ghana, and in March 1957 Marina was in Accra to watch the British flag come down and the red, gold and green flag with a black star of Ghana go up. In 1966 she again represented the Queen, this time as Bechuanaland became Botswana.

Australia had loved Alexandra, but Marina's visit in 1964

was considerably more poignant: for the first time she saw the country that would have been her home for a few years at least. Marina always took her job seriously, but, with memories of the pointless preparations she had made with George, she sat down once again with the briefings about Queensland. She invited Australians to her house again, including the man who had been Prime Minister in 1939 and now held the office once again, Sir Robert Menzies. Although less exotic than Latin America or Malaya, Australia held a particular interest for Marina. She was eager to see signs of Alexandra's earlier visit, saying, 'It's interesting to see what the family's been doing.' Most poignant of all, when she visited Government House she saw signs of George in the decorations he had chosen, and which had already been put in place before his death. There were the blue satin sofas, the silk tweed rugs, and, still in use all those years later, the pink sheets he had insisted upon.

Marina's new role as a travelling ambassadress for the Queen did not preclude her continued work at home, for her own charities and regiments as well as as part of the working royal family as a whole. She worked for the RNLI, for her regiment, for Alexandra Rose Day. She entertained the King and Queen of Siam and lent jewels to the Antique Dealers' Fair at the Grosvenor Hotel. She visited schools (often insisting on talking to the children rather than listening to speeches) and attended the OBE service at St Paul's Cathedral. She did not, however, attend any function given in hour of Mr Kosygin, the first Russian leader to come to England since the fall of the Tsars. Her closeness to the Russian rulers exempted her from offering any homage to the political descendants of their killers.

One of the jobs of which Marina was proudest was her chancellorship of the new University of Kent in 1966. In a ceremony at Canterbury in March, Marina was given an honorary degree as Doctor of Civil Law and became the university's first graduate. Then, having taken the chair as the first chancellor, she distributed various other honorary degrees, including one to the Archbishop of Canterbury, and had lunch with some of the students.

As with her other jobs, Marina threw herself wholeheartedly

into her new (and admittedly somewhat unlikely) role as head
of an academic institution. Indeed, one of her last public duties –
albeit one she had imposed on herself – was a garden party for
sixty University of Kent students at Kensington Palace.

Marina's life was made considerably easier in 1954 with the
gift from the Queen of a flat in Kensington Palace, which gave
her the London base which she had lacked since leaving Belgrave
Square during the war. She had had rooms in Marlborough
House, but these were never more than offices. Kensington
Palace was a London base and later, after Eddie's marriage,
became Marina's home.

Suite One, as it was then called, had been the home of Princess
Louise, Queen Victoria's daughter, who had lived until 1939.
The palace was bombed in the war, but survived, and although
George VI had offered Marina the flat early in her widowhood
the move had never quite been made. The Queen then repeated
the offer and at first Marina was hesitant – Princess Louise had
said that there was a room for each of her ninety years in the
suite and Marina did not need anything so large. Finally it was
decided to divide the suite into two flats, one of which was to
be Marina's (the other was later given to Princess Margaret and
Antony Snowdon). The rooms had been empty since Princess
Louise's death and were damp and in bad repair, but after
restoration they became an elegant home for Marina and Alexandra. Marina had never decorated a house before: George had
always loved that job, so she looked on the empty rooms with
something approaching despair. Princess Alexandra, though,
proved that she was more than just a good companion to her
mother and, with a flair inherited from father, helped her mother
organise all the rooms, moving pieces from Coppins or buying
new ones as she saw fit. Finally, after the restoration and decoration were finished, after the fitted carpets and central heating
had been installed and the antiques put each in its own place,
Marina moved into the flat in October 1955.

The children were growing up. Alexandra and Eddie were
taking their places in the 'Family Firm', which did not mean
that Marina was becoming obsolete but did mean that she saw
less of them. She knew, of course, that the next step would be

the marriage of one or other of them: if it were Eddie, Marina would cease to be the Duchess of Kent; if it were Alexandra she would lose her companion.

Rumour had long allied Alexandra and Constantine (Tino) of the Hellenes, but it was a rumour fabricated for its romantic aptness rather than based on any truth. And in the event it was Eddie, not Alexandra, who was the first to marry.

The Duke of Kent first met Katharine Worsley in 1957 when he was twenty-one. Until then he had earned a reputation as something of a playboy, smashing cars and dancing late. Then the army sent him to Caterick in Yorkshire and Sir William Worsley, a local landowner, regularly invited batches of young officers to lunch at his house, Hovingham Hall. For the next two years the courtship progressed. Katharine was a commoner, but came of a very good family. Her father was Lord Lieutenant of Yorkshire, and his family tree certainly went as far back as the Normans. Katharine was nearly three years older than Eddie, which was another reason (apart from his youth) that Marina thought the match was not altogether suitable, and of course she was not royal. Nobody who knew Marina denies that royalty meant a great deal to her. In one sense she was like Queen Mary; but while the old Queen's perception of royalty had been shaped in part because of her faulty blood-line, Marina's pedigree was exemplary. Her years in exile had moulded her: when she had nothing else left to her she had the knowledge that she was royal, that her forbears were royal and that they might take away her passport (as the Greeks did), but they could not take away her heritage. On the other hand she had always believed in the value of love-matches, and the years since Olga's brief engagement to Rico of Denmark had not changed her mind. However, she was genuinely worried that Katharine would not be up to the task of life as a royal Duchess, finding her warm but perhaps too gentle.

The press latched on to the romance and kept a keen eye on the couple from the early days. It was suggested as early as 1958 that Marina disapproved, although Sir William denied this to be the case. Whenever Eddie was on leave his movements were watched – did the couple meet or not? When, in the early days of their romance, Eddie left Sandringham on Boxing Day to be with Katharine, the public was delighted. Marina, though, was not. She had forbidden Eddie to leave Norfolk and he had gone over her head to ask, and receive, the Queen's permission to go.

It was decided that before an engagement was announced the couple should spend some time apart. Eddie refused to give Katharine up, but agreed to a year's separation: he went to Germany with the army and she went to Canada to stay with her brother. the year apart did not have the effect that Marina had half hoped for, and when they were reunited in 1959 the couple was as determined as ever to wed. Marina's next excuse was that Princess Margaret had recently become secretly engaged to Antony Armstrong-Jones. The engagement was to be announced in the New Year and there could not, said Marina, be two royal weddings in one year. Finally, just after his twenty-fifth birthday Eddie finished his tour of duty in Germany and then at last Marina agreed to an announcement, which was made in March 1961. Marina wrote to a friend, 'We are all very happy about it as he has loved Katharine for four years. It is a good beginning I feel, and she is a pretty, sweet person, so I thank God for another great blessing. But how the years pass. It seems only the other day he was a little boy.'

Prince Michael, still very much the junior member of the family, was living with a professor in Tours, working to improve his French before going to Sandhurst, when the engagement was accepted by Marina. It had already been announced that Eddie was to go to Sierra Leone, and the Queen was going to Italy for a state visit in May, so the wedding date was finally fixed for 8 June.

It was decided that the wedding should be held in York Minster. The Worsleys were an old Yorkshire family, it is traditional for a bride to be married from her home and (perhaps the most telling reason of all) there was to be no Archbishop of Canterbury between 31 May and 27 June (Doctor Fisher was retiring and Ramsay would not be enthroned until the end of June). So the marriage was to be solemnised by the Archbishop of York and the Archbishop-Designate of Canterbury.

Three weeks before the wedding Princess Marina had a Wrens

engagement at Lossiemouth in Scotland. It was only 40 miles from the site of George's death. After the Wren work her two eldest children joined her. They drove together to the hill on which George had died and visited the granite memorial cross. The three Kents flew back to London that same night, their pilgrimage made and the awareness of the beginning of a new life enhanced by the trip. Marina had continued to visit George's tomb on their wedding anniversary, but that was a private affair: this visit with her children was in its way more important.

The wedding day, 8 June, was wet, but the ceremony – the first royal wedding to be held in York Minster since 1328 when Edward III married Queen Philippa – was as splendid as only an English royal wedding can be. Foreign royalty came in force. They included Queen Victoria Eugenie of Spain, the Duke of Gerona and the Count of Barcelona; Prince and Princess George of Denmark; Princess Ileana of Rumania; Crown Prince Constantine and Princess Sophie of the Hellenes; Prince Harald of Norway and Princess Margretha of Denmark and Princess Irene of the Netherlands. As well there were members of other royal houses of Europe: Prince Charles of Luxembourg, Prince Frederick of Prussia. The Toerrings and the Yugoslavs were of course present, and the English aristocracy was there in force, Hamiltons and Ogilvys and Edens and Beresfords.

Despite the importance of the guests who came to see Eddie and Kate marry, this was not a state wedding and managed to keep an air of informality about it: more than anything this was a family affair. There were many more morning coats than dress uniforms on view. Eddie and his brother Michael were of course in uniform, Eddie wearing the ceremonial dress of the Royal Scots Greys with the blue ribbon of the GCVO and Michael in the ceremonial uniform of an officer cadet at Sandhurst. Princess Alexandra was in pink organdie, the Queen in lilac satin, the Queen Mother in turquoise lace and organdie. Marina wore caramel organdie embroidered with gold silk thread and diamonds and topazes. Her hat was a huge cartwheel of osprey feathers. The Minster was decorated in yellow, white and cream roses and the bridesmaids (led by Princess Anne) and pages wore yellow and white.

Marina (who stayed for the wedding with Lord Halifax's daughter Lady Feversham at nearby Helmsley) and Alexandra were notable for being the only members of the royal family to kneel for a few moments in prayer before they took their seats in the Minster: it did not matter to them that the television cameras were in place or that for many a wedding is more of a social than a religious occasion. Marina had continued practising her faith and although she did not talk much about it, her friends agree that she was, in a quiet way, a Christian woman. Marina did not always attend the Greek Orthodox Cathedral in Bayswater, she as often went to St Mary Abbots at the bottom of Kensington Church Street, a five-minute walk from Kensington Palace, but to the end of her life she was a church-goer. For the major festivals of the Church she usually did attend the Greek Orthodox rite, and would go to church twice on Good Friday, observing the strict fast of olives, boiled beans, bread and water.

The bride appeared, wearing a silk gauze dress that had taken 273 yards of silk and the ceremony went without a hitch: Marina wept a little, but with her customary dignity recovered herself in time for the walk down the long aisle with Sir William Worsley. And then all two thousand guests, Yorkshire neighbours, tenants, reigning and dethroned monarchy alike, repaired to the bride's home, Hovingham Hall, for the reception. Beaton took the pictures, while Marina and Eddie shared a moment's peace over some cigarettes. Afterwards Eddie and Kate (and her poodle and his golden Labrador) flew to Scotland where they were to spend the beginning of their honeymoon.

Eddie's marriage marked a new phase in Marina's life. She was no longer the Duchess of Kent and she did mind that fact. The Dowager Duchess of Kent was not a title that she wanted, so she decided that she would revert to her own title, and become Princess Marina, Duchess of Kent. Marina was, however, only fifty-five when Eddie married, not old enough to think of retirement or even of easing up on her share of the royal workload. Nor did she want to: her work had become important to her emotionally, something much more than the mere fulfilment of duty.

The most significant wrench was not so much the handing over of her title to the daughter-in-law she had at first resisted as the handing over of her home. Coppins had been made for her by George, and it was at Coppins that they had shared their happiest times. Marina had last seen George at Coppins, as he said goodbye on his final journey. His possessions were there, his taste was reflected in every room. Nevertheless, as always Marina knew how to behave correctly and on Eddie's marriage she left Coppins and made her home permanently in Kensington Palace.

Two years later Alexandra married, and this marriage was perhaps in some ways more of a wrench for Marina than Eddie's. Eddie had already left home, had lived in Germany as a soldier by the time he married. Alexandra was still living with her mother.

Angus Ogilvy was the grandson of Mabell, Countess of Airlie, Queen Mary's lady-in-waiting and close friend. His father was Lord Chamberlain to the Queen Mother. The Ogilvys had been intimates of the royal household for years, and Alexandra knew all the family to varying degrees. Angus had had a mixed career: the Scots Guards, followed by a degree at Trinity Oxford in PPE, then a spell in the merchant navy, had even qualified as a ski instructor while in Austria with the army. By the time of his wedding he was working in the City, where he was to remain and become highly successful: by the time of the engagement he was already director of twenty-nine companies.

But he was not royal. Those with hopes of Alexandra's becoming Queen of Greece or Norway had to see them dashed. She would of course have made a good Queen – her training and background made sure of that – and perhaps, it is not after all unlikely, Marina had harboured these hopes for her daughter. However, at least marriage to an ~~English~~man meant that Alexandra would remain near her. SCOTS

Alexandra's engagement was announced on 29 November 1962, which would have been her parents' twenty-eighth wedding anniversary. The Queen's formal approval had been given, as well as her mother's blessing. Seven weeks later Constantine of Greece's engagement was announced to the sixteen-year-old Anne-Marie of Denmark. So ended the tabloid writers' – and maybe the family's – hopes of a royal match.

The wedding on 24 April 1963 was, though, a royal occasion. The Queen gave a state ball at Windsor Castle the night before, and the guests included such friends and relations as the King of Norway, the Queens of the Hellenes, Denmark and Sweden, Queen Victoria Eugenie of Spain and Queen Helen of Romania, the Crown Princes of the Hellenes and Norway, Princesses of the Netherlands, the Hellenes, and Denmark ... it might have been a couple of generations earlier, when the royal families of Europe had gathered regularly at each other's courts to celebrate one another's weddings.

Alexandra's bridesmaids and pages were not all drawn from the ranks of royal cousinship. Princess Anne and Princess Elizabeth of Austria (Elizabeth Toerring's granddaughter) headed a list which included Philip Hay's son Simon and Angus Ogilvy's nieces and nephews. Both Eddie and Alexandra's weddings were televised, but although Alexandra's was held in Westminster Abbey, it was stressed that this was a civil, not a state occasion. Alexandra wore a dress designed by John Cavanagh around a piece of Valenciennes lace which Alexandra's grandmother, Princess Nicholas, had worn at her own wedding. The lace was used to edge the train – the same train Marina had worn on her own wedding day.

Five hundred guests were entertained at the reception, of which a hundred were royal and a hundred and fifty tenants and staff from Kensington Palace, Coppins and the Airlie estate.

Marina was always respected and loved by the British public, but with the royal family under increasing pressure to perform from that public she was also occasionally the subject of gossip. It was rumoured that she was to marry Anthony Eden, and another rumour that took stronger hold was that King Olaf of Norway wanted to marry her. This was first murmured about in 1954, five months after King Olaf was widowed, and took such a strong grip on the public imagination that Buckingham Palace went so far as to issue an official denial of the engagement. Three years later the gossips started again, but this time the palace remained silent. However, it is interesting to see that when King Olaf paid an official visit to Balmoral Marina was the only immediate member of the royal family not in Scotland. Her excuse was that she wanted to welcome the Duke and Duchess of Kent back from their visit to Uganda and Kenya – they were due back on 18 September, and did not in fact arrive until a day later, by which time the King of Norway had left.

Whatever the truth about Olaf's intentions, it is clear that Marina did not contemplate leaving England. It had become her home. Her children were there, and would remain there, her job was there and, by now, her heart was there. Daska Maclean, her friend and another expatriate from the land of her birth, explained the feelings that she and Marina shared. Both remained clearly 'foreign' in their accents, but both felt themselves to be British. In times of crisis or war their sympathies, of course, lay with their homelands, and both knew that parts of them would always be different from the British. But unlike George I of Greece, who warned his children never to forget that they were foreigners in the land they ruled, Marina and Mrs Maclean did forget and the forgetting helped them both.

As we have seen, the main influence of Marina's post-war life was Philip Hay, but this is not to rule out the possibility of other romantic attachments during her widowhood. Lord Bruntisfield's family believes that he and Marina were romantically involved after George's death and before his marriage. Her name was also linked by gossips with bandleader Edmundo Ross. Angela Fox, mother of the theatrical Fox's dynasty, avers that her husband had an affair with Marina. Robin Fox was very good-looking, very unfaithful and a theatrical agent. Marina did have many friends in the theatrical world and certainly knew Fox. However, the author was warned that Mrs Fox sees her husband's mistresses everywhere (there were indeed a great many) and that her word is not sufficient evidence for the affair. Mrs Fox says that she turned on the television one day to watch Wimbledon to see her husband, who was supposedly at a meeting in London, in the royal box with Princess Marina. 'She was beautiful and pathetic and absolutely beastly to me,' she told the *Daily Express* years after both Fox and Marina's deaths. She claims the affair was long-standing and that Marina was 'odious to me ... the most hateful of all his mistresses'. (This is unlikely if only because everyone comments on Marina's good manners, and nobody well-mannered would deliberately be rude to her lover's wife.) Mrs Fox also told the *Daily Mail* about a dinner party at Douglas Fairbanks's house, where Marina received in the drawing room. 'I felt really ugly, totally defeated, I tried to get out through the servants' entrance but a plain clothes policeman said the gates were shut. I had to go in and be presented to her. She was wearing the most wonderful white organza dress with diamonds, she was so beautiful she made one feel tiny. When we went into dinner Robin was sitting on her right, he knew everybody but there was nowhere for me to sit. I'll never forget Peter Cotes [Chips Channon's friend known as Petticoats] noticing me and saying, "Angela, you're sitting here," and making room for me. If I had any money I'd leave it to him in my will.' This story does not have the ring of total truth, as it would be incredible to give a dinner party which included royal guests and not lay enough places or organise a proper *place à table*.

There were other criticisms of Marina in the press: one, which turned out to be unfounded, shows how the media had begun to question the royal family's expenditure. In 1961 it was claimed that Alexandra and Marina's holiday in St Moritz had been paid for by the Army Ski Association, which was run by the War Office. In fact Marina had paid her own expenses, and an apology was printed by the newspaper. Nevertheless the incident was symptomatic of the way attitudes towards the monarchy were changing. Again, in 1966, questions were asked in the House of Commons about the necessity of the public paying for a messenger for Marina to be escorted from Wimbledon to Buckingham Palace and Kensington Palace.

Again, when in 1967 Marina sold a cottage at Iver for £4,000, the press had a view. It was a tied cottage, and living in it at the time of the sale was the retired head gardener from Coppins, Hugh Rideout. He was told that he must go, and lost his home. This is the sort of thing that tabloid journalism does not like, but it is to be remembered that Marina did not have a great deal of money, that there is no law against selling your own property, and that by then she herself had had to leave Coppins to make way for her son and daughter-in-law.

Press comment was as a rule more favourable than otherwise. When Rachel Pepys showed Marina's Pekingese dog for her at the Arundel dog show (and it won fourth place) the dog-loving British public was delighted. And, even as Marina grew older, she retained her position as the royal family's most elegant woman. When she had arrived in England her elegance had captured the British public, and she held the public's attention until her death. Fashion pieces were written about her clothes, about how she shopped at the department stores of London (thus making a virtue of a necessity) and even about how she led the fashion stakes in the spectacles world – in 1963 one newspaper commented on her half-moon glasses, adding that the Princess Royal had just followed Princess Marina's lead of three years.

Marina had always liked foreign travel and her increasing official tours did not preclude her taking her holidays. She visited Madrid and Paris and Germany, she went with the royal family to Cowes (for the first time in 1961, taking Alexandra and Michael with her for a stay on HMY *Britannia* as the Queen's guest), she spent Christmases at Sandringham and went to the Derby.

There was also a period of royal jamborees which must have taken Marina back to the old days of her early childhood. In the autumn of 1961 she and Alexandra went to Greece to celebrate King Paul's sixtieth birthday and the engagement of his daughter, Princess Sophia, to Juan Carlos of Spain. They stayed with Olga at the Villa Herodes Atticus, a mansion near the palace used for royal hospitality. In May 1962 the royal families of Europe gathered in Amsterdam for the silver wedding celebrations of Queen Juliana and Prince Bernhard, and in the same year King Juan Carlos and Sophia were married in Athens. The year 1964 saw the wedding, again in Athens, of Constantine to Anne-Marie of Denmark and two years later Crown Princess Beatrix of the Netherlands married Claus von Amsbert in Amsterdam. On each occasion Marina was there with other members of her extended British and Greek family.

One outstanding feud remained to be settled: the Duke of Windsor, George's favourite brother, was still more or less an outcast from his family. It took a long time for George VI to realise that his popularity was secure enough that his older brother's charm was no longer a threat to himself, and thus to the monarchy. The new Queen would never go against her mother but she had more room for forgiveness. To her, after all, the Abdication Crisis was a memory, and was now history. For most of her childhood she had been brought up knowing that she was Heir Presumptive to the throne.

In February 1965 the Duke was sent to London for an operation on his left eye. He was accompanied by his wife, and while he was in hospital they were visited by a series of senior members of the royal family. The Queen came first, escorted by her PPS Michael Adeane. Two days later, on 17 March, the Princess Royal went. It was only her second meeting with her sister-in-law since the Windsor's marriage. Eleven days later she died, and the Duke and Duchess were still in England and able to go to her funeral. They also returned for her memorial service. Marina was another visitor to the hospital. At last it seemed as though there was to be some *rapprochement*, if not a full reconciliation.

Two years later, on Derby Day, 7 June 1967, Queen Elizabeth unveiled a plaque on the wall of Marlborough House in memory of Queen Mary. It was the hundredth anniversary of her birth. The Windsors were both there: it was the Duke's first official appearance with the royal family since his mother's funeral, and the Duchess's first ever. It was also her first invitation as Duchess of Windsor to Buckingham Palace. In front of the fascinated eyes of the press it was noticed that the Duchess of Kent did not WINDS curtsy to her sister-in-law, the Queen Mother, although she did to the Queen.

After the brief ceremony the Queen, the Duke of Edinburgh, the Queen Mother and the Duchess of Gloucester hastened off to Epsom for the Derby. The Duke and Duchess of Windsor had not been invited to join the party, but Marina gave them lunch at Kensington Palace. The Duke and Duchess of Kent and Prince Michael were the other guests there.

Again, it was not an enormous step, but there had been some thawing towards the Duke. The younger members of the family took to visiting their uncle when they were in Paris, and he was no longer the total outcast he had been for so long.

By the mid sixties Princess Marina had become an important part of the royal family, trusted totally by her husband's family and respected equally at home and abroad, publicly and privately, for the effort and professionalism she put into her work.

Despite the deaths of so many close to her, Marina had a full and content if not happy life. Her family increased with the birth of grandchildren: Katherine and Eddie had a son, George (Philip Nicholas), Earl of St Andrews in June 1962 and a daughter, Helen (Marina Lucy) in April 1964; Alexandra and Angus had a son, James, in February 1964 and daughter, Marina, in July 1966.

Marina seemed fit and well and to be enjoying herself. There could be no reason why her life should not continue in its well-ordered pattern for another fifteen years.

CHAPTER NINE

The End

Marina celebrated her sixtieth birthday in the way she liked best: there was a family lunch at Kensington Palace, and in the evening she went to the theatre to see *A Girl in My Soup* with her closest relations – Eddie and Katharine Kent, Alexandra and Angus Ogilvy and Olga. If it was a quiet celebration it was designed that way. All her life Marina had feared the onslaught of old age. Her mother, the indomitable Princess Nicholas, had been a woman of outstanding beauty, reputedly outshining all three of her beautiful daughters, but those who only knew her in her old age testify to the loss of that beauty, to the scars that the years and her life had left on her face. Marina was not vain, and although everyone who knew her mentions her looks almost before anything else, all add that she wore her beauty as casually as she wore her elegant clothes. However, she decided that the photographs taken by Beaton to celebrate her sixtieth birthday were to be the last official photographs she would allow. When she thought about the future, she dreaded it. 'She was not made for old age,' Hugo Vickers told the author. 'Life was not going to get any better or easier.' 'Her life was an empty one and she had little more to live for,' Beaton wrote in his diary as he mourned her death.

She was not to be allowed a long and tranquil old age. In the summer of 1968 she began to notice a weakness in her left leg. She had always limped slightly – a legacy of the twisted foot of her childhood – but this was a different problem. Her leg would sometimes falter beneath her, making her stumble. The doctors advised her to cancel her regular summer visit to Paul and Olga at Pratolino, their villa near Florence. She had already had one holiday that year – a three-week safari with Michael in Kenya, Uganda and Tanzania – but by now something was clearly wrong with her, something more serious than rheumatism or exhaustion. The weakness spread to her left arm, and when she fell badly one day she realised she should seek specialist help.

On 18 July she went to the National Hospital for Nervous Diseases for tests to be made to discover the cause of this weakness. The next day she cancelled a public engagement for the first time in her career. It was discovered that she had an inoperable brain tumour. She was sent home to Kensington Palace from hospital: there was no point in keeping her there, and she was kept in ignorance about the seriousness of her condition. The doctors had given her only a few months to live.

The end was swift. On 23 August she visited Alexandra and Angus and sat with them and their children in the garden. They drove to lunch with her two days later, on Sunday 25th. During the service that morning prayers were said for George, who had died twenty-six years before on that day. After the Ogilvys left Marina and her old friend Zoia Poklewska, who had also lunched at Kensington Palace, sat in the garden reading the newspapers and attempting the crossword. That evening they watched television. The only sign that anything serious was about to happen was that Marina stumbled and fell on her way to bed.

Marina rose as normal on 26 August, but soon after breakfast she said she felt tired and would go to bed for a rest. That sleep turned into a coma, and Marina never woke again. It was only then, with Marina lying unconscious, that the British public was told that the Princess was seriously ill.

Alexandra rang Olga, who arrived from Italy that evening and spent the night beside her sister's bed. Marina opened her eyes once but never regained consciousness. Late in the morning the Archbishop of Canterbury, Dr Ramsey, visited the palace and prayed by her bedside with the family for fifteen minutes. At ten to twelve in the morning of Tuesday 27 August, in her room at Kensington Palace, she died. Her children and children-in-law were with her, as were two doctors, Sir Ronald Bodley

Scott and Dr MacDonald Critchely, who issued a statement, saying, 'The Princess had for some weeks been suffering from an inoperable tumour of the brain, and her condition had rapidly deteriorated during the past 24 hours.' The Queen ordered court mourning for a week, and flags flew at half-mast on government buildings on the days of her death and funeral. Eddie never smoked again from that day.

Marina's children had been told that she would die, but they had expected more time in which to prepare themselves for the inevitable. However, they were wise enough to realise that her quick death had spared her from the pain and indignities that a longer illness would have forced upon her. 'Thank God my sweet Mama knew no pain or suffering. And now she is at peace,' Princess Alexandra wrote to Marina's old friend Cecil Beaton, thanking him for an article he had written in the *Sunday Times* about the Princess. 'The Sunday article I liked so much as it was humorous and unpompous and she would have enjoyed it.'

Beaton recorded his memories in his diary when he heard of her death:

When I think of Princess Marina I remember her deep, serious voice, and her sad smile of compassion. I remember her shock at being greeted in the street in Florence where she was never recognised as at home in England, and she was suddenly reminded that she was not just an ordinary private individual. I recall the many photographic sessions in the garden at Coppins with her husband and children, and, at the studio, when she would arrive with a picnic lunch-basket and boxes containing Greek national dress and her formal gown complete with orders and decorations. I can see now the expression of intense concentration as, with dust sheet on the sitting-room floor, she worked with crayons and pencils at her easel. I remember her amusement at Vaynol in North Wales when slowly and ridiculously I fell into a lake fully dressed; and after a dance at her country house when she and her sisters, in nightgowns, laughed with the other house guests about the incidents of the evening.

Brought up by her mother with a deep regard for tradition, and steeped in ritual, she was the most simple of human beings, at her happiest in informal surroundings. It was characteristic that, throughout her life, she preferred to serve her friends herself at lunch at Kensington Palace, or better still at an outdoor picnic. Her parties lacked grandeur and possessed a delightful atmosphere of the impromptu, although there was never anything casual or offhand about her. She paid impeccable attention to details. In spite of all she had to do, she never permitted herself to be hurried or thoughtless.

Her sense of fun sometimes made it difficult for her on official occasions, and she was the first to laugh at herself in some situation which she considered 'och, so stupid!' She loved to give herself up to uncontrollable laughter. Sometimes her amusement was caused by jokes of a quite basic nature.

Beautiful and romantic princesses are a rare phenomenon today, and their mere existence enhances. Even those who saw her only a little were warmed by the knowledge that she was there; with Princess Marina's death that particularly lovely glow has gone from the land.

On 29 August, two days after her death, George's body was moved from the vault where it had lain for twenty-six years and reburied at Frogmore. This move had been announced in September 1942, the month after George's death, but had never taken place. One theory is that George VI had put off moving his brother's remains as Frogmore was of easier access than the vault in Windsor, for which Marina always had to ask for a key. He had wanted Marina to begin her new life as soon and as easily as possible, and did not believe that too much visiting the grave would help.

The curtains of Windsor were drawn as the hearse carrying George's coffin drove from the castle to the private burial ground in Windsor Great Park. There, George was reburied under a plane tree beside a second freshly dug grave. Marina's coffin was taken from Kensington Palace to Windsor Castle, where it was to await the funeral.

Once again the royalty of Europe gathered. The Duke of Windsor left his wife in Paris (although she had been asked to the funeral) and flew in to London, where he was met by Eddie. King Constantine and Queen Anne-Marie came with Queen Frederika from their exile in Rome. Another ex-King, Umberto of Italy, also came. So did Queen Helen of Rumania and Marina's cousin Margarita, Prince Philip's sister. The English royal family returned to London from Balmoral, where they were on their summer holiday.

The funeral took place in St George's Chapel, Windsor, on

Friday 30 August at three in the afternoon. Marina's coffin was carried into the chapel by eight non-commissioned officers in the dress uniforms of Marina's three regiments – the Queen's Regiment, the Devonshire and Dorset Regiment and the Corps of Royal Electrical and Mechanical Engineers. It lay covered with her standard and with the blue and white Greek flag. Two wreaths, a large one of pink, red and yellow roses from her children, and a smaller blue and white one from Olga and Paul, lay on the flags.

The mourners were led by the Queen and Prince Philip who were joined by the Queen Mother, the Duke of Windsor and all the other senior members of the royal family. In the front row of the church sat Marina's children and Paul and Olga. On the other side of the aisle were the most important members of her household: Lady Rachel Pepys, Lady Balfour, the Earl and Countess of Pembroke (Lady Pembroke had been Marina's first lady-in-waiting on her arrival in England) and of course Philip Hay and Peter Clarke, who had joined Marina in 1964 as Comptroller of her and Alexandra's households. Marina's two old friends Zoia Poklewska and Turia Campbell were with them.

Although Marina had continued in her Greek Orthodox faith, she was buried as a member of the British royal family with the rites of the Church of England. There was, however, also an officiating priest from Marina's church, the Archimandrite Gregory Theodorus, Chancellor of the diocese of Thyatira and the anthem was the collect hymn from the burial service of the Greek Orthodox Church, 'Give Rest, O Christ, to Thy Servant with Thy Saints'. Other hymns were 'He Who Would Valiant Be', 'Lord of our Life', and 'God of Our Salvation'. Psalm 23, 'The Lord is my Shepherd', was also sung. The lesson was from the Gospel of St John and began 'Let not your heart be troubled: ye believe in God, believe also in me.' The Dean of Windsor conducted the thirty-minute ceremony, assisted by two other prelates, and the blessing was said by the Archbishop of Canterbury. The final anthem was 'God Be in My Head'.

After the funeral the coffin, followed by mourners, left for Frogmore. There was a moment as the royal family stood, grouped in the door of the chapel, watching the coffin being carried down the steps to the waiting hearse, when the waiting press and public caught a glimpse of the mourners. Otherwise the ceremony was as private an occasion as the royal family had wished. Then Marina was laid beside George. During the burial service the Duke of Windsor chose his own burial spot, near his favourite brother George. He and his Duchess now lie there, the Duchess finally united with her husband's family.

Several hours after the mourners left the doors of the chapel were opened and the public was allowed in, although there was little to see.

Although so many people had come so far to be at the funeral, it was a completely private affair, and an announcement from Kensington Palace had 'particularly requested' that only family flowers should be sent. The hundred and fifty mourners, led by Marina's niece the Queen, were all close friends and family members. Outside, over a thousand people had silently lined the streets of Windsor for two hours before the service, and the flags all flew at half-mast.

The old cliché 'a nation mourns' was never truer than on the death of Princess Marina. The *Times* obituary did Marina justice when the writer said that she 'was greatly admired for her remarkable personal beauty, and respected and loved for her high sense of duty, her modest charm, her dignity in sorrow, and her devotion to her family'. It continued, 'Princess Marina was the most recent of a long line of foreign princesses to marry into the British Royal house, and none of her predecessors was more successful in winning the affection of the British public.' After a brief description of her life and a listing of her public duties, it concluded that 'her interest in painting and music was genuine and eager. She was warm-hearted and generous, always a little diffident and to the last nervous before she had to make a public speech or even a public appearance, but perfectly controlled. She was a fiercely loyal friend and a delightful companion, full of interest and of humour, with natural dignity but no self-consciousness of her rank.'

Kenneth Rose wrote about Marina in the *Sunday Telegraph*

just after the funeral. 'In her presence, few other lights shone brightly,' he said, adding that 'this was only one facet of her life. Her serene elegance was matched by a down-to-earth realism as sturdy as the huge and unbecoming pair of spectacles she would wear when working at her writing-table.' And he paid tribute to her upbringing of her children, saying, 'The most adoring of mothers, she watched over her children with a fidelity that was not wholly maternal. She taught them that their lives belong as much to their country as to themselves.'

'She was beautiful up to the last,' said the Queen Mother later.

The first memorial service held for Marina was at the Greek Orthodox Cathedral in Bayswater, at the beginning of October. It was followed at the end of the month by another service in Westminster Abbey. The memorial service was televised, and, as millions had listened to the wireless broadcast of her wedding from the same place thirty-four years earlier, so now millions watched and thought of the Princess who had come to England a beautiful bride so many years before.

Cecil Beaton, 'importantly placed in the nave', noted the 'tremendously impressive proceedings – the Charles II copes in mint condition of silver embroidery on grape velvet – and today the addition of the Greek clergy, the Bishop in jewelled crown, an old priest shuffling like the Fairy Carabosse with loud heavy tread, a stick and protruding bottom'. As well as her English friends, the great and good of Europe collected to honour Marina's memory. Greek, Yugoslav, Danish and Bulgarian royalty mixed with the ambassadorial representatives of the Dutch, Swedish, Norwegian, Nepalese and Belgian monarchies. There were also two representatives from the garage at Iver, officials connected with her work and total strangers who had thought well of her.

The Archbishop of Canterbury was joined in the blessings at the memorial service by the Metropolitan Archbishop Athenagoras of Thyateira. Among the clergy assisting was the Vicar of Kensington, Marina's home parish. Dukes and duchesses rubbed shoulders in the congregation with politicians, including five Prime Ministers: Wilson, Douglas-Home, Macmillan, Eden and Menzies. Ladies-in-waiting were there alongside Norman Hartnell and Noël Coward. It was perhaps the first time that all the strands of Marina's life were drawn together: she had been a woman who had kept her friends in separate spheres, but now the exiled Russians and Yugoslavs were there with the English aristocracy and meritocracy, the politicians and (those she preferred) the showbusiness stars.

During the service the Dean of Westminster, Dr Eric Abbott, gave the address:

'Into the hands of Almighty God ... we commend his servant Marina, with thanksgiving upon our remembrance of her grace and beauty, her spirit of spontaneity, her courage in adversity, her unswerving service to this land of her adoption, her faithfulness in friendship, her percipient sympathy with sufferers, her love and knowledge of music and the arts, her knowledgeable patronage of so many human activities; not least do we thank God for the mutual affection which was established between her and our people and for her own loving family.'

It is not always that an address at a memorial service can sing its subject's praises and yet be truthful, but in Marina's case no words could overstate the effort she had put into making her role and her place in the country successful.

A few days later, on 8 November, another memorial service was held, this one in Rochester Cathedral where the people of Kent remembered their Duchess with sorrow and gratitude.

On 17 October 1968 it was announced that Marina had left £54,121 net in her will and that probate had been granted 'without annexing copy of will' to her son, the Duke of Kent, to Seymour J. L. Egerton, banker and John P. Charles, solicitor. After death duties, the sum left was only £17,398. It was an astoundingly small sum of money for a royal duchess to leave, and proved to any who doubted it that Marina had not been as rich as her position might lead one to suppose.

And so Marina passed from the public consciousness into the collective public memory. She left behind her her three children, and as they grew older and ever more adept at their jobs within the royal family they became a living tribute to her conscientiousness and affection. Katharine Kent took over some of Marina's jobs – notably the presidency of the All England Lawn Tennis and Croquet Club. Gradually her memory faded from the British public's awareness. To many she became just another minor member of the royal family, a foreign Princess ('from where exactly?') who had brought a dash of glamour to England.

But those who remember not more than the craze for Marina Blue and a whimsical, crooked smile, do Princess Marina wrong. She was an important part of an important process. In her way, she played an integral role in the survival of the British monarchy while so many others in Europe tumbled into the dust.

EPILOGUE

The business of the monarchy, always, is to survive; the survival instinct is as strong in humans as it is in animals. Form a collection of human beings into an institution and it will feel the same basic need to survive. For centuries England's monarchy has seen its survival as supremely important. There have been moments when that monarchy has been in danger, but to date the throne of Britain is still filled with an occupant born to the job.

The early years of this century were of particular danger to monarchies throughout Europe. Many did not survive. The thrones of Greece, Russia, Rumania and Bulgaria are among those which now lie vacant, or are claimed by exiled heirs. Yugoslavia is no longer even one country.

Those that survive have done so by adapting to the changes in the world around them. The world has become more egalitarian, the public is better educated than at the beginning of the century and the rise in the power of the media – newspapers, television and radio – has given the public greater access to more information. It should not be forgotten for how long most of England was kept in ignorance of Edward VIII's Abdication Crisis. Now the Princess of Wales has only to be seen playing tennis with someone and the speculation begins. It even appears that the media has won that battle and she, exhausted by the strains the perpetual intrusion has placed her under since her marriage, is withdrawing from public life.

The image of the monarchy has of course been different under each monarch. Each generation finds an individual making his own struggle to conform to the ideal, and some are more successful than others. Edward VII's approach was very different from his mother's – but he had been a long time in waiting, when the habit of enjoying himself took a firm hold. His court was glamorous, pleasure-seeking, warm and full of light. Marina's first experiences of English royal life were her childhood visits to her great-aunt Queen Alexandra: much had changed by the time she married George.

Marina's father-in-law George V still believed that one method of keeping the public's respect was to continue in the old ways: his court was as formal as had been his grandmother's. 'Dull perhaps, but certainly respectable,' as he himself would say. He believed firmly in the virtues of punctuality, formality, rules. Marina and George trod the fine line between being dutiful members of the family and enjoying a way of life that Edward VII would have understood.

By the time Edward VIII succeeded he already appreciated the dangers of sticking too closely to the old ways: the spectre of the Tsar and his family was constantly before the eyes of the British royal family. It had been George V who had finally blocked the offer of asylum to the Tsar and his family: he feared the effect this might have on his own position as King Emperor. His heirs continued to have a 'wholesome dread of Bolshevism' as author and member of the Foreign Office Sir Robert Bruce-Lockhart put it: what had happened in Russia could happen in England. The Duchess of Windsor claimed in her autobiography that when her husband succeeded to the throne he was 'excited and challenged by what he took to be his mission to modernise the monarchy within its traditional glory and strength'. On the face of it she was giving him too much credit. However, Edward VIII's awareness of the problems of monarchy in a modern world led to his carefully designed appeal to the working man. He was vastly popular as Prince of Wales for his visits to depressed parts of the country, for his seeming understanding of and compassion for the poor. The popular view is now that this was totally assumed as part of his campaign to gain popularity. Russia had after all shown the power of the working man and it was a power neither Edward VIII nor anyone else close to him wished to see exercised against the British King. Nevertheless, it is only fair to say that he did carry out this part of his work effectively: if the working man was won over by him, that was an element of his job that was successful. He was always well informed on the subject. Let it not be forgotten either that Bertie, as Duke of York, was notable for his own hard work and the empathy he showed for the workers when he toured industrial plants.

Edward VIII also took other steps in his brief reign to bring the monarchy up to date. He banished official court dress, for instance. Again, this may have been in part due to his own obsession with informality. He loved America more than anywhere else, and by the time of his accession even spoke with an American accent. (Chips Channon wrote in his diary that all the royal family except for George Kent spoke with German accents.) He was also, like so many of his forebears, overly interested in clothes, even going so far as to write a book devoted almost entirely to that subject.

The most modern element of his approach to the monarchy was of course the manner in which he left it. Unlike his predecessor Henry VIII he found in the end that he could not do just as he chose with regard to women: his family and the government were prepared to close their eyes to almost any indiscretion but that of making the wrong marriage.

Edward VIII's successor, George VI, was completely different in character. Where Edward VIII had charm, George VI was shy and stammering. Where Edward VIII's ready wit could ease almost any situation, George VI was hard-working and diligent. Where Edward VIII was gallant and romantic, George VI was a family man with a round wife and two small daughters. Like his father, George VI was happiest at Sandringham, loving the shooting and relaxation (George V had once shot a thousand birds, part of a four-thousand slaughter in a day, but even he was worried they had gone 'a little far.') He also had the difficulty of a living predecessor, and of keeping the mysticism of the monarchy alive despite the all too human behaviour of that predecessor. Walter Bagehot wrote in his seminal work *The English Constitution*, 'If a king is a useful public functionary who may be changed, and in whose place you may make another, you cannot regard him with mystic awe and wonder: and if you are bound to worship him, of course you cannot change him.' Bagehot was writing of the making of the Hanovers, but the problem was as great for George VI as it had been for George I.

Marina and George represented once again a middle line: they had been closest to David, Marina rather despised her sister-in-law Elizabeth (although not nearly so much as she came to disapprove of her Windsor sister-in-law), but they were always prepared to take the correct party line.

At first George VI was underestimated, but he too realised the importance of moving with the times and knew that the monarchy must adapt to survive. When King George and Queen Elizabeth returned from their 1939 tour of North America, George announced that 'There must be no more high-hat business, the sort of thing that my father and those of his day regarded as the correct attitude – the feeling that certain things couldn't be done.' He wanted to be a 'people's King'.

He was also a family King – the image of a King with a wife and children, like so many of his subjects, drew him closer to them. He loved shooting and Sandringham, was a country man at heart. Although, like his father and grandfather before him (and indeed his brother George) he had a temper, the atmosphere at court was much happier than it had been in the past. 'The new atmosphere of Sandringham was very much more friendly than in the old days, more like that of any home,' writes Mabell Airlie. 'We still assembled in the drawing-room in the traditional way, but no orders or medals were worn, not even badges. One sensed far more the setting of ordinary family life in this generation than the last.' Bagehot commented on the idea of a royal family:

A *family* on the throne is an interesting idea also. It brings down the pride of sovereignty to the level of petty life. No feeling could seem more childish than the enthusiasm of the English at the marriage of the Prince of Wales [Edward VII]. They treated as a great political event, what, looked at as a matter of pure business, was very small indeed .... a Royal family sweetens politics by the seasonable addition of nice and pretty events. It introduces irrelevant facts into the business of government but they are facts which speak to 'men's bosoms' and employ their thoughts.

Or, as Jim Thomas, General Secretary of the National Union of Railwaymen, put it to Harold Nicolson in February 1936, ' "Ere we 'ave this little obstinate man with 'is Mrs Simpson. Hit won't do, 'arold, I tell you that straight. I know the people of this country. I *know* them. They 'ate 'aving no family life at Court." '

One of the reasons for Marina's popularity in her lifetime, both before and after George's death, was her obvious love of her family. The English continue to hold this view: even when the tide of popularity is against the Princess of Wales, we always 'give her her due' and mention 'how much she loves her boys'. One of the Duchess of York's weapons in her low-key attempt to return to favour is how important her girls are to her. The English not only want a family life at court, they want an idealised family.

A monarch who is the head of the family also begs some questions about morality. Of course the monarch is the Supreme Head of the Church of England, but there are many who care nothing for religion but do care about the monarchy. It may indeed be true that for many the monarch took the place of God in the structure of their lives: above the rest of us, untouchable, unassailable. Bagehot (writing of course in the reign of Victoria) noted that 'we have come to regard the Crown as the head of our *morality*. We have come to believe that it is natural to have a virtuous sovereign, and that domestic virtues are as likely to be found on thrones as they are eminent when there.' Our Queen continues to hold this moral platform, but some of her relations are not so untouched. Although we have seen that Princess Marina's widowhood was not entirely chaste, she succeeded in keeping her private life private and was seen as virtuous (which indeed she was).

Some of the greatest Kings of England have been those with the least glamour. Every schoolchild knows of Henry VIII, his disasters and his successes, his dead and divorced wives. But do they care much for Henry VII, whose hard work laid the foundations for the great Tudor triumph? George VI may have

lacked glamour but with Elizabeth as his strength and inspiration, he had the staying power which his brother lacked.
Realising that a constitutional monarch's job was fairly limited
in a democracy, he carried on the work his father had begun.
He wrote in his diary that one of his 'main jobs in life is to help
others, when I can be useful to them'. That is a very humble job
description, but he did prove that a monarch and his consort
could be loved as much for their sense of duty, could even appeal
to the sentiment of the nation by their very lack of romance, as
they could be loved for their charm and gaiety. George VI and
his Queen saw themselves in some measure as father and mother
to the nation. Queen Elizabeth wrote to Lady Astor after the
bombing of Plymouth in 1941:

One feels it all so bitterly, and so personally .... That is one of the hard
things about being King and Queen of a country that one loves so much.
Every time this sort of murderous attack is made, one feels it, as if our
own children were being hurt. All we can do, is to do our very best, and
leave the rest in God's hand.

Ramsay MacDonald told Harold Nicolson that Edward VIII
had 'done more harm to his country than any man in history',
but much of that harm was undone by the war, and in that sense
at least George VI was lucky. By the end of the war the whole
nation respected and loved him as they had loved his charming
older brother. 'The war has drawn the Throne and the people
more closely together than was ever before recorded and Your
Majesties are more beloved of all classes and conditions than
any of the princes of the past,' Churchill wrote to Bertie in
January 1941, and he spoke the truth.

Two years later the *Times* leader of 18 May 1943 said that
'Mr Churchill's telegram, revealing the help that one of the
strongest Prime Ministers has received from his sovereign, is a
powerful reminder that King George VI is doing a work as
indispensable for English governance as any of his predecessors,
just as he has set his peoples from the first day of the war an
unfailing public example of courage, confidence and devoted
energy'.

The war helped set the much needed changes into motion,

although according to the Queen Mother they happened spontaneously: 'We never consciously set out to change things; we never said "Let's change this or introduce that." Things just evolved. It's just that life was getting more informal,' she told writer Theo Aronson when discussing the modernisation of the monarchy that happened during the war years.

The real art in George VI's kingship lay in moving with the times and yet succeeding in retaining that air of mystery, of separateness, which keeps the monarch respected and, more important still, held almost in reverence by the public. Marina, with her looks, her romantic background and her tragic widowhood, had all the ingredients for a mysterious Princess. King George had to work hard to achieve the same effect, but Marina also worked hard to deserve it.

Bagehot wrote that 'Royalty is a government in which the attention of the nation is concentrated on one person doing interesting actions. A Republic is a government in which that attention is divided between many, who are all doing uninteresting actions .... Its [Royalty's] mystery is its life. We must not bring in the daylight upon magic.' George VI was not romantic, but he understood the principal. In 1943 his Principal Private Secretary, Sir Alexander Hardinge resigned due to 'ill health'. He had been ill, but he did not get on with the Assistant Private Secretary, Tommy (Sir Alan) Lascelles, nor really with the King. He had served George V and Edward VIII before George VI and was very old-fashioned indeed in his approach. Lascelles, who was more flexible, took his place and played his own, not unimportant part, in bringing the monarchy into the modern age.

It was in keeping the magic and mystery of the monarchy alive that Queen Elizabeth (the Queen Mother) and Princess Marina were so successful. The Queen with her romantic, diaphanous dresses and radiant grin, Princess Marina with her smart chic, romantic history and wistful smile reminded the people why they had and why they still loved the monarchy. And neither ever let their guard drop in public. None of her friends, however long they had known her, addressed Marina by her Christian name. (Cecil Beaton called her 'Ma'am Darling' but was not allowed to kiss her cheek until 1964.)

Once, not long after their marriage, Princess Alexandra and Angus Ogilvy were dining with Marina. It was a small party, not official, and during the course of it Angus referred to his wife as 'Alexandra'. Afterwards his mother-in-law told him he should never do that, no matter how intimate the company. It is a tiny example, and to some may seem pernickety, but it illustrates Marina's attitude. She brought her children up to take their part in the modern royal family, but that did not mean they or she should ever forget the essence of their royalty. That Marina could do this while still having that most important gift of modern royalty – the common touch – is proof of her aptitude for her job. Marina took the monarchy, but not herself, seriously. she used to tell a story of an American tourist approaching her in Kensington Gardens, holding out a camera. She assumed he was asking permission to take her photograph and was ready to agree graciously. In fact he asked her to take a picture of him with his wife and sister in front of Kensington Palace. She took the picture, did not tell him who she was, and later laughed at herself for assuming he was interested in her.

By the time George VI's daughter Elizabeth succeeded to the throne the monarchy was respected, loved and admired by the vast majority of the British public. The royal family had carved out a new niche for itself, made itself once again indispensable. It had moved closer to the people, but when it did so it was in such a way as to make its separateness almost tangible.

One notable sign of the monarchy's greater popular approach is the walkabout, a modern invention which owes much to Queen Elizabeth the Queen Mother. She caused the security men endless worries when, in America in 1939, she mingled freely with the crowds who had come to see her. But it touched the people, and was an inspired piece of publicity. Princess Marina also took up the walkabout, and people still say with awe that they once shook Princess Marina's hand. That small contact is something which 'ordinary' people treasure.

Elizabeth II followed the lead her father had given. Like him, she is committed to duty. She also showed from the beginning of her reign that she wished to draw closer to her people: 'I want to show that the Crown is not merely an abstract symbol of our unity but a personal and living bond between you and me,' she said in her Christmas broadcast in 1953. She also tried – although the task appears to have been impossible – to bring her children up in as normal a way as possible. Princess Anne was the first daughter of a monarch to go to boarding school (Princess Alexandra had of course already blazed that particular trail, but not being the daughter of a monarch was less in the public eye). Princess Anne's first husband, Captain Mark Philips, did not accept a title on his marriage, another new departure. Princess Anne was also the first member of the royal family to compete in the Olympic Games for Britain (and nobody denies that her place in the team was gained entirely on merit). Let it not be forgotten, though, that George VI (as Duke of York) competed at Wimbledon. However, this spirit of togetherness, or whatever it might be called, was later taken too far. The spectacle of the Princess Royal, the Duke and Duchess of York and Prince Edward competing in fancy dress in the television programme *It's a Knock-Out* was not edifying. Princess Alexandra once said, 'Don't forget that nowadays we have to compete with Elizabeth Taylor and the Beatles.' Perhaps in the long run it would have been better had the royal family occasionally forgotten, or risen above, the need for competition.

Our monarchy has seen some troubled times recently. It has become clear to the most ardent, the most unthinking, royalists that the royal family is made up of real people with problems much like ours. As a result the mystery is, alas, slightly tarnished.

The Queen's sister and three of her four children have broken marriages. Her first cousin, son of the Princess Royal (Princess Mary) and the Earl of Harewood, was the first of the Queen's close relations to be divorced, and for a long time he was ostracised from his mother's family for his decision. He had first married Marion Stein, but later began an affair with Patricia Tuckwell. By the time he finally left his wife for his mistress, he already had an illegitimate son. He was divorced in 1967 and later married Miss Tuckwell. As a close relation of the Queen, Harewood could not marry without her consent, and for the first time Queen Elizabeth was shown the difficulties of her joint position as monarch and Supreme Head of the Church of England. The difficulty was surmounted by the government advising the Queen to give Harewood permission to marry and she, as a constitutional monarch, had to take that advice.

In 1956 Princess Margaret decided not to marry Peter Townsend because he was a divorced man, even though he had been the innocent party in the divorce. (His wife Rosemary had left him, and he had been awarded custody of their two sons.) When the public realised that she was in love with Townsend they awaited the outcome with baited breath. The Duke and Duchess of Windsor, from their exile in Paris, must have followed the events with a certain malicious glee, must also have hoped that if Princess Margaret went ahead with the marriage they would at last be allowed home. However, unlike her uncle Princess Margaret put duty before everything else and renounced Townsend. He has since proved his worth by his consistent refusal to discuss the matter. The Princess later married Antony Armstrong-Jones, who was given the title Earl of Snowdon, but that marriage ended in separation in 1976, followed by divorce two years later. It had been an empty sacrifice. Her name was later linked with a young gardener and playboy and the Queen had to hold her head, and that of the monarchy, high as the media wallowed in the news.

In more recent years both the Duke and Duchess of York, and the Prince and Princess of Wales have officially separated. The break-up of the Yorks' marriage was particularly unsavoury, involving as it did the publication of some intimate photographs of the Duchess with a Texan. The current Princess Royal has not only divorced, but has married again, albeit in the Scottish Church.

That this should happen only one generation after King Edward VIII rocked not only England but the whole Western world with his decision to marry a twice-divorced woman shows how rapidly the royal family has had to rethink its attitudes in order to remain part of the modern world. Or perhaps it shows how the modern world, with its various temptations and vices, has intruded into what, to those who believe in the institution, should be something holy, set apart from other ways of life. The

Queen herself certainly believes that her job is something she has been called to do: for this reason alone it is unlikely that she would ever abdicate in favour of her son or grandson, as some commentators have suggested she might. She would not rehearse the vital moments of the coronation, as she felt to rehearse something sacred was almost sacrilegious.

Other members of the royal family have married divorcees: Marina's son Michael was to marry Marie-Christine von Reibnitz (ex-wife of banker 'poor Tom Troubridge'), an Austrian whose family had settled in Australia. They met while she was working in London as an interior designer. Friends of the family very much doubt whether that marriage would have taken place had Marina been alive: Princess Michael is a strong woman, but Marina would almost certainly have succeeded in stopping the match. Eddie's elder son George St Andrews also married a Roman Catholic divorcee, Sylvana Tomaselli, who is four years older than he.

Marina's granddaughter, also called Marina, has been involved in scandal and behaved in a way that would have broken her grandmother's heart. Daughter of Princess Alexandra and Angus Ogilvy, she was brought up with the same open affection as the three Kent children had been. Unfortunately, she had her grandmother's strong will and took her own path. This led her to conceive a baby out of wedlock (she married the child's father before the birth), being interviewed for the papers ('Why I Don't Give a Damn'), being awarded the dubious accolade 'Rear of the Year' posing in leather with corgis and a crown for national newspapers (in an effort to boost her photographer husband's career) and writing a regular column for a downmarket newspaper. Her cousin Nicholas Windsor, Eddie Kent's son, has also found himself in trouble: in 1986 he and a friend were arrested for being in possession of cannabis and taken to Bow Street Police Station. They were let off with a caution, but the press heard and used the story.

When the royal family began to move closer to the people it was thought to be a matter for congratulation, a step in the right direction. Whether, in the long run, it turned out to be a good idea is a matter of opinion. For a while at least it certainly seemed to work. But the only way for royalty, in Britain at least, to survive is for it to keep at least some of its separateness. Queen Mary, viewed by so many as the last bastion of the old-fashioned way of monarchy, understood more than most how the world was changing. Mabell Airlie reported that when Prince Philip became engaged to Princess Elizabeth, a member of the family said to her that the only thing against her prospective grandson-in-law was that he had been to 'a crank school with theories of complete social equality where the boys were taught to mix with all and sundry, and that it would remain to be seen whether the effects of this training would be useful or baleful to the King's son-in-law, she had replied decisively "Useful". "And it will be, Mabell," the Queen added. "The world has changed since you and I were born into it, and it will change still more." ' She was of course right, and would have been horrified at many of the excesses of both the press and indeed her own family.

Some of the changes seen in the modern monarchy are still beneficial. When the Duke of York, then Prince Andrew, went on active service in the Falklands War it was the first time for two centuries a Prince had seen military action. The mothers of soldiers and sailors throughout Britain could identify with the Queen in a way they had not been able to since the bombing of Buckingham Palace.

One of the biggest changes to happen in Marina's lifetime was of course the collapse of the British Empire (George VI was the last King-Emperor and his widow is still entitled to sign herself Elizabeth RI), and this was something with which Marina became personally involved. She represented the Queen at the independence celebrations of Ghana, the first African country to leave the umbrella of the Empire. George V's friend Sir Charles Cust once said, 'There are three kinds of people in the world: blacks, whites and Royalties.' We should be shocked to hear anyone say such a thing now, but that does not mean that it was not the way a vast number of even the educated upper classes thought and spoke until comparatively recently. Remembering that Princess Marina came from a way of monarchy which, however benevolent, stuck coins on to the sweating foreheads of the musical peasantry, it is the more remarkable that she made the transition to the new way so effectively. Her very appearance at independence celebrations was symbolic in itself: the Queen could not have chosen a more apt ambassadress to show how willing she was to change the spirit of monarchy.

In her own speeches Marina showed her awareness of the changing times. As early as 1952, on returning from her Malay tour, she spoke of her surprise at the affection shown for the royal family in 'times of spiritual change and unrest'. In the same speech she also referred to the Commonwealth as 'this great family of nations', exemplifying the shift in attitude between an empire and a commonwealth.

Edward Hay, son of Philip Hay, says that to Princess Marina and his father, her closest advisor, it was the monarchy as a whole that was important, not the individuals within the family. For that reason she held that members of the royal family should never give their own views on anything from politics to gardening. Both she and Hay would have been shocked at the new development in the monarchy whereby members of the family have begun for the first time to say what they think. So Marina, although not close to any of her relations-in-law, played her part as a member of the family to perfection. She firmly believed that the survival of the monarchy was of supreme importance and was prepared to take whatever role was needed to help that happen. When she died the monarchy was at its most respected and loved: it was some years before over-familiarisation began the slide downhill, and it was a familiarisation with which Princess Marina would have had no truck.

Marina was not an intellectual, but her instinct and her training taught her all she needed to know about her calling as a Princess of the House of Windsor. Bagehot wrote that 'So long as the human heart is strong and the human reason weak, royalty will be strong because it appeals to diffused feeling, and Republics weak because they appeal to the understanding.' Marina's heart was strong in just the way that appealed to the hearts of her niece's subjects: were more members of the royal family like Marina, there would have been infinitely less trouble for the monarchy. Could the young, modern members of the House of Windsor remember their aunt, have the humbleness to follow her example and the dignity to carry their trials as lightly as she, the royal house could regain its lost position in the lives of the British.

BIBLIOGRAPHY

Harold Acton, *More Memoirs of an Aesthete*, Methuen, 1970
Mabell Airlie, *Thatched with Gold*, Hutchinson, 1962
Theo Aronson, *The Royal Family at War*, John Murray, 1993
Theo Aronson, *Royal Family, Years of Transition*, John Murray, 1983
Walter Bagehot, *The English Constitution*, 1867
Neil Balfour and Sally Mackay, *Paul of Yugoslavia*, Hamish Hamilton, 1980
The Earl of Birkenhead, *Walter Monckton*, Weidenfeld and Nicolson, 1969
Michael Bloch, *The Secret File of the Duke of Windsor*, Bantam Press, 1988
Michael Bloch, *Wallis and Edward, Letters 1931–1937*, Weidenfeld and Nicolson, 1986
Hector Bolitho, *Edward VIII His Life and Reign*, Eyre and Spottiswoode, 1937
Sarah Bradford, *George VI*, Weidenfeld and Nicolson, 1989
Sir Robert Bruce-Lockhart, *Diaries I: 1915–1938*, Macmillan, 1973
(ed.) Richard Buckle, *Self Portrait with Friends, Selected Diaries of Cecil Beaton 1926–1974*, Weidenfeld and Nicolson, 1979
J. Bryan III and Charles J. V. Murphy, *The Windsor Story*, Granada, 1979
Helen Cathcart, *Princess Alexandra*, W.H. Allen, 1967
H.R.H. Prince Christopher of Greece, *Memoirs*, The Right Book Club, 1938
J. Wentworth Day, *H.R.H. Princess Marina*, Robert Hale Ltd, 1962
Frances Donaldson, *Edward VIII*, Weidenfeld and Nicolson, 1974
Anne Edwards, *Matriarch*, Hodder and Stoughton, 1984
Jennifer Ellis, *The Duchess of Kent*, Odham Press, 1952
Fairbanks Jnr, Douglas, *The Salad Days*, Collins, 1988.
Princess Alice, Duchess of Gloucester, *Memories of Ninety Years*, Collins and Brown, 1991

Unity Hall, *Philip, The Man Behind the Monarchy*, Michael O'Mara, 1987

Tim Heald, *The Duke: A Portrait of Prince Philip*, Hodder and Stoughton, 1991

Richard Hough, *Born Royal, The Lives and Loves of the Young Windsors*, Andre Deutsch, 1988

Helena von-der Hoven, *Intimate Life Story of H.R.H. The Duchess of Kent*, Cassell, 1937

Stella King, *Princess Marina, Her Life and Times*, Cassell, 1969

Robert Lacey, *Majesty*, Hutchinson, 1977

Elizabeth Longford, *Elizabeth R*, Weidenfeld and Nicolson, 1983

Compton Mackenzie, *The Windsor Tapestry*, Rich and Cowan, 1938

Grand Duchess Marie of Russia, *Things I Remember*, Cassell, 1930

Prince Michael of Greece & Alan Palmer, *The Royal House of Greece*, Weidenfeld and Nicolson, 1990

ed. Hugh Montgomery-Massingberd, *Burke's Royal Families of the World, Volume I Europe and Latin America*, Burke's Peerage Limited, 1977

Penelope Mortimer, *Queen Elizabeth, A Life of the Queen Mother*, Viking, 1986

ed. Charlotte Mosley, *The Letters of Nancy Mitford*, Hodder and Stoughton, 1993

Diana Mosley, *The Duchess of Windsor*, Sidgwick and Jackson, 1980

H.R.H. Prince Nicholas of Greece, *My Fifty Years*, Hutchinson, 1926

H.R.H. Prince Nicholas of Greece, *Political Memoirs*, Hutchinson, 1928

ed. Harold Nicolson, *Nigel Nicolson, Diaries and Letters 1930–1939*, Collins, 1967

ed. Harold Nicolson, *Nigel Nicolson, Diaries and Letters 1939–1945*, Collins, 1967

Hannah Pakula, *Queen of Romania*, Weidenfeld and Nicolson, 1984

ed. Graham Payn and Sheridan Morley, *The Noel Coward Diaries*, Weidenfeld and Nicolson, 1982

James Pope-Hennessy, *Queen Mary*, Allen and Unwin, 1959

ed. Robert Rhodes James, *Chips, the Diaries of Sir Henry Channon*, Weidenfeld and Nicolson, 1967

Kenneth Rose, *George V*, Weidenfeld and Nicolson, 1983

Kenneth Rose, *Kings, Queens and Courtiers*, Weidenfeld and Nicolson, 1985

Michael Thornton, *Royal Feud, The Queen Mother and the Duchess of Windsor*, Michael Joseph, 1985

Major F.E. Verney, *H.R.H. A Character Study of the Prince of Wales*, Hodder and Stoughton

Hugo Vickers, *Cecil Beaton*, Weidenfeld and Nicolson, 1985
Christopher Warwick, *George and Marina*, Weidenfeld and Nicolson, 1988
Evelyn Waugh, *Diaries*
John. W. Wheeler-Bennett, *King George VI*, Macmillan, 1958
J. Lincoln White, *The Abdication of Edward VIII*, Routledge, 1937
Whiting, Audrey, *The Kents*, Hutchinson 1985
Duchess of Windsor, *The Heart Has its Reasons*, Michael Joseph, 1956
Duke of Windsor, *A King's Story*, Cassell, 1951
Duke of Windsor, *A Family Album*, Cassell, 1960
C.M. Woodhouse, *Modern Greece, A Short History*, Faber & Faber, 1968
Philip Ziegler, *King Edward VIII*, Collins, 1990

NEWSPAPERS
The Times, The Times Literary Supplement, Aeroplane Monthly, Daily Mail, Daily Express, Sunday Express, Sunday Chronicle

INDEX